AFTER THE WAR IN IRAQ
DEFINING THE NEW STRATEGIC BALANCE

AFTER THE WAR IN IRAQ
DEFINING THE NEW STRATEGIC BALANCE

Edited by **SHAI FELDMAN**

sussex
ACADEMIC
PRESS

BRIGHTON • PORTLAND

JAFFEE CENTER FOR
STRATEGIC STUDIES

2 4 6 8 10 9 7 5 3 1

First published in 2003 in Great Britain by
SUSSEX ACADEMIC PRESS
PO Box 2950
Brighton BN2 5SP

and in the United States of America by
SUSSEX ACADEMIC PRESS
920 NE 58th Ave   Suite 300
Portland, Oregon 97213-3786

British Library Cataloguing in Publication Data
A CIP catalogue record for this book is available from the British Library.

Library of Congress Cataloging-in-Publication Data
After the war in Iraq : defining the new strategic balance / edited by
Shai Feldman.
p. cm.
Includes bibliographical references and index.
ISBN 1–903900–74–3 — ISBN 1–903900–75–1 (pbk.)
1. Iraq War, 2003—Influence. 2. United States—Foreign relations—Middle East.
3. Middle East—Foreign relations—United States. 4. National security—
United States. 5. Middle East—Politics and government—1979–
6. World politics—1989– I. Feldman, Shai, 1950–

DS79.76 .A36 2003
956.7044'3—dc22

2003016849

Typeset and designed by G&G Editorial, Brighton
Printed by TJ International, Padstow, Cornwall
This book is printed on acid-free paper.

Contents

Preface and Acknowledgments

After the War in Iraq: Defining the New Strategic Balance is a collection of essays intended to provide a comprehensive and timely analysis of the implications of the war. Begun not long after Baghdad's central square fell to coalition forces, the book represents a joint effort undertaken by most of the research staff of the Jaffee Center for Strategic Studies and comprises a study of the war's ramifications from different disciplines and vantage points. The book also presents a uniquely Israeli perspective, as some of the analysis included addresses the direct and indirect impact of the war on Israel: its prospects for peace, its regional standing, its public opinion, and its home front defense.

This book evolved from a number of brainstorming sessions and an elaborate quality control process in which all members of the Jaffee Center's research staff have taken part. We are grateful to our colleagues for their diligent work and for cooperating in a manner allowing the completion of this manuscript in record time. Thanks go to Yoel Kozak for his assistance in obtaining research materials, and to Moshe Tlamim and Hever Metargemim for their translation work. Moshe Grundman, Assistant to the Head of JCSS and director of JCSS publications, coordinated and oversaw all aspects involved with preparation of the text. We are particularly indebted to Judith Rosen, the Center's English editor, for doing such a wonderful job, allowing us to produce a book that is not only important but also readable.

SHAI FELDMAN
July 2003

Introduction

Shai Feldman

After the War in Iraq: Defining the New Strategic Balance explores different dimensions to the war in Iraq launched in March 2003 by the United States. The essays collected here offer concise, penetrating analyses that examine the major implications of the war and their strategic, political, and military contexts.

The book is analytical in character: it does not attempt to provide a detailed description of the events leading to the war, the various phases of the war, and the developments observed in Iraq and in neighboring countries in the war's immediate aftermath. Instead, it seeks to ascertain the principal global and regional implications of the war as well as its effects on Israel.

Part I comprises eight essays that analyze the international context of the war. **Mark Heller** addresses the impact of United States foreign policy *vis-à-vis* the war on the international system, focusing on its unipolar and multipolar dimensions. He examines the tension between the United States as the world's sole superpower and its inability nonetheless to remain independent of international diplomatic pressures. His essay is followed by **Abraham Ben-Zvi's** chapter on the manner in which the Bush administration's foreign and defense policy has evolved from its inception through the terrorist attacks of September 11, 2001 and up to and beyond the war in Iraq. According to Ben-Zvi, September 11 became a watershed in foreign policy doctrine, boosting the neo-conservative voice within the Bush administration that advocated preemptive strategies.

Yair Evron and **Emily Landau** present essays that address specific dimensions of US policy. Evron's analyzes the extent to which the different strategic concepts of deterrence, prevention, and compellence are reflected in current US defense strategy. He also explores the role of deterrence in Iraq and in Israel during the events leading up to the war. Landau's essay examines how US arms control policy evolved before and in light of the war in Iraq, and probes the way in which US arms control policy is not unilateralist, but tends to consider individual states and the regional contexts in which they figure in the arms control debate.

Yoram Schweitzer examines the connection between the war in Iraq and the campaign against international terrorism. Schweitzer argues that terrorism did not play a major role in the war, and in effect, Iraq as a target represented somewhat of a divergence from the initial course charted by the Bush administration to combat international terrorism.

Isaac Ben-Israel reviews the military lessons of the war in Iraq, focusing on the dramatic military operation in light of the Revolution in Military Affairs. His essay is followed by **Shmuel Even's** analysis regarding the impact of the war on the global oil market. Finally, **Hirsh Goodman** and **Jonathan Cummings** consider the press coverage of the war and the policy of embedding as a case study in military–media relations.

Part II includes six essays that center on the regional ramifications of the war and the impact on Israel and its neighbors. **Ephraim Kam's** essay spans scenarios of "the day after" in Iraq as well as the impact of Saddam's fall on the Middle East at large and its major players. **Shai Feldman** analyzes the extent to which the war in Iraq has affected the prospects of Israeli–Palestinian peace, focusing on the manner in which the war accelerated developments favoring peace that evolved prior to the war. **Ephraim Asculai** addresses the heated subject of weapons of mass destruction in Iraq, outlining Iraq's history with non-conventional weapons and suggesting two scenarios as to what might have happened to these weapons just before the war erupted. **Shlomo Brom's** analysis portrays the manner in which the war has affected the strategic balance in the region, and suggests how the overwhelming military advantage enjoyed by the United States and Israel encourages neighboring states to develop an asymmetric response to conventional military resources.

Anat Kurz and **Tamar Malz** follow with an essay on the Israeli public's behavior before and during the war. They suggest that the public's overwhelming adherence to its routine reflected a low perception of the Iraqi threat and was related to the Israeli tendency not to challenge security policies and directives outside of institutionalized settings. **David Klein's** essay examines Israel's home front defense policy and suggests implications for future policies in light of the changed post-war strategic threat.

Two additional texts complete the book. The first is a chronology of the international inspection regime in Iraq from 1991 to 2003. The second is the full text of *The National Security Strategy of the United States of America*, published in September 2002. This document, referred to specifically by Ben-Zvi and Evron, may be regarded as the basis of the Bush administration's strategic rationale for the war in Iraq.

Offering analyses so quickly after the war is necessarily a risky proposition: it exposes the manuscript as a whole and the individual essays included to the possible criticism that "it is far too early to tell . . . " But the significance of the war in Iraq is urgent enough and compelling enough to attempt such analyses even in the absence of what some would consider a requisite distance and perspective. The writers have made every effort to balance their creativity and daring in attempting to ascertain the war's implications with caution against jumping to conclusions that are unlikely to meet the test of time. The coming months and years will expand the perspectives offered here and invite new analysis and research.

The International Dimensions

The International System After the War in Iraq

Mark A. Heller

America After the Cold War: Last Man Standing?

America's preeminent position in world affairs does not derive solely from its military power. The United States is also the largest single-country economy and consumer market in the world, making it the premier target for exports of most other countries. Compared to its nearest putative rival – united Europe – its economy has grown faster during periods of expansion and declined more slowly during periods of contraction. Its population is younger and growing, while that of Europe is aging and dwindling. It is the largest underwriter of higher education and of public and private sector scientific and medical research and development, and it is the biggest source of technological innovation. It is even the greatest producer and exporter of mass culture, ranging from literature and film to pop music and junk food. But it is in the military sphere that its preeminence is most pronounced.

The coalition victory in Iraq provided graphic evidence of what was already widely acknowledged before the war began: that the United States bestrides the globe as a military colossus. In terms of its ability to develop and apply military force and to project power abroad, the United States has no rivals and practically needs no partners. American military preponderance is not only uncontested in the contemporary world; it is virtually unprecedented in recorded history. Even the British Empire at the height of its power did not possess the overwhelming advantage over any potential adversaries currently enjoyed by the United States. Measured by military power alone, the gap in military capabilities that prevails today between the leading actor and others probably outstrips anything at least since the time of the Roman Empire, when the "known world" was a much smaller entity. For example, the US already spends more than twice as much on military procurement as does the entire European Union. Moreover, every indicator suggests that the military divide between the US and the rest of the world will only grow in the foreseeable future. American investment in military research and development, particularly in exotic areas such as cybernetics and nanotechnology, far outstrips that of any other country or probable coalition of countries; it is more than four times the total R&D investment of all EU members. This virtually assures that America's technological advantage will only increase in the coming years.

None of this means that American preeminence is permanent. In the long run of history it is almost certain that such preeminence is transitory and that others will eventually challenge the American advantage (though underlying trends suggest that the challenge, when it comes, is more likely to come from Asia than from Europe). But it does mean that the United States, for the foreseeable future, will truly qualify as what former French Foreign Minister Hubert Védrine once termed the "hyperpower." And it does mean that the current international system is as close to being structurally unipolar as any that has ever existed.

Constraints on American Power and the Need for Partners

Even so, the exercise of American power, even military power, is not unconstrained by other actors in the international system. For one thing, the United States, unlike previous international hegemons, is a democracy. That means that executive decision-making processes are influenced by public opinion and legislative action, one component of which is the need for legitimacy. Part of that legitimacy derives from the support or at least tacit approval of other international actors, which is why the US stressed so strongly that it was acting in Iraq with a "coalition of the willing," even if coalition partners were actually dispensable for military operations. Put differently, it means that the rest of the international system, even when it cannot directly prevent the use of American force, can indirectly constrain it by providing input into the domestic American debate.

The willingness of other actors to support or object to American action is conditioned not only by their material stakes in the issue at hand, but also by their general level of comfort or discomfort with the preeminence in global affairs of the United States, or, indeed, of any other actual or aspiring hegemon. Historically, the emergence of such power has prompted others to try, almost instinctively, to mobilize balancing or countervailing power, if not alone then through the building of counter-coalitions. The combination of resentment, envy, and fear that explains this instinct was given expression in one of French President Jacques Chirac's explanations for his opposition to the use of American force in Iraq: "Any community with only one dominant power is always a dangerous one, and provokes reactions. That's why I favor a multipolar world, in which Europe obviously has its place."

A second constraint has to do with the sorts of security threats that military force is intended to address. American military power is undoubtedly sufficient to deter or defeat any orthodox, state-based military threat to itself or its allies, i.e., a direct military attack. But since the end of the Cold War, the US has increasingly broadened the definition of its threat agenda to include and in fact emphasize threats of terrorism by non-state actors and state supporters of terrorism, and the proliferation of weapons of mass destruction to rogue states and terrorists. The applicability of military power to these sorts of threats is far more problematic.

Non-state actors, even in an era of cybernetics and virtual reality, need to occupy some physical space in order to plan, train, equip, finance, and launch operations. That physical space exists within the frontiers of states, and terrorists can freely use it only if governments support or tolerate their presence or else are unable to assert control of the territory nominally under their jurisdiction, e.g., in "failed states." In some circumstances, military power can be applied to contain state supporters of terrorism or else take control of failed states. That is what the United States did in Afghanistan and also (as at least part of the rationale for war) in Iraq. But even in these circumstances, the use of military force is politically feasible only if some degree of legitimacy has been established through a prior effort to address the threat through methods short of war and a successful search for some degree of approval by other actors in the international system. Such political preconditions do not mean that the US will subordinate its own assessment of when all other means short of war have been exhausted or that it will accept that only institutionalized bodies, such as the UN or the EU, can confer the "seal of approval." But they do constrain the extent to which the United States can act militarily in a truly unilateral fashion.

Thirdly, to be effective, counter-terrorism measures short of war depend in large measure on international cooperation. In assessing and evaluating information about the capabilities and intentions of terrorists and state sponsors of terrorism (and especially in tapping human intelligence), in tracking and controlling the movement of suspect individuals, suspect funds, and suspect materials and components, in police operations, and in judicial proceedings, American security agencies have no choice but to rely on coordination and cooperation with their counterparts in other countries.

Finally, and most critically, American military preponderance is not easily adapted to dealing with what is increasingly seen as the "root cause" of the international terrorist threat – the conditions of political, economic, and social dysfunction that create both a large corps of highly motivated terrorists and an even larger corps of supporters and sympathizers who contribute to the material infrastructure and provide the psychological foundation for terrorists. Particularly since September 11, the US administration has focused on the nexus between terrorism/WMD proliferation, on the one hand, and the lack of political, economic, and social freedom among those posing the chief threats, on the other. What this logically implies is that the United States will adopt what is essentially a subversive foreign policy agenda: to promote the liberalization of political and economic systems in the Third World.

In one sense, there is nothing new about this. Both the United States and most European countries have been ostensibly committed to development and modernization in the Third World for many decades, and both have gone through spasms of commitment to the promotion of human rights. Indeed, the European Union actually preceded the United States in appreciating the security threat to itself stemming from political repression, economic regression, and social stagnation in neighboring areas. That appreciation gave rise to the Euro-Mediterranean Partnership (EMP), an initiative undertaken by the EU in 1995 to promote democratization, civil society, and human rights in the Mediterranean through dialogue and economic incentives, including a Euro-Mediterranean free trade area.

What is different about the American approach now, therefore, is not the mere conviction that the ills associated with the failure to move the modernization project forward – ills vividly documented by the 2002 Arab Human Development Report of the United Nations – constitute a direct threat to its national security. Instead, it is the apparent determination to push the modernization project with greater vigor, even if that no longer means only working with existing regimes but also working against them. In other words, the United States has apparently concluded that it can no longer rely exclusively on inducements such as security support and economic assistance to elicit greater domestic liberalization, but that it must be prepared to apply some degree of coercion and run the risk of confrontation with authoritarian regimes, even those otherwise deemed "friendly" or "moderate." If this truly reflects the intent of the United States, then it will diverge in its behavior from the practice of the Europeans, who, at least thus far, have confined themselves to working with existing regimes.

Yet outside of the military sphere, it will be very difficult for the United States alone to make coercion truly effective. This is not because the US lacks non-military instruments of its own. After all, American diplomatic and economic levers are not inconsequential and the costs of defying strong American preferences, even if they are pursued unilaterally, cannot be blithely dismissed as negligible. But these instruments do not begin to "dominate the market" in the same way that American military power does. Consequently, the threat of American political and economic sanctions, unless coordinated with a critical mass of other international actors, cannot have the same impact. In short, non-military unilateralism by the United States is not nearly as feasible an option as is military unilateralism. Thus, in situations where the threat of military force is not credible, the United States will continue to need the support of others. That means that the international system, in many important respects, remains multipolar.

Building a Coalition on the Middle East

Both the need for cooperation with others and the difficulty of obtaining it will almost certainly be most evident with respect to the Muslim world, especially the Middle East. The need derives from the fact that this is where the greatest socioeconomic dysfunction is found and from where the greatest new security threats emanate. By nearly all indicators of political and economic openness, the Middle East lags behind most other regions of the world, in some respects even behind sub-Saharan Africa. With a few notable exceptions, such as North Korea, Myanmar, and Cuba, almost all the remaining authoritarian governments and state-controlled economies are concentrated there. Again with a few exceptions, it is also the region that generates the most intense concerns about proliferation of weapons of mass destruction and long-range delivery systems, where the most virulent anti-Western sentiment is cultivated, and from which (at least according to the US State Department list of state sponsors of terrorism) the most numerous and destructive perpetrators of terrorism draw their support, inspiration, financing, and recruits.

The difficulty of securing cooperation stems from the fact that this is where the other major international actors find the greatest opportunities to assert their independence from the United States and the fewest reasons to align themselves with the US in pursuing confrontational policies with local regimes. To some extent this is merely a local/regional manifestation of a global problem. There is a general aversion of other states and international organizations to be seen as accomplices or tools of an America suspected of hegemonic aspirations – an aversion that applies to states as geographically remote from the region as China or Brazil. Most other international actors, especially in Europe, do not endorse the American view that coercion, especially military force, is a legitimate instrument of foreign policy except in direct self-defense (even if they themselves resort to coercive actions). That difference in values, rather than any disparity in available resources, explains the Euro-American gap in military procurement and R&D (indeed, the combined domestic product of EU members actually outstrips the GDP of the United States).

But beyond this general aversion there are specific reasons why other actors will be reluctant to alienate regional governments and vocal publics in Arab or Muslim countries. These include dependence on oil, the absence of visible and effective liberal opposition movements in most of these countries, and sensitivity about participating in what will inevitably be described by the targets of American-led action as an anti-Muslim or anti-Arab crusade. This latter consideration is particularly compelling in countries with large Muslim minorities.

Both the general and the specific reasons have particular resonance in Europe, especially in some of the larger countries where participation in American-led enterprises is believed to compromise independent stature in global affairs, and in Russia. The European Union as well as some of its leading members, notably France, believes that Europeans have an even greater stake in Middle Eastern/North African/Mediterranean affairs than does the United States because of geographical proximity, closer economic links (including a larger share of Middle Eastern import markets, which they are reluctant to lose, and greater dependence on Middle Eastern sources of energy, which they are reluctant to jeopardize), and a larger domestic Muslim/Arab population. They also believe that they have a better understanding of these regions because of longer – if not always happier – experience dealing with former colonies as well as closer ongoing economic and cultural ties with them. Some of them even claim a more nuanced appreciation of terrorism due to longer exposure to it at home. For these reasons, several of these countries have invested considerable diplomatic resources in the region, and the EU as a whole has made the Middle East the centerpiece of its Common Foreign and Security Policy.

Indeed, EU and European national preoccupation with the region has served as a major vehicle for promoting an international identity distinct from the United States, which they accuse of being excessively partial to Israel and excessively focused on military–security issues. France, for example, was motivated to elaborate its "politique Arabe," implying a special and especially indulgent French relationship with the Arab world, for much the same reason that drove its decisions to develop an independent nuclear capability, withdraw from NATO's unified military command structure, and more recently, promote the establishment of an EU military planning headquarters separate from NATO, namely, to assert its international uniqueness and autonomy from the United States. The persistent tendency to seek international identity and prominence through acts of expressive policy does not augur well for the prospects of sustained and effective coordination under American leadership in policies likely to arouse resistance from regimes and vocal opinion leaders in the Arab/Muslim world.

This means that it will be difficult for the United States to assemble broad coalitions to promote American-defined solutions to various challenges. With respect to Europe, this will be particularly true in the unlikely event that the European Union manages to fashion a truly unified and coherent foreign and security policy dominated by countries uncomfortable with American activism in areas of traditional European preeminence. But even if European states retain a large measure of autonomy in foreign/security policy, the challenge of finding coalition partners for future solutions construed by Middle Eastern regimes as intrusive or aggressive may well be even more daunting than was the case with Iraq. In the most extreme cases involving large-scale military intervention, that does not necessarily pose a problem insofar as the conduct of military operations is concerned. In most cases, American power alone is sufficient to eliminate hostile regimes of rogue states or, where regimes barely function, to take physical control of failed states (or parts of them).

But if the purpose afterward is to transform the societies that harbor terrorists and/or weapons of mass destruction, then there must be sustained follow-up in the form of humanitarian assistance, peacekeeping, law enforcement, the entrenchment of political institutions, and the propagation of different political values – in short, "nation building." American military forces are not trained or equipped for these sorts of tasks. Nor are they inclined to undertake them. Postwar transformation relies on different sorts of skills, resources, and experiences. It is not clear that any externally sponsored project in nation building can ever really succeed anywhere. But early indications from Afghanistan and even more preliminary evidence from Iraq make it clear that for the project to have any chance of success, skills, resources, and experiences are needed that the US, alone, does not possess in sufficient quantities. In other words, for a military action, even a unilateral one, to accomplish its political purpose, the US will need to mobilize the willing involvement of other states and international organizations, including the United Nations, which have those critical support systems and resources.

The need for international cooperation is also apparent in less extreme situations, where the purpose is not to replace a regime or create one where it effectively doesn't exist, but rather to influence through coercive means the domestic and international behavior of functioning regimes. In moderate cases, this implies diplomatic and/or economic sanctions (for example, boycotts or embargoes). Here too, the United States has some unilateral capacity to act, and it is rarely possible for any other individual country to step in and adequately fill whatever diplomatic, economic, or security role the US plays. But it is also rarely possible for the United States, acting alone, to apply enough pressure or sufficiently comprehensive sanctions to bring about change in the behavior of regimes, particularly when that change represents a threat to the long-term survival of a regime. For such pressure or sanctions to be effective they need to encompass a critical mass of other diplomatic and/or economic actors, so that any remaining cracks in the wall of containment are not wide enough for regimes to wiggle through.

The problem is that sanctions almost always also imply some diplomatic and/or economic costs to the states that apply them, or to important domestic elements within those states, and they almost always provoke opposition on humanitarian grounds, because they punish innocent civilians rather than the government they are intended to target. Even the post-1991 sanctions regime against Iraq, which enjoyed indisputable international legitimacy in the form of UN Security Council resolutions, was not immune to these sorts of counter-considerations. Given the nature of vested economic interests and domestic political calculations, especially in Europe, any future call for sanctions against other Muslim or Arab states is likely to elicit even less cooperation and compliance. And given the fact that Europe, not the United States, is the largest trading partner for most states in the region, any refusal to exercise potential European leverage will constitute a particularly wide crack in any wall.

Finally, even the mildest form of American coercion – assistance made contingent on compliance with donor-defined criteria – cannot be effective if it is only unilateral. There is a whole range of performance standards that do not immediately produce democracy but do pose longer term, if not immediate, threats to the viability of authoritarian systems. Some of these are explicitly political, such as independent judiciaries, tolerance of civil society, free press, and uncontrolled movement of ideas. Some are them are implicit in economic restructuring, such as financial transparency, sanctity of contracts, campaigns against corruption, and reduction or elimination of monopolies, licensing arrangements, indirect taxes, and other controls on the movement of people, goods, services, and capital. But all of them go to the heart of how bureaucratic–patrimonial regimes survive. The European Union made an effort to promote some of these standards in the EMP through material inducements – accession agreements, assistance funds, technical support, encouragement of regional economic cooperation and cultural dialogue, the promise of a free trade area – but it never threatened to withhold these "carrots" in case of failure to comply. Nor did its individual members make their own assistance programs contingent on conformity by regional recipients with their own standards of governance. In part, they probably hoped that any incidental economic improvement would reduce the pressures causing illegal immigration into Europe. In part, they were responsive to complaints that such action would constitute unwarranted interference in domestic affairs and contempt for the sovereign rights of recipient states. By and large, American policy in the past has operated in a similar manner. But even if post-9/11, post-Afghanistan, post-Iraq thinking augurs a change in American behavior in this regard, that change cannot have a truly decisive impact unless it is simultaneously implemented by a sufficient number of other providers of financial, technical, and/or security assistance.

Uni-Multipolarity in the International System

All in all, the implications are clear. In the international system, the United States is not even "first among equals" because there are no presumptive equals. Instead, it is the preeminent actor in almost every respect, particularly in respect of military power. As a result, it has the capacity along with the will to act unilaterally when it feels that its vital interests are threatened and to resist the demands by others eager to constrain it in the hope of transforming the international system into a kind of European Union writ large, in which some components of identity and sovereignty are transferred to supranational institutions, all disputes are settled peacefully on the basis of supranational consensus or international law defined by multilateral consultation and negotiation, and force (except in totally unambiguous and highly unusual instances of self-defense against direct aggression by other states) is effectively banished from the repertoire of foreign policy.

At the same time, however, American power alone is far from sufficient to accomplish ambitious goals of conflict resolution between and political–social transformation within states that are the source of the most palpable political–security threats. To act effectively against these threats, the US will need to convince others of the nature and immediacy of these threats and of the legitimacy of the actions it proposes to take against them. "Others" does not necessarily mean global or even regional institutions and organizations. There can be no delusion about the near impossibility of mobilizing universal support based on general principles for anything the US wishes to do anytime or anywhere (especially in the Middle East). Nor is it likely that the United States will agree to condition its actions on such support and thus find itself in a situation of Gulliver-like paralysis. In this sense, the demand by some that the US subordinate its foreign policy to the United Nations Security Council is highly unrealistic (as it is even for some far less powerful countries).

Still, the United States will continually have to engage in some kind of ad hoc coalition building. Tailoring the coalition to the mission is less diplomatically demanding than tailoring the mission to preexisting coalitions, because the lowest common denominator of "coalitions of the willing" is, by definition, higher than that of broader target audiences. Even so, any coalition of more than one will oblige the US to take some account of the concerns of potential coalition partners, including their concerns about the objective of the mission and the means employed. Building a sufficient base of international sympathy and support therefore inevitably means some dilution of or compromise on American preferences, not just on the immediate issue at stake, but also, perhaps as part of a trade-off, on other specific issues or general matters like environmental codes of conduct or universal criminal jurisdiction.

If this is the course that events take, then American policy, though probably impelled by an underlying unilateralist impulse, will necessarily include elements of substantial multilateralism. Of course, there is no assurance that the US administration will recognize this necessity and act according to its logic, or, even if it does, that it will be able to mobilize the degree of international support it seeks. But even in the aftermath of military operations in Iraq, there are indications that this reality is imposing itself on all parties. In UN Security Council deliberations and other consultations about post-war Iraq, the US has attempted to involve other states and the United Nations in post-war reconstruction, though not at the price of forfeiting ultimate control; and other powers – individually and within the framework of the UN – have shown a willingness to be involved, even if that implies *post factum* legitimation of a war they had previously opposed.

This situation simply reflects a distribution of power dictating an international system that is neither truly unipolar nor truly multipolar, but rather some kind of hybrid that might be termed uni-multipolarity. In a bow to the vocabulary of European Union discourse, it might also be described as "variable geometry." However, the engine at the center of this variable global geometry will be the United States, and the primary authority and responsibility for determining its success or failure will remain in American hands for a long time to come.

The Foreign and Defense Policy of the Bush Administration

2

Abraham Ben-Zvi

An Overview of Twentieth-Century US Foreign Policy

The history of American foreign and defense policy from the beginning of the twentieth century is characterized by dramatic fluctuations between divergent theoretical and practical approaches. Intensive involvement in the international arena, originating in the desire to reshape the external environment on the basis of new premises, contrasts with periods of disengagement, relative or complete, from the outside diplomatic world, without any effort to influence developments abroad – as indeed happened between the two world wars.

President Woodrow Wilson sought to build a new world order on the basis of his "Fourteen Points" and viewed American entrance into World War I as the necessary springboard for promoting his comprehensive political, ideological, and territorial vision, which was predicated upon his conviction that the entire international system could be fundamentally reformed on the basis of democratic ideas and principles. In contrast, the administrations that followed his presidency largely avoided such a sweeping definition of the changes required in the domestic structure and modus operandi of the national units comprising the international body politic. And although at the outset of the Cold War several American leaders such as John Foster Dulles, who from 1953 to 1959 served as Secretary of State in Dwight Eisenhower's administration, did occasionally allude to the need to roll the Soviet empire back from Eastern Europe, their actual policy was largely rooted in the defensive premises of containment, deterrence, and coercion.[1]

To this end, a comprehensive ring of regional security alliances was formed, among them NATO, which sought to encircle the Soviet Union with a tight chain of countervailing forces in the hope of preventing the Soviet Union from threatening or disrupting the territorial status quo. In the Middle East this defensive strategy was evident in the joint American and British effort to forge the Baghdad

Pact for the purpose of aborting Soviet encroachment into the region in light of the British decision to disengage from most of their strategic strongholds, including their bases in the Suez Canal area.

It is true that from time to time offensive initiatives and stratagems supplemented this predominantly defensive posture. These initiatives attempted, through political, economic, and military means, to bring about regime change in certain states, for example, Cuba. However, in most instances these attempts fell considerably short of a direct and undisguised challenge to the leadership in power and largely involved clandestine, behind-the-scenes, and proxy operations (as was the case in Iran in 1953, Guatemala in 1954, Syria in 1957, Cuba in 1961, and Chile in 1973). In the case of the military measures that were taken by the Clinton administration against the Serbian regime of Slobodan Milosevic, the initiation of air strikes in Kosovo in March 1999 was an integral part of a collective operation conducted under the auspices of NATO, and enjoyed broad international support and legitimacy.[2]

Furthermore, even in cases of massive military intervention such as in Korea and Vietnam, the logic of the American operations (except in the second phase of the Korean War) was purely defensive. The initial Korean War objectives of 1950 were to repel North Korea's invasion into the South; and a decade later, the US objectives were to prevent North Vietnam from occupying the South through its Vietcong forces already in South Vietnam, that is, from establishing a Communist regime in the entire Vietnam peninsula. In the second stage of the Korean conflict, President Truman decided to abandon his initial strategy of containment, and to embark instead on an offensive strategy designed to bring about a unification of the entire Korean peninsula under a pro-Western regime. With Vietnam, however, Presidents Kennedy, Johnson, and Nixon sought to preserve or restore the territorial status quo rather than to initiate change in the structure and modus operandi of adversarial governments.

An examination of the first eight months of George W. Bush's tenure as president indicates that they were predicated upon the traditional premises of containment and deterrence (which, during the Clinton era, were incorporated into the "dual containment" doctrine). While the Bush foreign and defense policy elites were initially predisposed to pursue a unilateralist, largely exclusionist posture, they sought to minimize the risk of military entanglements in Third World areas such as Haiti and Somalia, where the US became militarily involved during Clinton's tenure as president, and instead to rely upon the tools of deterrence and coercive diplomacy in confronting challenges and threats to American security. Thus, while betraying a generalized and unbounded skepticism toward international organizations, frameworks, and agreements – such as the Kyoto Climate Change Agreement – President Bush initially looked upon the "big stick strategy" as a less costly alternative to his predecessor's posture of selective diplomatic and military engagements.

Against this backdrop, it is clear that while the administration's determination to advance its plans for National Missile Defense (NMD) program, even at the cost of withdrawing from the 1972 Anti-Ballistic Missile (ABM) treaty, exacerbated tension within the American–Russian framework and thus quintessentially reflected its unilateralist approach, it was also indicative of its defensive orientation, since the NMD program was intended to protect the US mainland from a missile attack. Similarly, notwithstanding the fact that American–Chinese relations during the early months of the Bush administration were fraught with tension in the wake of the collision in April 2001 of an American EP-3E aircraft and a Chinese F-8 fighter and the subsequent detention of the American crew by the Chinese authorities, the administration's behavior during the crisis was characterized by utmost caution and consistent reluctance to resort to the strong retaliatory economic and trade sanctions against the Chinese government demanded by Congress.[3]

The Impact of September 11 on Foreign Policy

A similar picture of caution and determination to control the risks of escalation in acute adversarial crises emerges when the first eight months of the Bush presidency are examined through the Iraqi prism. Indeed, although since its inception the Bush administration was highly critical of President Clinton's de facto acquiescence in Baghdad's rejection of intrusive, on-site inspections of weapons-making facilities, prior to September 11, 2001, this criticism was not accompanied by measures designed to restore the inspection regime or to implement Bush's policy of "smart sanctions."[4]

Indeed, during the period preceding the September 11 attacks, the neo-conservative belief that American foreign policy should be prepared to take the initiative and not merely react in confronting national security threats was decidedly a minority view. As such, the case for launching preventive strikes unilaterally by using American military hegemony as the means of destroying the recalcitrant forces of international terrorism, if broad global support for this measure was not forthcoming, amounted to nothing more than an intellectual platform. In general, the insistence that the US should incorporate in its defense posture the principle of preemption as the most appropriate tactic in the war against the hidden world of terrorism remained in this early period outside the operational code of the Bush presidency.[5]

It is true that the neo-conservative agenda had increasingly permeated and influenced the thinking of several policymakers and defense analysts at the Pentagon over the preceding decade. Furthermore, the enthusiastic recommendation published in 1996 of two of the most prominent advocates of the neo-conservative vision, Robert Kagan and William Kristol, fully coincided with the strategic thinking of several members of the Pentagon's high policy elite. Their position argued that overwhelming power should be used against either tyrants or terrorist organizations worldwide as the necessary springboard for replacing such states or networks with peaceful democratic regimes.[6] Yet it was only in the aftermath of September 11, 2001, when the warning issued by Kagan and Kristol five years earlier of the immediate danger inherent in international terrorism backed by a group of rogue states proved valid, that advocacy of the doctrine of preemptive military strikes against even potential and embryonic threats to American security gained credence. Thus, although long before the trauma of September 11 unfolded Pentagon officials such as Deputy Secretary of Defense Paul Wolfowitz and then Chairman of the Defense Policy Board Richard Perle strongly supported the neo-conservative military prescription for forcefully eliminating international terrorism and its supporting axis of evil as an avenue to realizing the Wilsonian dream of an unimpaired global democratic order, in the wake of this watershed they could form the nucleus of a majority coalition within the administration, which enabled them to promote this vision actively, first through Afghanistan and later Iraq.

The official and operational guide for action, which quintessentially reflected neo-conservative premises and beliefs as to the most appropriate way for coping with national security threats of great magnitude, was published on September 17, 2002 as a compilation of several presidential statements and addresses, and was named "The National Security Strategy of the United States of America" (NSS).[7]

Given the evolution in policy orientation, and after the military campaign in Afghanistan was concluded successfully, it was only natural for the Bush administration to focus on the oppressive regime of Saddam Hussein as the target for its next onslaught. Not only did the Iraqi leader expel UN inspectors in December 1998, but Iraq's compliance with UN resolutions over the last decade was partial at best, a fact that gave rise to a growing American fear – which perhaps ironically has so far not been even partially substantiated – that Baghdad was in possession of chemical and biological Weapons of Mass Destruction (WMD).

The national trauma of September 11 provided an impetus for reinforcing yet another pre-existing predilection of the Bush administration, namely, its willingness to deviate from the multilateral legacy of the Clinton presidency, a willingness that was fully manifested in its decision to initiate war against Iraq even without the support of most members of the UN Security Council.

In the final analysis, therefore, it was the convergence between the events of September 11, whose scope and magnitude overshadowed the administration's initial reluctance to intervene directly and militarily in international crises, and its innate skepticism toward multilateral institutions, organizations, and frameworks, that paved the road toward the Iraqi campaign. This road was fundamentally different in terms of the nature of the strategic decision it implied from the broad consensual road along which the US and the international community jointly and steadily advanced toward the Gulf War in 1991. As such, this unilateral, exclusionist route reflected the victory, at least in the Iraqi context, of the neo-ideology and its proponents within the Bush foreign and defense policy apparatus. These advocates, and particularly Wolfowitz and Perle, ultimately managed to win the support of virtually all representatives of the traditionalist–conservative line of thinking – who were initially motivated by a cluster of unilateralist balance of power considerations, but without any desire to radically transform the international system – including President Bush, Vice President Richard Cheney, Secretary of Defense Donald Rumsfeld, and National Security Advisor Condoleezza Rice, for the offensive approach of initiating war against Iraq as an impetus for regime change and democratization across the Middle East in a quintessential Wilsonian fashion.

The decision of the traditionalist–conservative members of the administration to set aside their initial caution and to join forces with proponents of the neo-conservative strategy guaranteed that advocates of a third foreign policy orientation were sharply outnumbered at the end of the intra-governmental bargaining over the appropriate course to be adopted not only in the Iraqi theater, but toward the Security Council as well. Specifically, those who competed for influence in the shaping of the American foreign and defense posture with a strategy based upon liberal–multilateral premises carried much less weight than before. And indeed, faced with a powerful coalition comprising the neo-conservatives and the traditional or "old" conservatives in support of a unilateral posture once the initial effort to consolidate a broad margin of support in the Security Council for a de facto war resolution against Iraq proved abortive, Secretary of State Colin Powell, the chief advocate of the multilateral approach, had little choice but to acquiesce.[8]

From the vantage point of the global international system, the adoption by the Bush administration of an exclusionist strategy in the Iraqi context reaffirmed the fact that the US was, in the aftermath of the collapse of the Soviet empire, the only superpower with overwhelming and unassailable military and economic capabilities. This fact remained largely obscured during the Clinton era, where the administration tended in most instances to predicate its foreign policy behavior upon multilateral premises. Seeking to promote international order and economic growth and stability through a broad network of regional and global institutions such as the World Trade Organization (WTO), the North American Free Trade Agreement (NAFTA), and Asia Pacific Economic Cooperation (APEC), the Clinton presidency was in fact prepared to downplay or obfuscate its hegemonic nature in the international system and thus relinquish a broad range of unilateral advantages that were inherent in its status as the undisputed hegemonic power.[9]

From its inception the Bush administration had been highly skeptical of various forms of multilateral behavior, particularly in the context of certain pending international agreements such as the Kyoto Agreement and the Biological Weapons Convention. The events of September 11 provided the catalyst to abandon the era of multilateral economic and security order and assume instead a strong, undisguised, and offensive exclusionist posture that superseded a commitment to international institutions.[10] This posture surpassed the specific objective of fighting international terrorism in general and al-Qaeda in particular, and incorporated sweeping objectives such as the desire "to extend the American vision of freedom across the globe"[11] by forcefully challenging, and ultimately uprooting, dictatorial and autocratic regimes, whose intrinsic nature posed a threat, potential or actual, to American security in a variety of ways – such as developing WMD or providing support to terrorist groups. According to Perle, one of the chief advocates of the neo-conservative doctrine that underscores its exclusionist core, "It is wonderful to have the support of our friends and allies, but our foremost consideration has to be to protect this country and not to take a vote among others as to how we should do it."[12]

And indeed, by virtue of its magnitude and impact upon American strategic thinking, the tragedy of September 11 can be viewed as a traumatic, formative event that precipitated a profound and immediate change in the longstanding, traditional modus operandi of American foreign policy, from the conservative pole of an effort to defend the status quo to the revisionist extreme of seeking to transform the entire international system so that it conforms to American ideas, values, and institutions. Thus, contrary to President Clinton's definition of American strategic interests and objectives in terms of an accelerated and peaceful democratization process, which was patterned on the need to integrate non-democratic actors (such as China) into global economic frameworks, and contrary as well to the defensive logic of the containment doctrine throughout the Cold War, the September 11 attack generated a new and vastly expanded definition of the scope of national security threats, which called upon the administration to abandon or downgrade, at least temporarily, traditional tools of diplomacy such as deterrence and concentrate instead on the strategy of military preemption as the means of establishing a peaceful, democratic, and durable world order. As President Bush stated in his West Point address of June 1, 2002 and as was later incorporated into the NSS, since the US was now confronted with rogue states, whose leaders were "willing to take risks, gambling with the lives of their people" and to use weapons of mass destruction as "tools of intimidation and military aggression against their neighbors," it had a "compelling" case for acting preemptively in order "to forestall or prevent such hostile acts by our adversaries."[13]

Clearly, whereas the strategic vision of President Clinton was highly optimistic, based on his conviction that all major global powers could be induced to liberalize their economies and eventually their societies and political systems as well, no such optimism characterized the post-September 11 thinking of the Bush foreign policy and defense entourage. Motivated by an acute and sudden sense of vulnerability, the Bush administration therefore decided that, "given the goals of rogue states and terrorists," it could no longer "solely rely on a reactive posture as we have in the past." Hence, "the inability to deter a potential attacker, the immediacy of today's threats, and the magnitude of potential harm that could be caused by our adversaries' choice of weapons, do not permit that option. We cannot let our enemies strike first."[14]

In the Aftermath of the War

For all its inherent simplicity and internal logic, the new preemptive doctrine, which was formally inaugurated in September 2002, has yet to provide the operational impetus for a broad range of regional moves and developments beyond the limited Iraqi context, except perhaps in the Palestinian sphere. In other words, the actual linkage between the Iraqi campaign and the envisioned transformation in the structure of other social and political systems, particularly those approximating the axis of evil model, remained largely tenuous in the immediate aftermath of the war. Not only has the effort to link the Iraqi regime to international terrorism and the possession of WMD failed so far to furnish any compelling, definitive proof, but the expectation that the destruction of the Saddam regime would instantly and profoundly affect the foreign policy behavior of such regional actors as Iran and Syria has similarly faded into the background as a long-term ideal at best.

Furthermore, in relying in Afghanistan and Iraq exclusively on the premises of preemption and war initiation, the new strategy embedded in the September 17, 2002 presidential document seriously downgraded the traditional tools of coercive diplomacy, namely, the strategies of deterrence and coercion. Clearly, while these defensive strategies may well prove ineffective "against suicidal terrorist organizations," they were quite successful during the Cold War in containing the threat of rogue states and might, therefore, be no less effective in containing secular and non-ideological adversaries.[15]

Under these circumstances the adoption of the offensive strategy of preventive war as a panacea for uprooting adversarial regimes that are devoid of any militant ideological fervor "can entail considerable . . . political risk, depending upon local, regional, and international circumstances,"[16] including the risk of a long and costly military occupation. Such a course can, therefore, deprive the US of the needed margin of maneuverability in the pursuit of a flexible and expedient foreign and defense policy, which would seek through the use of traditional diplomatic methods, including the strategy of accommodation, to promote American interests without becoming entangled in protracted conflicts and disputes.

Moreover, even in the Iraqi context, it is still far from clear whether or not the successful conclusion of the war has indeed laid the groundwork for the establishment of viable and effective democratic institutions. Nor is it likely that the Iraqi precedent would soon precipitate a similar military course *vis-à-vis* additional parties, be they states or organizations that either support international terrorism or are engaged in the development of WMD.

What is particularly striking in this respect is the fact that the harsh criticism directed by the administration in the course of the war at the Syrian regime of Bashar Assad did not focus mainly on its continued support for Hizbollah in South Lebanon and for such Palestinian terrorist organizations as Hamas and Islamic Jihad (or on its chemical WMD), but rather on its military and strategic collaboration with the regime of Saddam Hussein on the very eve of its downfall. The fact that Secretary of State Colin Powell included Damascus in his Middle Eastern visit of May 2003 further indicates that, despite its belligerent rhetoric and offensive doctrine, the administration did not altogether abandon the traditional components of diplomacy, including the use of "positive sanctions" and inducements along with the less benign albeit defensive tools of deterrence and coercion, as the means of restraining adversaries without resorting to war.

A similar picture of a lapse or at least partial incompatibility between the administration's pre-war rhetoric and doctrine and its actual post-war behavior is provided by a brief examination of its conduct in the Israeli–Palestinian sphere. During the period preceding September 11, American policy within the Israeli–Palestinian framework was closely predicated upon the notion of incrementalism, with the Palestinian Authority (PA) expected to make the first move en route to conflict reduction and eventual accommodation with Israel. Specifically, the Mitchell Report of April 30, 2001 envisioned the entire peace construct as contingent upon a series of strictly unilateral moves incumbent on the PA as a precondition for any future reciprocal Israeli measures. In this report, the confidence-building phase, which calls for Israel to freeze its settlement activity, had to be preceded by seven days of complete tranquility, followed by a six-week cooling-off period. Then, and only then, would Israel be called upon to confront head on the highly-charged settlements issue.[17]

This perception of the peacemaking process as gradual and incremental, with the Palestinians depicted as the party required to provide Israel with the initial reassurances that they were indeed determined to combat terrorism, surfaced once again in the aftermath of September 11, and reflected President Bush's acute sensitivity to the dangers inherent in unabated terrorism. Thus, in a June 24, 2002 address, the President (following the logic and basic premises of the Mitchell Report), portrayed the impetus for progress in strictly unilateral terms, with the Palestinians required to undertake sweeping constitutional, financial, leadership, and security reforms before Israel had to contribute its share in the eventual trade-off.

However, a juxtaposition of the President's June 24, 2002 peace vision and of the roadmap that was released by the Quartet – of which the administration is a member – exactly two years after the Mitchell Report was published (on April 30, 2003), indicates a significant deviation from the premises of asymmetrical progress and incrementalism to which the Bush administration previously had been fully committed. Specifically, whereas President Bush's June 24, 2002 vision was predicated upon one unilateral precipitant, namely, the accomplishment of a far-reaching reform of Palestinian institutions, leadership, and modus operandi, the Quartet roadmap envisioned the path toward accommodation as a sequence of simultaneous reciprocal Israeli and Palestinian moves, including at the initial phase of fighting terrorism. Indeed, at each phase of the process Palestinian confidence-building measures must therefore be matched by concurrent and fully compatible Israeli steps, such as the affirmation of the Israeli commitment to the vision of an independent Palestinian state alongside Israel.[18]

Apparently motivated by a complex mélange of pragmatic considerations, including the desire to persuade Middle East states that the administration is not anti-Arab or anti-Muslim, to compensate such parties as Saudi Arabia for quietly supporting the US in the war, and to accommodate the domestic and inter-European needs of British Prime Minister Tony Blair, President Bush's most committed and loyal coalition partner, the administration opted to set aside at least some of its previous positions in the Israeli–Palestinian sphere. By endorsing the roadmap, and by insisting that it be fully and unequivocally accepted by Israel, it clearly decided to reduce its demands concerning the scope of the necessary reforms in the PA. Further encouraged by the election of Mahmoud Abbas (Abu Mazen) as the Palestinian Prime Minister and by the decision of Israeli Prime Minister Ariel Sharon to endorse the roadmap, the American leadership ultimately decided de facto to abandon, or at least to set aside, several components of its initial vision of Palestinian reform that were incorporated into President Bush's speech of June 24, 2002.

Notwithstanding these tactical deviations, and seen from a strategic vantage point, the administration's post-war diplomacy in the Palestinian sphere can still be legitimately regarded as essentially related to the neo-conservative doctrine and compatible with its basic premises. Since this doctrine envisioned a direct and almost automatic linkage between the Iraqi campaign and the subsequent trans-formation in the structure of other regional, social, and political systems and entities, it was only natural for President Bush to look for additional windows of opportunity for progress along the road toward accomplishing the Wilsonian dream of democracy.

It is indeed at this juncture that the Quartet roadmap, despite deviating in several critical components from the president's June 24, 2002 peace vision, joined the election of Abu Mazen as prime minister to become the main springboard for the administration in the reinvigorated effort to translate its strategic and ideolog-ical thinking into a new, more benign, and democratic reality in the Palestinian arena.

The initial effort to reclaim and exert US leverage as an undisputed super-power that was demonstrated in Iraq by the readiness to use force to combat the threat of rogue states and international terrorism and lay the groundwork for a fun-damentally revised regional environment, may appear successful in the Israeli–Palestinian context in the immediate aftermath of the Sharm el-Sheik and Aqaba summits of June 2003. It does not guarantee, of course, that the roadmap will be smoothly implemented even with the encouragement and prodding of a deter-mined hegemon (as indicated by the wave of renewed Palestinian terror that erupted in the immediate aftermath of the Aqaba summit). With the parties still separated by irreconcilable views concerning core issues, and with the president about to become increasingly preoccupied with the exigencies of the 2004 presi-dential campaign, the road toward accommodation and reconciliation may still be long and rocky.

Ultimately, then, if he is unable to proceed quickly beyond the first phase of the Israeli–Palestinian ceasefire, President Bush may well decide to postpone his dream of comprehensively transforming and resolving this predicament for the sake of concentrating on a considerably less ambitious enterprise: winning reelec-tion. If this scenario indeed materializes it would mark the beginning of a new swing of the pendulum of American foreign policy back from the pole of inter-vention and engagement toward the axis of selective involvement and even occasional disengagement, inspired by the desire to minimize the risks inherent in a prolonged entanglement in an area where the administration has already become – as in Iraq – deeply engaged, both militarily and politically.

Finally, beyond its intrinsic significance in the context of the Middle East, a swing of this sort would become yet another chapter in a long tradition of ideo-logical fluctuations and policy shifts between idealism and realism, or between the utopian and the practical, with the architects of American diplomacy and strategy repeatedly forced to shift gear and thus recognize the inherent incompatibility between psychological and operational environments, between the envisioned and the real, and between the desired and the feasible.

Notes

1 John Lewis Gaddis, "A Grand Strategy of Transformation," *Foreign Policy* 133 (November–December 2002): 50–55.
2 Andrew Bennett, "Who Rules the Roost? Congressional-Executive Relations on Foreign Policy After the Cold War," in Robert J. Lieber (ed.), *Eagle Rules? Foreign Policy and American Primacy in the Twenty-First Century* (Upper Saddle River, NJ: Prentice Hall, 2002), pp. 47–69.
3 Bennett, "Who Rules the Roost," p. 69.
4 Abraham Ben-Zvi, "The Bush Administration, the Middle East and Israel: In the Shadow of September 11," *Strategic Assessment* 4, no. 4 (2002): 12–17.
5 Ben-Zvi, "The Bush Administration, the Middle East and Israel," p. 13. See also Michael Hirsh, "Bush and the World," *Foreign Affairs* 81, no. 5 (2002): 18–43.
6 William Kristol and Robert Kagan, "Toward a Neo-Reaganite Foreign Policy," *Foreign Affairs* 75, no. 4 (1996): 18–32.
7 National Security Strategy of the United States, www.whitehouse.gov/nsc/nss.pdf, hereafter NSS.
8 Hirsh, "Bush and the World," p. 25.
9 G. John Ikenberry, "American Grand Strategy in the Age of Terror," *Survival* 43, no. 4 (2001): 19–34. See also Stanley Hoffmann, "The United States and International Organizations," in *Eagle Rules?* pp. 342–52.
10 Edward Rhodes, "The Imperial Logic of Bush's Liberal Agenda," *Survival* 45, no. 1 (2003): 131–153. See also Ikenberry, "American Grand Strategy in the Age of Terror," p. 26.
11 Rhodes, "The Imperial Logic of Bush's Liberal Agenda," p. 135.
12 Quoted by Ikenberry, "American Grand Strategy in the Age of Terror," p. 27.
13 NSS, p. 15.
14 NSS, p. 15.
15 Jeffrey Record, "The Bush Doctrine and War with Iraq," *Parameters* 33, no. 1 (2003): 4–21.
16 Record, "The Bush Doctrine and War with Iraq," p. 14.
17 Abraham Ben-Zvi, "Playing Different Melodies," *The Jerusalem Post*, March 14, 2003, p. B2; Ben-Zvi, "The Bush Administration," p. 15.
18 Ben-Zvi, "Playing Different Melodies," p. B2.

Deterrence, Prevention, and Other Strategies

Yair Evron

In the National Security Strategy (NSS) published in September 2002, references were made to several basic strategic concepts that actually have been in use in the security studies literature for many years: deterrence, prevention, preemption, and anticipatory action. While the document reemphasized the centrality of deterrence as a strategy designed to defeat various threats to the United States, it presented the need for the US to rely also on additional strategies in order to deal with the range of new threats, primarily international terrorism, a threat that would be even more acute if bolstered by Weapons of Mass Destruction (WMD).

As Francois Heisbourg pointed out, the formulations in the NSS appear to have developed gradually in the administration over quite some time.[1] Thus, for example, in his State of the Union address on January 29, 2002, President Bush declared, "We must prevent the terrorists and regimes who seek chemical, biological, or nuclear weapons from threatening the United States and the world. . . . I will not wait on events, while dangers gather." In his commencement speech at West Point on June 1, 2002, he said, "For much of the last century, America's defense relied on the Cold War doctrines of deterrence and containment. In some cases, those strategies still apply. But new threats also require new thinking. . . . If we wait for threats to fully materialize, we will have waited too long. . . . We must take the battle to the enemy . . . and confront the worst threats before they emerge."

Heisbourg also quotes Deputy Secretary of Defense Paul Wolfowitz, who developed the same subject in an address to the International Institute for Strategic Studies on December 2, 2002: "The notion that we can wait to prepare assumes that we know when the threat is imminent. . . . When were the attacks of September 11 imminent? Certainly they were imminent on September 10, although we didn't know it. . . . Anyone who believes that we can wait until we have certain knowledge that attacks are imminent, has failed to connect the dots that led to September 11."

The emphasis on the new and various strategic approaches appears in Chapter 5 of the NSS (entitled "Prevent Our Enemies from Threatening Us, Our Allies, and Our Friends with Weapons of Mass Destruction"), which elaborates on the concepts of preemption and anticipatory action, while implying as well the need for a strategy of prevention. Significantly, the American attack on Iraq had several rationales, objectives, and implications that can be characterized as falling into these categories as well as into the category of deterrence.

The concept of deterrence as directly related to one dimension of the war was defined in another administration document. Before the outbreak of military action, yet clearly with the war in mind, the administration referred to the possible use of WMD against American forces or allies and friends. In a deterrent posture, the administration warned publicly in its National Security Presidential Directive No. 17 of December 11, 2002 – an unclassified version of a previous document – that the United States "reserves the right to respond with overwhelming force – including through resort to all of our options – to the use of WMD against the United States, our forces abroad, and friends and allies." The wording was such that it could easily be interpreted as allowing the use of nuclear weapons in response to chemical and biological attacks. (Indeed, one source quoted from the classified version of the same document a direct reference to the possible use of nuclear weapons as part of the threatened response.[2]) In some respects this was not a new formulation. It had been defined already in the warning that the Bush Sr. administration communicated to Iraq on the eve of the Gulf War of 1991, was endorsed by the Clinton administration as part of its strategy in the 1990s, and was reemphasized by the new Bush administration, although even then the formulation left the actual response of the US to adversarial use of WMD rather vague. Whether the US would in fact resort to a nuclear response remains an open question, and in view of the enormous American conventional capabilities that could be used in a response and the dangerous international precedent created by the use of nuclear weapons, many observers doubt it. Certainly, however, this deterrent threat remains in the American strategic posture.

Thus, the Bush administration debated several strategic alternatives. For the purpose of the analysis that follows, therefore, it is important to differentiate clearly between the various strategies detailed in the policy documents and public statements.

An Analytical Framework

Deterrence is a strategy designed to affect the intentions of an adversary that plans to challenge the status quo. Its core comprises threats issued by the deterring party, whose objective is to prevent the challenger from pursuing a military action. The threats could fall into the category of *denial*, that is, a threat that the anticipated action would be met with such force that would prevent the challenger from materializing its goals, or the category of *punishment*, i.e., warning the challenger that its anticipated action would result in severe punishment. In many cases deterrence signals interweave both denial and punishment threats.

Another exercise in threats to use force is that of *compellence*, a term that does not appear in the NSS. It revolves around demands by the compeller that its adversary undertake a certain course of action, i.e., make concessions. While sometimes confused with deterrence, its goal is not to press the adversary to avoid a course of action, rather to force it to undertake positive steps, to force it to change the status quo.

Prevention, on the other hand, refers not to threats to use force in the future, based on the behavior of the challenger, but rather to the actual use of force. The purpose of preventive war is not to affect the intentions of the adversary, but rather to destroy its capabilities. Preventive war is launched when the "preventor" suspects that its adversary is committed to the use of force in any event. What gives the adversary pause is a lack of capabilities. Thus, concerned about the possibility of a future change in the balance of power, the use of military force is executed by the preventor.

Preemption refers to the use of force not in anticipation of a possible future change in the balance of military forces and a possible resulting attack by the adversary, but to an immediate military development. Thus, when the adversary is already in the very last phase of preparations for a military attack, or in more graphic terms, when the adversary has already begun "rolling the tanks" or its strike aircraft have already warmed their engines for take-off en route to their attack missions, the preemptor launches a preemptive strike designed to blunt the effects of the imminent attack. One of the implications of the Wolfowitz speech is that within the context of the war against terrorism, any preventive activity could be seen as an act of preemption. This is because one can never be sure that an act of terrorism is not in the process of being planned or even about to be executed.

All four strategies are exercises in military power and involve the potential or actual use of force, although there are clearly critical differences between them. In most cases, deterrence does not imply the immediate use of force. It transfers the burden of responsibility for the potential military clash to the challenger, and its basic purpose is to prevent the use of force. As such, deterrence can be perceived as basically defensive, though of course there are situations when deterrence threats, if used in a provocative manner and especially in situations when the assumed challenger did not in fact plan an attack, could lead to unintended escalation. Similarly, compellence is an exercise in threats rather than in the actual use of force. But because the purpose is a forced change in the status quo, it is much more offensive than deterrence.

In contrast to deterrence, prevention and preemption involve the actual use of force. The differences between them, however, are quite substantial. The rationale, let alone the justification, for preventive war is always problematic. There is an inherent doubt about the intentions of states, which can easily change over time. Furthermore, the accumulation of military capabilities is also an unclear process and thus the threatening change to the balance of military power suspected (by the preventor) may not occur. Finally, other strategies might be employed to deal with the future threats as perceived by the potential preventor.

Preemption appears to be much more justified. It can actually be seen as part of a defensive war: the war in fact has already been launched by the adversary. Preemption is thus an operational move designed to limit the effects of an attack that has already begun.

Rationales for the Iraq War

The American administration justified the attack on Iraq on several grounds: disarming Iraq of WMD; obstructing terrorism sponsored by or linked to the Iraqi regime; preventing Baghdad from transferring WMD to terrorists who might use them against the United States, possibly even on home territory; regime change; and democratization. All these rationales were debated at great length in the US and throughout the world, sparking much controversy.

Before considering to what extent these rationales for the Iraq operation fall into the analytical categories listed above, it is worthwhile to consider briefly the validity of the administration's stated agenda. The administration has been extremely concerned about the possibility of WMD terrorism inside the US or directed against US targets abroad, a concern that has driven much of overall American strategy since September 11. In order to prevent the materialization of this threat, the US has sought to limit the ability of states hostile to the US to accumulate WMD that might potentially be transferred to terrorists. However, while the administration repeatedly referred to the presumed links between Iraq and international terrorism and even to Bin Laden's organization, the supporting evidence was weak and circumstantial. Even more dubious is the supposition that Iraq would transfer WMD to a terrorist organization. States usually do not transfer such weapons to third parties, let alone to terrorist organizations, who are too often uncontrollable and unpredictable. Moreover, this is particularly the case with regard to the Saddam regime, which was obsessed by the overpowering drive to have absolute and exclusive control over all the means of destruction it possessed. Finally, the notion represented in the Wolfowitz speech that referred to the preemptive nature of any activity against international terrorism certainly did not apply to Iraq, which by all accounts was not on the verge of launching terrorist operations against the US.

In addition, the existence of WMD in Iraq has been a cause for American concern far beyond the possibility of transfer to terrorists. The aggressive and strongly anti-American Saddam regime was perceived as a potential regional threat, and renewed Iraqi military pressure against neighboring states was deemed eminently possible, if not probable. Were such a move backed by WMD, then the balance of costs of possible American intervention might change for the worse. Of special concern was the long-term possibility of the continued development of nuclear weapons capability. Such a capability might have presumably enabled Iraq to try to deter the United States from any intervention in the Middle East against Saddam's expansionism. Thus, as the administration could not furnish a convincing foundation to link the Iraqi regime with international terrorism, especially al-Qaeda, the arguments over Iraq's possible use of WMD in a regional context appeared more solid.

The administration's interest in democratization and the defense of the Iraqis' human rights appeared genuine, but was rejected by protests that these are not sufficient grounds for a war. Thus, in the final analysis, the justification most plausible to most people was the WMD threat.

The War: Prevention, Deterrence, and Compellence

American Security Interests

As a global power with a deep commitment to "world order," American security interests are manifested on two planes. The first level is "standard" national interests, such as the defense of the homeland, its people, economy, and well-being. On this American interests do not differ from those of other states throughout the international system. As a world power with a semi-hegemonic role, however, the United States has a second set of interests that extend far beyond the mere defense of national territory and relate to the desire for world order. During the Cold War the US and the USSR together, though fiercely competing with each other, in fact injected a measure of stability in the world order of states. Even then, it was the US that was the principal guarantor of the status quo, and since the end of the Cold War, the United States has performed this role by itself or at the head of different coalitions. Thus, various exercises of military force by the US might fulfill different missions on two levels: the US as a protector of hegemonic interests (and thereby serving world order), and the defense of more limited American security interests.

A mix of limited national and world order security interests currently exists in the American strategy to counter nuclear proliferation and international terrorism. American nonproliferation strategy, which began almost from the early stages of the nuclear era and has gained momentum since the early 1960s, has always been motivated by a mélange of direct national security and world order concerns. During the Cold War one of the few cooperative policies conducted by the two superpowers was the nonproliferation effort culminating in the Non-Proliferation Treaty of 1968 (which came into force in 1970). Following the end of the Cold War cooperation with Russia on nonproliferation persisted, but the main responsibility for it shifted to the United States. The focus on international terrorism, however, is a recent development. While references to terrorism accumulated during the latter part of the 1990s, the overwhelming emphasis currently apparent began only after 9/11.

The war in Iraq was depicted by the administration as primarily an effort to combat both dangers, and it thus integrally linked the two threats. Though it was accepted in Washington that Iraq did not yet have a nuclear weapons capability, the assessment was that given time the Iraqi scientific and technological community would be able to overcome the obstacles placed by the international sanctions and achieve this capability.

Prevention

With the rationales for the war presented by the administration as background, it could be argued that the war was first and foremost a preventive war. The main objective was to disarm Iraq from its WMD, and to destroy a regime that Washington perceived as likely to endorse or directly conduct terrorist activities inside the US or against its forces or its allies. The disarming of Iraq from WMD was deemed important not only because of possible terrorism activity but also, given the history of the Iraqi regime's past behavior, it appeared likely that it would not hesitate to threaten its neighbors with WMD. As such, the war would be construed as a preventive one both from the perspective of the narrow security interests of the US and also in terms of world order. Iraq was seen as potentially threatening the US itself, and in addition – and in tandem with its possession of WMD – as a cause for threats to the stability of the Middle East and the Persian Gulf region.

While preemption was mentioned in connection with the war, it is highly improbable that there was an imminent danger of terrorist activity conducted by the Iraqi regime, or the possibility of an immediate transfer of chemical or biological agents to terrorist organizations. Hence preemption regarding Iraq was not relevant.

Deterrence

In addition to the function of prevention, the war also played a deterrent role on several levels: first, as a message to various regimes considered possible sponsors of terror organizations and activities to desist from such efforts. The highly successful American military performance and the determination to use force even in the face of much international criticism have strengthened American deterrence against states that might have considered extending support to international terrorism. American deterrence against a direct attack by a state on the US has always been very powerful; more intricate is the potential state endorsement of terror activities against the US and its interests. A message of deterrence was already delivered with the war in Afghanistan, but its potency was considerably enhanced with the war on Iraq. While in Afghanistan the US encountered a weak and completely backward army, in Iraq it encountered what was considered a relatively strong military machine. Its quick and total destruction served notice about the ability of the US to punish severely states that might – even indirectly – challenge the US.

Second, the deterrent message was also an indication of the readiness of the US to defend regional order, and thus indirectly also world order at large. In the future, regional powers that strive to alter the status quo would have to consider the possibility of American military intervention. This is a very powerful deterrent signal against future challenges to the current international status quo.

Finally, the war sent a deterrent signal to rogue states trying to develop a nuclear capability. Here, however, this deterrent message may have much more complex consequences. Iran and North Korea began developing their nuclear capabilities because of what they considered to be serious security threats to their critical national interests: Iran primarily out of concern about the Iraqi nuclear effort, and North Korea primarily from fear of American power. Paradoxically, the war in Iraq may strengthen two contradictory impulses among the leaderships of these countries. Fear of American military power may enhance readiness to reach a compromise with the US concerning nuclear developments. On the other hand, precisely the demonstration of overwhelming American conventional capability might bring Iranian and North Korean strategic analysts (as well as analysts in other states) to the conclusion that only a nuclear capability can deter the United States. Upon initial consideration, the first alternative presented is the more likely. This is so because states might develop nuclear capabilities primarily because of regional threats and not because of the American hegemonic posture. The threat of American power, capabilities, and determination would likely diminish the readiness of such states to quarrel with the US.

Compellence

The goal of "democratization" brings with it an element of coercion. It involves the actual attempt to change the nature of the regime in Iraq. It also connotes a compellent message to other regimes in the Middle East and perhaps around the world concerning the American commitment to democratization, and possibly even to the readiness to use force in order to bring about such changes of government. The future efficacy of this strategy depends to a large extent on the success of the attempted democratization in Iraq, which at present appears increasingly questionable.

Iraqi Deterrence

With an American attack looming, Baghdad responded with a mix of strategies. Its primary response was a rejection of international and American demands as to the inspection of WMD, qualified by gradual, reluctant, and always belated acceptance of these demands. It also strongly denied American accusations of Iraqi connections with al-Qaeda. In addition, Iraq sought Arab and international diplomatic support, which it hoped could obstruct the American military operation.

The concomitant strategy was to discourage the US from a military attack by issuing several types of deterrent warnings. As a strategy of deterrence by denial, Iraq warned that American forces would suffer heavy losses on the battlefield, stressing the special difficulties that American forces would face in the battle for Baghdad. In the final weeks before the war, for example, the Iraqi regime presented to the media Arab and Muslim volunteers who ostensibly were planning to serve as suicide bombers against American forces. In addition, Iraq also warned that a wave of terror activities directed against American interests and people worldwide, including the use of chemical and biological agents, would follow an American attack.

The US remained undeterred by these warnings: confident of its superior military capabilities (which had been demonstrated yet again in Afghanistan if there existed any doubt) the Iraqi conventional forces were not seen as capable of causing a high rate of casualties to the American forces. Iraqi use of chemical and biological arms on the battlefield was indeed perceived as a possibility, but in view of the American deterrent warnings, it was assumed that this measure would take place only as a last resort, possibly in defense of Baghdad. Therefore, the American military did not consider this a major obstacle to its operations, and in any event the forces were highly equipped for such eventualities with defensive gear that was donned whenever it was suspected chemical and biological weaponry might be used, especially before the battle for Baghdad.

Terror attacks on American targets worldwide were indeed considered a serious threat, with one of the scenarios being the use of biological agents against populations in the US. Clearly, however, the administration could not allow itself to be deterred by that possibility, since retreating before a threat of this nature would seriously compromise American credibility. Moreover, the possibility of WMD in terror activity was already perceived as an ongoing peril. Indeed, the removal of the Saddam regime was billed as an important instrument in the campaign to quash precisely this threat. In addition, the American public's balance of costs and benefits to military activity changed radically following September 11, and since then the public has expressed much readiness to pay a high price in the overall campaign against international terrorism.

Israeli Deterrence Before and After the War

One of the recurrent themes before the war in the Israeli public debate as well as in different politicians' statements was that Israel would be forced to retaliate if Iraq launched a missile attack against Israel once the American campaign was underway, and particularly if the missiles were armed with unconventional warheads. The American interest, on the other hand, was decidedly to keep Israel out of the war, a message that was clearly communicated to Jerusalem. Yet concerned about the possibility of Israeli retaliation against Iraq, the administration promised a military effort to minimize, if not eliminate, the possibility of an Iraqi strike. The US also asked Israel to lower the profile of official references to a possible Iraqi attack, and indeed this request was largely heeded. However, both Prime Minister Sharon and even more so Defense Minister Shaul Mofaz intimated several times that if missiles did hit Israel, Israel would have to retaliate. At a later stage, the Prime Minister modified his position and said that if the missiles were armed with unconventional warheads and Israel suffered considerable casualties, *then* Israel would have to retaliate.

The American effort to preclude a strike against Israel was conducted on three levels. First, the United States issued unequivocal deterrent warnings about the use of WMD against US forces and its allies and friends. These warnings were conveyed not only on the state to state level, but also delivered through different channels to the Iraqi armed forces and its officer corps. Second, an unprecedented, high level American–Israeli coordination system was put into place involving intelligence cooperation and the deployment of American Patriot batteries of surface-to-air missiles in Israel. Finally, and most importantly, American special forces operated from the very beginning of the war (and possibly even before that) in western Iraq, the only location in Iraq from where launched missiles might reach Israel.

In fact, no Iraqi missiles were launched against Israel in 2003, although a number of short-range missiles were launched against Kuwait and the American forces there. It is still unclear why missiles were not used more extensively and why unconventional arms were not used at all. Perhaps, according to various advance estimates, the number of Iraqi launchers was indeed quite small; they and the missiles had not been tested for many years, thus degrading their operational use; and finally, the American operations in western Iraq might have preempted their use. The fact that thus far no surface-to-surface missiles (of the al-Hussein type) and no unconventional agents have been found might lead to the temporary conclusion that on the eve of the war, Iraq already had no operational al-Hussein missiles, let alone those armed with unconventional warheads, and thus neither American nor Israeli deterrent signals were put to the test.

Interestingly, the Israeli strategic behavior demonstrated that Israel itself was doubtful about the efficacy of its deterrent signals. It relied primarily on the military activities of coalition forces in western Iraq and on various "active defense" and "damage limitation" instruments available: the Arrow and Patriot batteries; the Israeli air force (against the threat of small Iraqi aircraft); and extensive civil defense measures such as bomb shelters, protected spaces against unconventional agents, and gas masks.

While Israeli deterrence was thus not an active element in the war, the Israeli debate raises several important issues that lie at the core of Israeli thinking about deterrence. Generally speaking, deterrence success or failure is based on the relationships between three balances: the balance of military power; the balance of political interests; and the balance of resolve. (There are of course several additional factors, especially in the failure of deterrence, including cognitive perceptions.) The literature on deterrence theory and practice – which is primarily American – has put much emphasis on the "balance of resolve." This focus derived from the centrality of the nuclear challenge, and the problem of "extended nuclear deterrence": in a situation of two adversarial nuclear powers, enhancing the credibility of a nuclear deterrent threat is a major problem, especially when issued in defense of an ally. Consequently, much of the literature focused on various ways designed to enhance the image of resolve of the deterring party.

Yet in most deterrence relationships between two adversaries (if outside of the context of extended deterrence, and particularly if limited to conventional weapons) failure or success of deterrence is based on the respective perceptions and calculations of the balance of military power and the relative vitality of the political interests at issue. The combination of these two balances affects the relative resolve of the adversaries. This has been the main lesson of the Israeli–Arab balance of deterrence over the years.

In practice, in trying to maintain a positive balance of conventional military power, the Israeli strategic leadership has partly apprehended this lesson. It paid much less attention to the importance of the balance of political interests, especially following the 1967 Six Day War. The result was the Yom Kippur War of 1973, which could have been avoided with a better Israeli understanding of the complexities of the balance of political interests with Egypt.

Overall, however, Israel has focused too much on the "balance of resolve," as if that were the main pillar of deterrence. This emphasis was evident in the debate over the question of retaliation against Iraq. Thus, for example, it has been argued that the Israeli failure to retaliate against Iraq in 1991 undermined its deterrence posture both against Iraq in particular and against its Arab adversaries in general. In fact, however, there is no evidence for that. No Arab state has attacked Israel since 1991 or has even undertaken steps that could be construed as signaling Israel's deterrence failure. Arab leaderships were aware of the special circumstances in which Israel refrained from responding to the Iraqi strikes. They continued to assess the political situation, and Egypt and Jordan, states with formal peace treaties with Israel, concluded that the status quo has not hurt their political interests. Syria, which has a strong interest in changing the status quo, correctly perceived the balance of military power as tilted in favor of Israel.

Indeed, the lesson of the non-response of Israel in 1991 bears evidence to the "non-transitivity" of demonstrations of resolve from one inter-state context to another. Seeming lack of resolve in one context does not affect the credibility of deterrent threats when an important security interest is threatened, and certainly not when the military balance favors Israel. The entire history of the military conflict (not including the outbursts of terrorism and guerrilla operations by non-state actors) attests to this general pattern. Hence also the non-transitivity of the image of resolve in the Israeli decision to withdraw from Lebanon in the mid-1980s down to the security zone. It had been argued within the public debate that this withdrawal would erode Israel's deterrent posture and encourage Arab states, primarily Syria, to attack Israel – predictions that did not materialize.

Finally, it was argued, based on the "transitivity" of deterrence resolve image, that had Iraq attacked Israel with unconventional arms, non-retaliation would erode Israeli deterrence against similar attacks by other Arab states, again Syria in particular. Yet this too is a problematic notion: first, Syria is surely aware of the special conditions of the 1991 Gulf War that would have recurred in 2003 had Iraq launched unconventional arms against Israel. American operations there removed a significant threat to Israel, and it would have been a strategic mistake for Israel to intervene and complicate the American operations. Second, Syria is no doubt well aware of Israel's significant military superiority. Chemical agents are only one component of the entire military balance that overall heavily favors Israel. Hence, Syrian use of this component in its arsenal would come only as part of a larger military operation that in any case would end with an Israeli victory. Third, the Syrian surface-to-surface missiles are seen by Damascus as a deterrent or possible response to Israel's overwhelming air superiority. The chemical warheads on these missiles are perceived as strengthening this assumed deterrent, almost a "poor man's deterrent" against Israeli nuclear capability. Since the effectiveness of both these means is so inferior to the Israeli capabilities they are designed to deter, their deterrence value is in doubt. Certainly, their use in a first strike appears totally unlikely.

The crossing of a symbolic threshold by the use of chemical agents is a cause for some concern. However, deterrence against it will not be based on the transitivity of deterrence images from one inter-state context to another, but rather on emphasizing the possible responses designed to counter such use within the context of a particular conflict with specific states.

Israeli deterrence, formidable before the war, has been enhanced by the war and its outcome. The American military performance in Iraq demonstrates that the Israeli forces – particularly the air force, which is widely assumed to be equipped with many of the technological assets of the US forces – are even more superior to the Arab forces than previously assumed. The destruction of the Iraqi military machine lessens any prospect for renewal of an "eastern front" against Israel (a possibility that was highly doubtful in any case). More importantly, it removed the threat of an eventual development of an Iraqi nuclear capability, which could have complicated the calculus of Israeli deterrence. Finally, the possible establishment of a *pax Americana* in the Middle East renders the possibility of any military challenge by a state to Israel even more reduced than was the case before the war.

Notes

1   Francois Heisbourg, "Work in Progress: The Bush Doctrine and its Consequences," *Washington Quarterly* 26, no. 2 (2003): 75–88.
2   *Washington Times*, January 31, 2003.

The US Approach to Arms Control

4

Emily B. Landau

From its first weeks in office, the Bush administration has emphasized the threat of Weapons of Mass Destruction (WMD) as one of the top security challenges confronting the United States. The primary states that have been targeted in this regard are Iran, Iraq, and North Korea. The subsequent policy decisions the administration adopted have arguably reflected a fair degree of uncertainty as to the value of arms control for dealing with the non-conventional threats it identified. However, while many analysts are quick to note that the US is displaying at best an ambiguous and at worst a negative attitude toward the arms control regime, the complexities of the US position are often glossed over. In particular, the months leading up to the war in Iraq tended to obscure the nuances evident in the US approach to WMD. What emerged instead were somewhat superficial depictions of the US as increasingly unilateralist, systematically rejecting international agreements and forums that curtailed its freedom of action, in favor of "taking matters into its own hands."

In fact, US skepticism regarding arms control has different rationales, sources, and policy implications. The following discussion will present the complexity of US calculations and positions, not only to provide a more complete picture of where the US stands with regard to arms control, including in the context of the war in Iraq, but also to assess the prospects for advancing both arms control and regional security in the Middle East in the coming years.

The Bush Administration Approach

To assess the approach taken by the Bush administration toward arms control, several issues must be clarified. The first is its attitude toward existing arms control *agreements* and the question of US unilateralism in the context of these agreements. The second issue is the understanding of the *concept* of arms control and its multiple interrelated aspects: the *focus* of arms control – whether it should best be placed on arms as such, or whether there is a need to focus on "arms in context," i.e., arms control in the context of and as a function of stable inter-state relations; the *nature* of arms control – whether it is viewed primarily as an inter-state process, or more as a series of agreements that target different aspects and types of WMD; and, finally, the preferred *framework* for concluding arms control agreements – whether in global, regional, or bilateral contexts.

These are neither simple nor trivial issues. They not only influence US assessments as to whether arms control is a reliable means of dealing with WMD-related security threats, but lie at the base of some of the criticism that has been directed against the US with regard to arms control. In fact, the often implicit differences that exist among states in their definition of these issues are a driving force for some of their disputes over respective commitments to arms control. Thus, in order to evaluate US attitudes toward arms control, it is important to understand the terms of reference.

A third essential issue that requires clarification is how arms control is viewed by the administration in relation to *other strategies* for dealing with the threat of WMD: in particular, deterrence, defense, diplomacy, and prevention/preemption. References to this larger issue will find expression in different parts of the discussion that follows, but it will not be the subject of comprehensive analysis.

Unilateralism

Indications of the Bush administration's *unilateral approach* to arms control have been evident in policy preferences both before and after 9/11. However, "unilateralism" is not synonymous with a tendency to intervene whenever and wherever the US pleases in order to confront a perceived threat forcibly. With regard to arms control, unilateralism means that the US will not allow what it views as its vital security interests to be undermined by an exclusive reliance on what it regards as inadequate arms control agreements. If necessary it will carve out alternative means for dealing with perceived threats. Significantly, however, this approach can assume very different shapes, as is evident when we compare the US approach before 9/11 to the dramatic change that took place in its wake.

Prior to the terror attacks in September 2001, the Bush administration attempted to promote the plan for a National Missile Defense (NMD) program in order to deal with the newly defined WMD threats.[1] Clearly, its intention was to go forward with this plan even if it came at the expense of a central bilateral arms control agreement, the Anti-Ballistic Missile (ABM) Treaty signed with the USSR in 1972. The solution it sought at that stage was of a defensive and isolationist nature, namely, creating an impenetrable "wall" against attack. Following September 11, however, and in the wake of the acute sense of vulnerability caused by the strikes on the US mainland, the approach changed. Most noticeably, it was no longer considered sufficient to try to encircle the US. If WMD threats were apparent, the US must actively work to eliminate them before they materialized into actual attacks. Significantly, active attempts to eliminate a threat could still assume different forms, ranging from diplomacy to military intervention. It is with regard to the latter that the option of preemption featured more prominently in the US security debate, as "self-defense" was broadened to include preemptive acts against states armed with WMD and was then applied to Iraq. However, this is only one possible option among many for a more active approach.

While the US unilateralist tendency, if not augmented by new diplomatic initiatives, may have undesirable long-term effects on the arms control regime, the approach to date is not indicative of a flat rejection of the regime as such. Specific decisions that related to some of the global treaties – most notably concerning the lack of US support for the draft protocol for enhanced verification of the Biological Weapons Convention (BWC) – are no doubt detrimental to the overall regime. But positions that have been adopted with regard to the so-called "axis of evil" states reflect more of a disappointment with the limitations of arms control agreements in their present form in light of new security threats, rather than a direct questioning in principle of the normative value of these agreements. The continued adherence of the US to the spirit of arms control comes out most clearly with regard to developments in US–Russian relations. In his November 2001 meeting with Putin in Crawford, Texas, Bush emphasized that the challenge of terrorism had made close cooperation between the US and Russia more important than ever. In this context, and against the backdrop of the tension that had been previously injected into US–Russian relations due to US determination to go forward with NMD at the expense of the ABM, he announced his intention to reduce unilaterally US operationally deployed strategic nuclear warheads to between 1,700 and 2,200 by 2012. While this seemed at first to be an indication of some type of new "unilateral arms control,"[2] it ultimately resulted in Bush and Putin signing the Moscow Treaty on Strategic Offensive Reductions on May 24, 2002. Under the terms of the treaty, the United States and Russia both agreed to reduce their warheads to these limits by December 31, 2012.

The key to understanding the current US arms control approach is thus not to be found in the notion of unilateralism as such (or some form of excessive interventionism or even imperialism), but rather in the newly perceived security threats that it faces in the post-Cold War period, primarily from the direction of Iran, Iraq, and North Korea. What makes the US approach unique is that is has enough power to attempt to reshape the rules of the game for dealing with these threats, and this is where the unilateral flavor emerges. At the same time, there are indications that the administration is in fact searching for new and more effective rules to guide its policy. The challenge is to try to understand the principles upon which the US seeks to base these rules in light of the threats it perceives, and to assess the implications of these emerging principles for the future of arms control.

Stabilization and Disarmament

While "arms control," by definition, ultimately aims to target the destructive potential of weapons, the common term is often used by analysts and policymakers alike to refer to very different types of agreements, different arms control processes, and

different understandings of how national security is to be achieved. More specifically, one can discern two quite distinct traditions that have developed over the
years under the common label of arms control: one that emphasizes "stabilization,"
and one that focuses on "disarmament."[3] While both were an outgrowth of the Cold
War years and the dangers associated with nuclear weapons in particular, the stabilization prong of arms control focused more on the dangers inherent in the
exclusive reliance on deterrence to manage relations between the already nuclear
armed superpowers. The aim was to *stabilize* relations (primarily in a bilateral
framework) in order to improve the ability of both sides to correctly assess mutual
intentions, and thus lessen the chances of misescalation to nuclear confrontation.
This tradition included the logic of confidence building, as evident in Confidence
and Security Building Measures (CSBMs), and tended to view arms control as a
process in which improved inter-state relations were cultivated. Some of the initial
arms control agreements between the superpowers were in fact CSBMs. The
disarmament tradition, on the other hand, was more fundamentally grounded in
multilateral practices, very often carried out under the auspices of the UN.
Disarmament practices focused more on the need to *eliminate* entire categories of
weapons, rather than merely control their effects, and tended to be viewed as agreements with conditions to be fulfilled, rather than inter-state relations to be
developed.[4]

There are indications that the US is moving in the direction of an approach
that places a greater premium on the relationships that exist among states directly
threatened by the presence (or suspected presence) of WMD, rather than relying
solely on existing broad-based agreements that (often unsuccessfully) seek to eliminate the weapons themselves, for example, the Non-Proliferation Treaty (NPT).
There also seems to be an emerging preference to cultivate such relations in bilateral or regional frameworks, in order to address specific interests that are lost in
the context of global agreements. Significantly, both of these tendencies exist within
the "stabilization" tradition of arms control. The question is whether these tendencies can be promoted without seriously undermining the effect of the broader arms
control agreements already in place.

The Principle of Equality

An intermediate approach between the two arms control traditions of stabilization
and disarmament, which also impacts on the question of whether emphasis is
placed on interests/relations or on weapons, has to do with what may be called the
principle of equality. This principle, or norm, maintains that all states should be
treated equally with regard to their WMD capabilities, technologies, and development, that is, as a function of the weapons themselves, and has been implicitly
embedded in the disarmament tradition.[5] It has also served as the justification for
complaints lodged against interest/relations approaches when these have incorporated a seeming double standard in their differential treatment of states that
should be "equal" on the basis of weapons development.[6] This fairly widespread
normative principle could seriously hamper the justification of an arms control

approach that advocates the need to address state interests, attitudes, and behavior within bilateral and regional relationships.

The norm of equality indeed has a moral appeal in the abstract. There is no apparent reason to presume that different states should be treated differently with regard to arms control and disarmament obligations. If WMD are highly dangerous and there is a desire to do away with them, this should apply equally to all. The difficulties begin when an agreement exists that signatory states don't adhere to (or are suspected of not adhering to), and when the agreement itself does not have the mechanisms to enforce their compliance. The cases of Iran, pre-war Iraq, and North Korea demonstrate most clearly that the three states have/had a common denominator in terms of their motivation to acquire WMD (irrespective of their different stages of actual development). Nonetheless, the three have displayed substantially and significantly divergent *attitudes* toward arms control and inspections, and to the contexts of their own WMD development. Indeed, in his State of the Union address of January 2003, Bush implicitly acknowledged these differences, modified the "axis of evil" theme, and advocated "different strategies for different threats" to deal with the three states. Specifically, in the case of Iran he noted favorably the support of the Iranian people for democracy, whereas Iraq's record of defiance and deceit was the dominant theme underlying the case made for war.[7]

In fact, looking back at the origins of the NPT we find that the principle of equality was not fully upheld, even within the disarmament tradition.[8] Inequalities were built into the NPT – the commitment of nuclear states in the framework of the NPT (Article VI) to reduce their nuclear arsenals is not a condition that was backed up by force. Thus, an international regime set up to deal with nuclear proliferation seemingly equally and across the board implicitly accepted established differences between nuclear and non-nuclear states. The differences in attitude were also evident when in the late 1990s India and Pakistan (outside the regime) conducted nuclear tests. While they were subjected to sanctions, they were not labeled as rogue states or part of an axis of evil. Assumptions regarding Israel's nuclear activity have also not elicited harsh measures given the acknowledgment of its security situation. In each of these cases we find allowance for unique circumstances, regional considerations, and security concerns.

In a recent contribution to *Foreign Affairs*, George Perkovich rejects the NPT on this very basis.[9] He argues that the NPT is flawed precisely because it does not adhere religiously to the principle of targeting weapons equally. Accordingly, as long as some states continue to possess nuclear weapons legitimately, others will want them. Therefore, "the proliferation threat . . . stems from the existence and possession of nuclear weapons . . . not merely from the intentions of today's 'axis of evil.'" What is missing in this approach, however, is a more realistic assessment of how to deal with the dangers that nevertheless exist. Even if it is true that the inequalities themselves may have been a driving factor for some states to strive to develop or acquire WMD, this is not the sole motivation. Moreover, while it is not realistic to expect that nuclear weapons will be eradicated from the world any time soon, additional nuclear proliferation continues to present a serious challenge for the short term. If the NPT is severely limited in the face of determined prolifera-tors, other options and arrangements may have to be pursued.

The emerging US approach seems to underscore that dealing with a prolifer-ator, actual or potential, must take into account the nature of the state, its stage of development in the realm of WMD, its intentions in this regard, its positions on arms control and previous agreements, and its relationship to other states, including the US. The focus of the Bush administration on inter-state relations as the basis for determining policy in the non-conventional realm has evolved over the past year in light of international realities in connection with Iraq, Iran, and North Korea. However, it can also be viewed as an outgrowth of previous inter-national tendencies: the stabilization tradition of arms control, as well as the disarmament tradition itself, which never really gave full expression to the prin-ciple of equality among states solely on the basis of weapons development.

Arms Control Before and After the War

How did arms control principles and constraints figure in US calculations with regard to Iraq? The case of WMD and Iraq reflected the assessment of the Bush administration that in some cases there is no alternative to the use of direct mili-tary force in order to eliminate a serious security threat. On the one hand, the US decision to employ massive force could be viewed in the context of upholding UN Security Council resolutions insisting on Iraq's obligation to disarm, and as a case where harsh measures had to be taken in light of the blatant non-compliance of the state. In this sense, it reflected more negatively on Iraq than on the NPT or Security Council resolutions as such. However, the experience with Iraq also spawned profound disillusionment with the arms control regime more generally, in terms of its ability to deal effectively with potential and actual proliferators. Concurrent developments in the past year surrounding the nuclear activities of Iran and North Korea (also signatories to the NPT) contributed to the skepticism.

Interestingly, the perceived failure of arms control to deal with the Iraqi threat was both a central pretext for the US going to war, and at the same time, almost irrelevant to the major pre-war dynamics that took place between the US and some European states. In their dispute with the US, France and Germany claimed that there was no hard evidence of WMD in Iraq; they maintained that the US was targeting Saddam Hussein for other reasons. The struggle between the two positions was more over political power and influence, with these European states attempting to secure an increasingly prominent role in global political deci-sions. France and Germany avowed, however, that had "hard evidence" been produced, they would have supported the US intention to employ force in the face of Iraq's non-compliance. If so, the disagreement was more over whether or not there were WMD in Iraq and how to act in light of that question rather than over the principle of arms control. In other words, the US was censured for deciding on its own that Iraq was in non-compliance, not for abuse of the arms control regime per se.

The situation is even more intricate regarding recent developments in North

Korea, where there are strong indications of very advanced nuclear weapons development, including North Korean statements to the effect that the state has developed a number of nuclear devices.[10] In this case, as opposed to Iraq, European states and the international community at large seem quite willing for the US to conduct negotiations in order to resolve the crisis, much as was the case in 1994, when the US and North Korea came to an agreement that kept North Korea's signature on the NPT intact. They are not pressing the US to deal with the situation through international bodies. The approach adopted by European states toward the North Korean case may thus signal a measure of acceptance of a US approach *vis-à-vis* potential and actual proliferators that relies more on the cultivation of inter-state relations, taking into account different state interests and behavior.[11]

As to current arms control trends, there is additional evidence that the US has an interest in continuing to maintain and even strengthen the arms control regime. One indication is the "National Strategy to Combat Weapons of Mass Destruction," an official US document published in December 2002, which defines strengthened nonproliferation as one of the three pillars of the national strategy to combat WMD. Moreover, neither with North Korea nor with Iran do we see the US ignoring international norms of arms control or following the prescripts of preemptive action. It is, rather, attempting to augment existing agreements through compellence and diplomacy. Interestingly, North Korea itself is demanding to negotiate directly with the US over its nuclear activity and development. Clearly, the example of North Korea demonstrates that broad international agreements are not sufficient in themselves to halt WMD proliferation, while bilateral relations (in this case, US–North Korea) have played a central supplementary role. The US has not rejected the NPT, but has rather worked to supplement it with a bilateral agreement. As to Iran, the US is attempting to deal with this state through international forums, pressing for the IAEA to pronounce Iran in violation of its obligations according to the NPT. In its mid-June meeting the IAEA did not impose sanctions on Iran, but it did criticize the state for failing to report some recently discovered nuclear activities, and strongly urged it to ratify the Additional Protocol and to cooperate more fully with the agency.

Finally, with regard to US–Russian arms control, the Russian Duma ratified the Moscow Treaty on May 14, 2003. The US Senate had ratified the treaty in March, but opposition to the war in Iraq delayed Russian ratification. While Russia's upper house of parliament must still approve the treaty, this vote is expected to be a mere formality, and the Treaty will soon enter into force. This is further indication of the fact that the value of arms control will be upheld, although it may be assuming new directions.[12] Less favorable perhaps for the arms control regime is the recent approval by Congress to lift a ten-year-old ban on research of smaller nuclear weapons (less than 5 kilotons). The Bush administration has sought to lift this ban in order to pursue research into options for deterring smaller powers, to defeat chemical and biological agents, and to penetrate and destroy deeply buried bunkers.[13]

All of these developments signal important changes in how WMD are being dealt with under US global leadership. The tendency that seems to be emerging is that the US will be taking a much more active role in shaping the nature of arms control agreements, dialogues, and arrangements in the coming years. It will be looking at the states behind the threats and will attempt to devise the means to impact on and improve inter-state relations in order to eliminate or at least control the effects of dangerous weapons development. The nature of arms control is likely to change somewhat and become more flexible, and in the future we may well see a much enhanced role for bilateral and multilateral (regional) inter-state relations as part and parcel of future arms control regimes.

This may be perceived as threatening the "equality principle" that for many years provided moral grounds for global agreements that strengthened the norm against development and use of WMD. At the same time, acknowledging that not all states are treated equally (purely as a function of their weapons development) does not necessarily have to undermine the norm against WMD. It merely suggests that controls will not always be negotiated equally or identically. In fact, perhaps it is this very recognition that is a necessary prerequisite for dealing more effectively with states that are highly motivated to proliferate. In the end, it is the *interests* of states rather than weapons alone that will need to be addressed. The WMD developments in Iran, Iraq, and North Korea, signatories to global arms control agreements, are testimony to the fact that the global arms control regimes alone will not stop determined proliferators. Nor were these states driven primarily by the lack of apparent equality in the agreements themselves. Clinging to a principle that does not functionally exist will prove increasingly detrimental to the effort to deal more effectively with the dangers that do exist.

Of course, the US will have to be wary of stretching its ability to act unilaterally too far. Excessive unilateralism will not be conducive to an effort to establish new rules of the game, but will only expose the US to criticism and increased antagonism. The US will have to present its goals as striving to enhance and supplement the arms control regime, not replace it.

Implications for the Middle East

With regard to the Middle East, here too the tendency to target interests and relations can be conducive to restarting some form of dialogue on arms control in a regional framework. Following the war in Iraq, states in the Middle East may once again be able to pursue arms control and regional security talks. These will have to include both Iran and Iraq, and they will clearly have to be oriented to the needs and interests of the participating states. Beyond discussion of weapon systems, dialogue will have to focus on the easing of tensions, the stabilization of relations, and the creation of accepted rules of the game. Understandings and agreements in this regard will enable states to exist in a relatively stable regional environment (with whatever WMD remain in the hands of regional states in the interim period), until more comprehensive regional arms control agreements can be negotiated and agreed upon. The restarting of regional arms control talks will depend to a large degree on the willingness of the US to press for them. The fact that *in theory* the US attention to inter-state relations could contribute to this effort does not guarantee that the US will have the political will to put its full weight behind this option. As yet, there are no indications that the US is thinking in these terms.

For Israel in particular there is an additional question of whether, in the wake of the war in Iraq, there will be renewed pressure on it to be more forthcoming on global arms control treaties and negotiations. So far there are no real indications of this, and there is reason to believe that the US will not significantly increase pressure on Israel in this regard, at least in the short term. First of all, the US itself is disappointed with the ability of global regimes to halt proliferation; secondly, there is a growing sense that Iran is at a more advanced stage of nuclear development than previously surmised and very likely in violation of its commitments according to the NPT; and finally, the present US administration seems to prefer dealing with Middle East issues one by one, and energies are presently directed primarily to the Israeli–Palestinian arena and to steps that must be taken for implementation of the roadmap.

Notes

1 On emerging US arms control tendencies in this period, see Emily Landau, "The NMD/Arms Control Balance: A Message for the Middle East?" *Strategic Assessment* 4, no. 1 (2001): 17–20.

2 Emily Landau, "Unilateral Arms Control? Post-September 11 Trends in US Arms Control and Non-Proliferation Approaches," *Strategic Assessment* 4, no. 4 (2002): 18–21.

3 This division should not be understood as the basis for categorizing all varieties of arms control agreements (there would be a question, for example, of how Nuclear-Weapon-Free Zones [NWFZ] would be classified). It is offered rather for analytical purposes to highlight a central distinction that while not always recognized, exists and in fact has central importance for a better understanding of debates over arms control.

4 See Emanuel Adler, "The Emergence of Cooperation: National Epistemic Communities and the International Evolution of the Idea of Nuclear Arms Control," *International Organization* 46, no. 1 (1992): 101–145; David Mutimer, *The Weapons State: Proliferation and the Framing of Security* (Colorado: Lynne Rienner Publishers, 2000); David Mutimer, "Testing Times: Of Nuclear Tests, Test Bans and the Framing of Proliferation," *Contemporary Security Policy* 21, no. 1 (2000): 1–22; and Emily B. Landau and Tamar Malz, "Assessing Regional Security Dialogue Through the Agent-Structure Lens: Reflections on ACRS," *Journal of Strategic Studies* (forthcoming, September 2003).

5 The term used in documents relating to global disarmament efforts is "non-discriminatory." This term is found, for example, in the Final Document of the 2000 NPT Review Conference with regard to the need to negotiate in the Conference on Disarmament (CD) a "non-discriminatory, multilateral, and internationally and effectively verifiable treaty banning the production of fissile material for nuclear weapons." In essence, the term advocates that states should be judged on the basis of criteria that are relevant to the treaty, so that it does not discriminate among states on the basis of irrelevant criteria, such as size, power, and so on. In using the term "equality," I refer to this basic idea – equality as a function of the weapons discussed. However, I prefer "equality" to the cumbersome "non-discrimination" in order to move away from specific UN terminology used in treaties and give a better sense of the more general and widespread demand for equal treatment of states on the basis of their weapons development and capabilities, rather than state behavior, attitudes, relationships to other states, etc. In this regard, we can discern an additional and related norm that underlies the norm of

equality: namely, that weapons are a more "objective" and therefore *better* criterion to be used in order to evaluate states; in turn, judgments about state behavior are necessarily subjective, and thus less worthy of constituting the basis for such evaluation.

6   Examples include the longstanding Egyptian rejection of the special treatment given to Israel in the nuclear realm on the basis of its seemingly unique security concerns. Egypt was not willing for this to be legitimized within the Arms Control and Regional Security talks held in the early 1990s, and advocated equal treatment of *all* WMD. The double standard argument has been a permanent feature of Iranian statements regarding its suspected nuclear weapons development – it denies that its nuclear activity is for military applications, and suggests that the international community direct its attention to Israel. Most recently, the double standard argument was raised with regard to the US differential treatment of North Korea and Iraq – when it demonstrated its willingness to deal diplomatically with North Korea, but resorted to war in the case of Iraq.

7   Emily B. Landau and Ram Erez, "The Nuclear Dimension of 'Axis of Evil': Different Strategies for Different Threats," *Strategic Assessment* 6, no. 1 (2003): 8–14.

8   Landau and Erez, "The Nuclear Dimension of 'Axis of Evil.'"

9   George Perkovich, "Bush's Nuclear Revolution: A Regime Change in Nonproliferation," *Foreign Affairs* 82, no. 2 (2003): 2–8.

10 The statements emerged in the context of the talks between the US, North Korea, and China in late April 2003. See, for example, "North Korea Presents Dilemma for U.S.," *New York Times,* April 27, 2003.

11 This seems not to be the case for the head of the IAEA, Mohamed ElBaradei, who believes that the world needs a uniform and consistent message for countries developing WMD, including North Korea (*New York Times*, April 27, 2003). ElBaradei's position is in line with the principle of equality discussed above.

12 The Moscow Treaty in itself is different from previous bilateral arms control agreements negotiated between the US and USSR/Russia – it is a relatively short document that relates only to the essence of the agreed reductions, without elaborating on means for verification, for example.

13 *New York Times*, May 21, 2003 and May 27, 2003.

The War in Iraq and International Terrorism

5

Yoram Schweitzer

The lurking fear that the war in Iraq would be accompanied by a wave of terror, and the ominous possibility that non-conventional (chemical or biological) weapons would be used, remained theoretical scenarios only. Furthermore, at least in the initial months since the end of the war, it appears that the immediate effect of the war on international terrorism has been marginal. This essay will suggest why the effect was minimal, along with the question of whether the war in Iraq truly constituted an integral part of the campaign against international terrorism declared by the United States following the September 11, 2001 attack, or whether it was a digression from the main effort. The effect on terrorism during the war will also be examined, as will the implications for the principal future objectives of the war against international terrorism.

The War and the Struggle against International Terrorism

The September 11, 2001 terrorist attack constituted a definitive moment in the history of international terrorism.[1] Its byproducts have impacted on international relations at levels far exceeding any previous weight accorded to terrorism. The large number of victims, over 3,000 civilian fatalities, the severe damage to both the United States and the global economy, and the exposure of the vulnerability of Western society, particularly the US, to terrorist attacks, constituted a watershed in American national security policy. The attack also redefined American relations with various countries around the world.

The president announced a global offensive against international terrorism, focusing first on a war against al-Qaeda and the Taliban regime, which had sponsored a terrorism industry led by Osama Bin Laden and his followers, "the Afghan alumni."[2] The horror and shock over the terrorist attack in the United States, and the realization among many countries that terrorism poses a strategic threat to themselves as well, helped the US form a broad international coalition with world-wide support for an offensive to oust the Taliban regime and destroy the al-Qaeda infrastructure in Afghanistan.

At the same time, the US administration formulated a national security policy, known as "the Bush doctrine,"[3] which redefined what constitutes imminent threats and the risks from these threats to the national security of the US and its strategic status as a superpower. The doctrine also outlined new methods for dealing with those risks. The campaign against international terrorism occupied a central role in this doctrine, although not an exclusive one.

The Bush administration conceived of the war against international terrorism as a clearly defined struggle between those favoring American policy against terrorism and those opposing it. It grouped together what it considered to be the main enemies of the United States as forming an "axis of evil," a term that encompassed both those who supported international terrorism and those involved with the proliferation of non-conventional weapons. The idea also reflected concern that rogue states supporting terrorism would transfer these weapons to terrorist organizations, which abide by no legal or moral restrictions regarding the use of these weapons.

The countries defined as the axis of evil by the Bush administration, Iraq, Iran, and North Korea – and hence the priorities in neutralizing the threats they constituted – were not selected according to the degree or intensity of their active involvement in international terrorism. The three countries were chosen based on the administration's assessment of the acuteness of the threats they and their leaders posed to essential American interests in the region, and the degree to which these leaders were willing to use non-conventional weapons or transfer them to terrorist organizations. From this assessment, Saddam Hussein and Iraq were selected as the initial targets. The choice of Iraq reflected the belief of President Bush and his senior advisors, Secretary of Defense Donald Rumsfeld, Vice President Richard Cheney, Deputy Secretary of Defense Paul Wolfowitz, and others, that in contrast to Iran and North Korea, the confrontation with Saddam Hussein was unavoidable. Indeed, given Saddam Hussein's advanced efforts to obtain nuclear weapons, his assumed possession of biological and chemical weapons, and his past behavior in international affairs, leaving him in power would almost certainly lead to a clash in the near future, and under much worse conditions.[4]

The administration took care to portray the war in Iraq as an integral part of the international campaign against terrorism. Among other statements, it characterized Iraq and al-Qaeda as two sides of the same coin,[5] and assumed that the removal of rogue regimes such as those in Afghanistan and Iraq would be a key element in deterring other states supporting terrorism in the Middle East, such as Iran, Syria, and others.

Iraqi Involvement with International Terrorism

The fact that Iraq under Saddam Hussein was involved in international terrorism is indisputable. From the outset of his presidency in 1979 the regime nurtured a large number of Palestinian terrorist organizations and supported their activities for many years. Terrorist organizations active on the international scene, such as Abu Nidal's Fatah Revolutionary Council, Abu Abbas's Palestine Liberation Front, Ahmad Jibril's Popular Front for the Liberation of Palestine – General Command, and George Habash's Popular Front for the Liberation of Palestine and its splinter groups, including Wadi Haddad's faction and its offshoots, Abu Ibrahim's May 15 Organization and Salim Abu Salim's Popular Front for the Liberation of Palestine – Special Command, all received from Iraq at various times and to various degrees assistance in planning and sometimes even in staging terrorist attacks. They were certainly granted bases and offices on Iraqi territory. Furthermore, Iraq committed terrorist acts through its own agents who murdered expatriate opponents of the regime and carried out terrorist attacks against Western and Arab targets in various European countries.

The United States and leading European countries conveyed numerous warnings and applied extensive pressure on Saddam Hussein to restrain the terrorist organizations operating internationally with help from Iraq. Cost-benefit considerations, particularly the urgent need for Western assistance and support in the war with Iran, led Saddam gradually to rein in his support for terrorism. Starting in the second half of the 1980s, Iraq reduced its direct involvement in international terrorism. The assassination of Iraqi exiles in Europe was halted, and Iraq forced terrorist organizations operating from its territory, such as Abu Ibrahim's group, to cease their activities entirely. Jibril's and Habash's groups had to look for aid from other countries, such as Libya and Syria, and focus their operations in Israel, instead of internationally.

At the same time, Iraq oversaw the offices of the Palestinian terrorist organizations on its soil, and continued to provide shelter to wanted terrorists, refusing to extradite them. The best known case is Palestine Liberation Front leader Abu Abbas, wanted in Italy and the United States for his role in the hijacking of the Italian ship *Achille Lauro* and the murder of wheelchair bound Leon Klinghoffer, who was thrown overboard during the ship's hijacking in October 1985. Abbas was granted asylum in Baghdad, and the Palestine Liberation Front and similar organizations continued to operate in Iraq. Saddam Hussein thereby retained a number of channels of activity on the Israeli–Palestinian front and the ability to wage terrorist activity through terrorist agents, if and when he chose to do so.

In general, it can be said that after the end of the Iran–Iraq war, and even following the 1991 Gulf War, Iraq continued to keep a low profile as far as its active involvement in international terrorism was concerned. To be sure, Iraq was accused of being behind the first terrorist attack on the New York World Trade Center in February 1993,[6] and even of helping the September 11, 2001 attacks, but these accusations are still unproven. The US administration has also tried to connect Iraq with al-Qaeda and the terrorist organizations and networks linked to it, such as Ansar al-Islam, which was based on the Iran–Iraq border, and another al-Qaeda-affiliated terrorist network, headed by Abu Musaab al-Zarkawi.[7] Documents captured in the war and the interrogations of senior Iraqi intelligence officials held by the Americans are still under evaluation to determine to what extent these organizations were indeed linked to Iraq. Yet unless more information comes to light, it would seem that Iraqi aid was not a key factor in the activity of al-Qaeda and its allies. Certainly Iraq lacked the control to channel these organizations' activities in order to promote its own interests, as it had formerly done with the Palestinian terrorist organizations operating under its sponsorship.

At the same time, in recent years, particularly after the outbreak of what is known as the al-Aqsa Intifada, Iraq once again became actively involved in the Israeli–Palestinian conflict and helped finance the "production line" of Palestinian suicide bombings in Israel. Iraq paid the family of each suicide bomber between $10,000 and $25,000,[8] and also trained and sent to Israel several Palestinian terrorist cells to commit large-scale terrorist attacks – which were successfully preempted – in the summers of 2001 and 2002.

Thus, while Iraq's involvement in international terrorism unquestionably demonstrates by any standard of proof that Iraq is a terrorism-supporting state, and though Iraq's policy on terrorism invited active measures on the part of the US and the West to change this policy, Iraq was certainly not the leading country in this field. Its neighbor, Iran, has been involved in international terrorism to this day, and much more actively so than Iraq. The choice of Iraq as the primary target of a campaign against international terrorism, therefore, represented somewhat of a divergence from the central course of dealing with the principal threats that international terrorism posed to the world after September 11, 2001.

Terrorism's Lesser Role in the War

A number of factors can be cited to explain the low level of terrorist activity during the 2003 war in Iraq. Significantly, even during the 1991 Gulf War, which was longer than the recent war, terrorism did not play a key role. During that war, which lasted from January 16, 1991 until March 16, 1991, there were 218 terrorist attacks around the world, 81 of which targeted Americans. Most of the attacks were protests by leftist organizations, which took advantage of the war to act against American policy. Their protests were primarily exhibitionistic and non-deadly, and very few left any impression at all.[9] The axiom "when the cannons roar, terrorism is silent" was essentially borne out. A likely explanation for this pattern is that the effect of terrorism on its target audience depends to large extent on the ability of the perpetrators to gain a high profile in the media. It is hard to attract such attention during a war, which is naturally laden with violence and pictures of death and destruction. These images overshadow the destruction caused by terrorist operations, thereby making them less "attractive" to the media.

The military strategy of the American and British armies in the 2003 war surprised the Iraqi army, exposing its own weakness and demonstrating the coalition's qualitative superiority, principally in firepower and complete control of the air. These factors led to a quick, decisive victory over the Iraqi army. The speed with which the fighting ended and the Iraqi regime lost control of its forces left the Iraqi commanders no chance to prepare and organize guerilla and terrorist operations, even had they wished to do so. In the perspective of the recent aftermath of the war, it appears that Saddam Hussein did not prepare in advance for this kind of fighting, and in any case the forces suitable for terrorism and guerilla fighting that could have helped him organize terrorist operations, e.g., Palestinian terrorist organizations, had no real capability and probably also lacked the will to defend the collapsing regime, despite the generous aid Saddam gave them in the past. Similarly, Saddam's brutal personality and habits, which allowed him to butcher his political enemies, Iraqi and foreign, religious and secular, were at least in part why his subordinates and his enemies' opponents did not bother fighting for him.

The Iraqi plan to use suicide attacks in the war, touted as the legendary winning tactic of Muslims in their war against the heathens, was also a failure. The threats voiced by Saddam Hussein's spokesmen that hundreds of Iraqi fighters were waiting to commit suicide attacks and sacrifice themselves for the leader in order to free Iraq from its occupiers were proven empty. The attempts by Bin Laden, one of the main exponents of the suicide weapon for defending Islam, to incite the Iraqi people and his supporters to volunteer for such a mission and use it to cast fear into the hearts of the "enemies of Islam," went largely unheeded during the battles themselves. The few suicide attacks committed during the war caused a fairly low number of casualties and were largely unnoticed among the total number of American and British casualties, with no actual effect on the course of the fighting or its results.

The events of the war suggest that the American attempt to allege a link between Iraq and al-Qaeda and its allies lacked a factual basis. Al-Qaeda refrained from direct involvement in the battles, confining itself to militant rhetoric aimed at inciting the Iraqi people to fight for their honor and that of the Islamic nation.[10] Moreover, in his speeches both before and during the war, Bin Laden was careful to distinguish between his support for the Iraqi people and his objections to Saddam Hussein's regime. Actually, except for sporadic operations by Ansar al-Islam, a Muslim organization close to al-Qaeda whose operatives were based in an enclave in northern Iraq that was attacked by American forces, al-Qaeda conducted no attacks during the war. As expected, however, Bin Laden used the Anglo-American attack in Iraq to strengthen the ideological justification for future attacks by his organization against the US forces in the Persian Gulf. He justified such attacks by claiming to defend Islam against Judeo-Crusader aggression designed to humiliate Islam and loot its treasures.[11]

A hint of what operations could be expected from al-Qaeda after the war can be found in an e-mail sent by an al-Qaeda spokesman to the London-based Saudi Arabian newspaper *Al-Majallah* a few days before the May 12 suicide attacks in Saudi Arabia. The message said, "The organization has completed its preparations for a major attack in the Gulf, striking at the rear of the American enemy." It continued, "Al-Qaeda plans to transfer all the forms and methods of its struggle to the heart of the Arabian peninsula and the Gulf region. . . . We are now in the state of preparing squads and weapons, and the world will see how we make the United States pay a price for invading Iraq. We are willing to attack the United States and the Gulf countries. The date of execution is very close, the rear of the Crusader army will be attacked, and in this way, we will help Iraq."[12]

The Post-War Campaign against Terrorism

The war in Iraq did not materially affect the international terrorist threat or the principal challenges facing the international community as it attempts to reduce the impact of terrorism as a significant factor in international relations.

The fairly short duration of the war in Iraq, and the absence of extreme and excessive violence in the war, notwithstanding the destruction and the casualties, largely silenced the pre-war wave of public criticism about the necessity and moral justification for the war. Even the leaders of France, Germany, and Russia, among the leading opponents of the war, took care to moderate their criticism once the fighting began. After the war ended, they initiated contacts to downplay the dispute between them and American and British leaders. Among other objectives, the opponents of the war wished to share in the expected economic and political benefits arising from post-war reconstruction in Iraq. Critical here, however, is that the issues in dispute and the accompanying political confrontation between key NATO countries and the United States not be ignored, because otherwise they are liable to hamper future efforts to forge a common policy for dealing with the main issues in the campaign against international terrorism.

The two main challenges in the current global campaign against terrorism are the efforts to neutralize al-Qaeda and its cohorts around the world by arresting or killing their operatives, and preventing the countries supporting terrorism from aiding terrorist organizations and giving terrorists a refuge in their territory.

Al-Qaeda and the terrorist organizations and networks it supports have constituted the most dangerous and acute threat posed by international terrorism since the beginning of the 1990s. This threat has increased since September 11, 2001. These organizations are motivated by an extreme ideology, and act consistently and with determination to commit terrorist mass murders. Since the 2001–2002 offensive against Afghanistan they have stepped up their efforts to commit mega-terrorist attacks around the world. They have proven that despite counter efforts by security forces around the world, they are capable of carrying out terrorist attacks on a number of continents and inflicting many casualties.[13] Operative flexibility, the numerous cadres trained by Bin Laden over many years in the Sudan and later in Afghanistan, and the decentralized nomadic structure of the Islamic front,[14] have enabled al-Qaeda to absorb the blows rained on it, and continue recruiting new operatives for terrorist activity around the world.

Al-Qaeda has taken advantage of the diversion of resources and attention on the part of security forces and political authorities to the crisis in Iraq to make thorough preparations for a terrorist campaign against its usual targets: the United States, its Western allies, and Arab countries whose regimes it regards as heretical. The war in Iraq also made it easier for al-Qaeda to portray itself as the only element defending Muslims, and to justify its terrorism and indiscriminate killing of civilians as the only legitimate way of paying the aggressors back in kind.

Shortly after the end of the war in Iraq, al-Qaeda carried out a number of terrorist attacks. Though others were foiled, Western security forces have warned that a further wave of attacks is under preparation.

In Riyadh, Saudi Arabia, on May 12, al-Qaeda staged a triple suicide attack on a residential complex for foreigners in the eastern part of the city. Twenty-five civilians were killed in the attack, some of them foreigners, and dozens more were injured. Four days later, a terrorist attack also took place in Casablanca, which included five simultaneous suicide attacks. The perpetrators were from an al-Qaeda-supported Moroccan terrorist network. Thirty-one people were killed and about 100 injured in this attack against Jewish and Western targets. In addition, an attempted mass terrorist strike against the American consulate in Pakistan was foiled after the Pakistani security forces arrested a number of al-Qaeda members and captured a large arms cache. In Thailand, an attack planned in June against Western targets and local tourist targets by al-Jamah`ah–al-Islamiya, a Southeast Asian al-Qaeda-affiliated network, was successfully thwarted.[15] Information about impending terrorist attacks in some countries in Africa was reflected in official warnings issued by the US State Department and the British Foreign Office to their citizens. Intelligence information pointed to the involvement of al-Qaeda operatives. These operatives are members of the same terrorist network involved in the Mombasa suicide attack on the Paradise Hotel and the launching of shoulder-fired missiles at an Arkia airliner during take-off from the nearby airport in November 2002, and the attacks on the US embassies in Kenya and Tanzania in 1998.[16]

For al-Qaeda and its supporters the increased American presence in the Persian Gulf region is not only a desecration of Muslim holy places, it is also an opportunity to escalate the struggle against it, in order to expedite the evacuation of American forces and claim a military victory for the forces of revolutionary Islam. The joint American–Saudi Arabian announcement in early May 2003 of the withdrawal of American forces from Saudi Arabia was seized by al-Qaeda as a golden opportunity to claim credit for the decision. Al-Qaeda portrayed the withdrawal as a defeat for American policy, and a sign of cowardice in the face of the expected future wave of terrorism. For Bin Laden, any damage to US forces in the Gulf is a valuable propaganda asset for what can be called "the time of the guerilla," i.e., when foreign forces are preparing to retreat, which creates an opportunity for local forces to attack them during their withdrawal. A likely consequence of an extended US presence in Iraq is anti-American guerilla and terrorist activity, whether committed by Afghan-affiliated Arabs or Saddam fedayeen. This may also spark a wave of domestic international terrorism, especially if the US is joined by other foreign forces in the reconstruction effort, and spill over to the greater international terrorist arena.

The ongoing struggle against international terrorism in the post-war era will require the US and its partners to upgrade their cooperation against al-Qaeda and its allies. The campaign must be conducted intensively, continuously, aggressively, and to a greater extent than in the past. As part of this effort, it will be necessary to step up both bilateral intelligence cooperation – often the most effective measure – and multilateral cooperation between various security forces around the world, and adapt the legal and penal systems to the magnitude of the terrorist threat. Only a joint comprehensive international effort can disrupt al-Qaeda's ability to maneuver and exploit the existing freedom of action available in the open Western democracies, as well as the weak control and absence of effective enforcement in African, Asian, and Middle Eastern countries. It is likely that despite the disagreement over Iraq it will be possible to find a broad common denominator and a coinciding of interests against this specific enemy which will enhance continued cooperation between the United States, European countries, and leading countries in Asia and Africa aimed at waging an uncompromising war against terrorism.

In contrast to the anticipated consensus on greater cooperation against al-Qaeda and its allies, however, the international activity required to prevent countries like Iran, Syria, Lebanon, and others from supporting terrorism can be expected to lead to disputes resonant of the friction between the US and its opponents over what methods were appropriate for handling the Iraqi situation. The economic relations of France, Germany, and Russia with Syria, Lebanon, and Iran are liable to lead the former to dissent from an aggressive joint policy against these countries, and they are particularly likely to oppose economic and diplomatic sanctions against these three Muslim states, let alone any military sanctions whatsoever, should the latter refuse to halt their support for terrorism. An example of this potential disagreement can be found in the question of Hizbollah's status as a terrorist organization. While the United States included Hizbollah on its list of foreign terrorist organizations (FTO), the main European countries, including France, Germany, and even Britain, refrained from including the organization on their list of terrorist organizations, arguing that its political activities should be distinguished from its "military" activities.

Syria's posture during the war in Iraq, which included provocative statements against the US, also highlighted the dilemma over how to deal with it in the post-war era. Following political pressure and threatening hints from the United States and diplomatic warnings from other Western countries, Syria fell into line, and even expressed readiness to take steps towards handing over senior officials in Saddam Hussein's regime. Syria also acceded to American requests to close the Damascus offices of terrorist organizations. It nevertheless appears that at this stage neither Syria nor Iran feels threatened to a degree that would force it to refrain from supporting terrorism; each will likely merely exercise more caution in this policy.

It is also likely that in order to achieve a genuine reversal in these countries' policies on terrorism the broadest possible international coalition will have to impose upon them a change in the rules of the game. This is true for other countries that offer "passive" support to terrorism, including Saudi Arabia, Yemen, Sudan, and even countries such as Somalia. Some of these lack full control over all their sovereign territory, while others vacillate and adopt only temporary or token measures against the terrorists on their soil. An international campaign against terrorism must formulate rules under which countries having difficulty in coping with terrorist infrastructures and, lacking the ability to exert their sovereignty against terrorist groups active in their territory, are assisted by an external international force to arrest or expel the terrorists.

In the post-September 11 era, when terrorism has become globalized, the free world must realize the necessity for adopting the rule that protecting the sovereign borders and international thoroughfares of every country is a crucial element in preserving the safety of the entire world. Failure to adopt this rule threatens international security and order, and will enable terrorists to continue their attacks in various locations around the world, thereby undermining international stability.

The elimination by military force of a totalitarian Arab regime that supported terrorism unquestionably constitutes a precedent, and is likely to serve as a warning to the various terrorist groups operating in the international arena. The mass suicide attacks that took place in Saudi Arabia and Morocco six weeks after the war ended, however, prove that the problem of terrorism will not disappear quickly from the international agenda. The continuation of the struggle against international terrorism requires formulating a broad system of agreements and cooperation between as many countries as possible, first and foremost the United States and the countries of the expanded European Union, against two main threats: al-Qaeda and the networks it supports, and the countries supporting terrorism. The controversy surrounding the war in Iraq between the "natural" or "likely" allies in a war against terrorism has not materially damaged the potential cooperation in fighting al-Qaeda. It has, however, highlighted the different approaches of the parties regarding a solution for the problem of countries supporting terrorism. The international community must now confront this problem, as it must concurrently assume responsibility for the growth in international terrorism to its present proportions, and redefine the rules of the game for countries using terrorism as a weapon to promote their political interests. The absence of such agreements is liable to limit the campaign against international terrorism to isolated and temporary successes, while leaving the principal strategic goal of downgrading terrorism's status as a key factor in international relations – especially after September 11, 2001 – unachieved.

Notes

1   Yoram Schweitzer and Shaul Shay, *The Globalization of Terror: The Challenge of Al-Qaida and the Response of the International Community* (New Jersey: Transaction Publishers of Rutgers University Press, 2003), p. 1.
2   The term refers to veterans of the war in Afghanistan (1979–89) and the "second and third generation descendants" who came to Afghanistan and were trained, indoctrinated, and sworn to loyalty by Bin Laden and his operatives, and then dispersed in countries around the world for terrorist purposes. See Yoram Schweitzer, "Middle East Terrorism: The 'Afghanistan Alumni,'" in Shlomo Brom and Yiftah Shapir (eds.), *The Middle East Military Balance 1999–2000* (Cambridge, Mass: MIT Press with the Jaffee Center for Startegic Studies, 2000), pp. 121–33.
3   Jeffrey Record, "The Bush Doctrine and War with Iraq," *Parameters* 33, no. 1 (2003): 4–21.
4   Record, "The Bush Doctrine and the War with Iraq."

5   Anthony Lewis, "Bush and Iraq," *The New York Review of Books*, 49, no. 17, November 7, 2002.
6   Laurie Mylroie, *The War Against America – Saddam Hussein and the World Trade Center Attacks: A Study of Revenge*, 2nd rev. ed. (New York: HarperCollins, 2001).
7   David Johnson, "Senior Officials Tell Lawmakers of Iraq–Al-Qaeda Ties," *New York Times* internet edition, February 11, 2003.
8   NewsMax.com, America's News Page, April 3, 2001.
9   Anat Kurz, "The Persian Gulf Crisis, International Terrorism, and the Armed Palestinian Struggle," in Joseph Alpher (ed.), *War in the Gulf: Implications for Israel*, Report of a Jaffee Center for Strategic Studies study group (Tel Aviv: Papyrus, 1991), p. 191.
10 Bin Laden's cassette tape, broadcast by al-Jazeera, February 2003.
11 Bin Laden tape, February 2003.
12 AFP, May 13, 2003.
13 Yoram Schweitzer, "The Age of Non-Conventional Terrorism," *Strategic Assessment* 6, no. 1 (2003): 26–31.
14 Schweitzer and Shay, *The Globalization of Terror*, p. 46.
15 Dan Murphy, "Southeast Asia's 'Mini Al-Qaeda' Nests in Thailand," *Christian Science Monitor* internet edition, June 12, 2003; and Yossi Melman, "Terrorist Network Discovered in Thailand Intended to Attack Israelis," *Ha'aretz* internet edition, June 11, 2003.
16 Yossi Melman, "The United States Warns against Terrorist Attacks Around the World, Britain Halts its Flights to Kenya," *Ha'aretz* internet edition, May 18, 2003.

The Revolution in Military Affairs and the Operation in Iraq

6

Isaac Ben-Israel

Three weeks elapsed from the opening shots of the war on the night of March 19–20, 2003 until the capture of Baghdad's central square. Within this brief period the United States, with limited assistance from British forces, toppled Saddam Hussein's regime, routed his army, and captured a vast geographical area with far less manpower and fewer tanks than possessed by the Israel Defense Forces (IDF). This feat was accomplished with fewer than 160 casualties, nearly half of which were the result of accidents and "friendly fire."

In many ways the campaign in Iraq ushered in a new age. The era when victory is gained only by outmaneuvering the enemy and dominating over it by capturing dominant terrain and "high ground" is over, and a new era has dawned when decisive victory can also be obtained by eliminating the enemy's main forces with (conventional) *precision standoff fire*, that is, beyond the enemy's range of fire. The war in Iraq constitutes a crystallization of a long process that began with introducing a new concept in warfare, Revolution in Military Affairs (RMA), which emerged at the end of the Gulf War (January–February 1991), continued during the fighting in Kosovo and Afghanistan, and reached its climax in Iraq in 2003.

The following essay deals primarily with this aspect of the war, especially its relevance to Israel's security doctrine. Naturally, an attempt to derive military lessons so soon after the conclusion of the war should proceed cautiously. Much more remains hidden than is known, and deeper research will be necessary before insights that will stand the test of time can be gained.[1]

Background and Principal Moves

Balance of Forces

Numerically the Iraqis were far superior in ground forces and inferior in the air *vis-à-vis* the Americans (tables 6.1 and 6.2), but when the *quality* of both equipment and manpower is taken into account, the Americans' advantage was clear in every area.

First, the majority of Iraqi equipment was outdated, in contrast to the Americans' state-of-the-art military hardware, some of which had no parallel on the Iraqi side (including aircraft carriers, spy satellites, cruise missiles, and precision weapons able to function at night and in any weather). Second, in the twelve years since the 1991 Gulf War, the Iraqi Army was limited by a strictly enforced arms embargo, which led to its equipment being in poor technical state (although, as is often the case with Soviet-made equipment, it proved more serviceable than expected).

Table 6.1   Comparison of Military Forces – Ground Forces

	Iraq	Coalition Forces
Number of troops	400,000 (plus an additional one million paramilitaries)	225,000 Americans; 30,000 British
Number of tanks	2,200–2,400 (including 750 T-72s)	Approximately 500
Main ground force	23 ground divisions of various types including 6 armored and 7 Republican Guard divisions (3 armored, 3 mechanized, 1 infantry)	3rd Infantry Division (18,000 troops, 200 tanks) and units from the 5th Corps (total – nearly 50,000 troops); one brigade of the 82nd Airborne Division (4,000 troops); the 101st Airborne Division (approximately 20,000 troops, 275 Apache attack helicopters); the 1st Marine Expeditionary Force and units from the 2nd Marine Expeditionary Force (total – 2 divisions, 60,000 troops, 120 tanks); a reduced British armored division (26,000 troops, 120 tanks).

The Goals of the War

The war's political–military aims were decided in Washington:[2]

1   A stable Iraq, with its territorial integrity intact and a broad-based government[3] that renounces WMD development and use, and no longer supports terrorism or threatens its neighbors.

Table 6.2 Comparison of Military Forces – Air and Sea Forces

	Iraq	Coalition Forces
Fighter planes	310 (including 45 Mirage F-1 and MIG 29)	650 (F-14, F-15, F-16, F-18, and A10 aircraft); and an additional 80 British and Australian planes
Attack helicopters	100	Approximately 500[4]
Bombers	1 Topolov-16	43 (B-1, B-2, B-52 bombers and an additional 12 F-117 stealth aircraft)
Surface-to-air missile batteries	40 (SAM 2 and SAM 3 batteries); 10 SAM 6 20 SAM 8, and 70 Roland batteries	Not relevant[5]
Aircraft carriers	—	6 American aircraft carriers ("Lincoln," "Kitty Hawk," "Constellation," and "Nimitz" in the Persian Gulf and Arabian Sea; "Roosevelt" and "Truman" in the Mediterranean Sea); 1 British aircraft carrier ("Ark Royal")

2 Success in Iraq leveraged to convince or compel other countries to cease support to terrorists and to deny them access to WMD.
3 Destabilize, isolate, and overthrow the Iraqi regime and provide support to a new, broad-based government.
4 Destroy Iraqi WMD capability and infrastructure.
5 Protect allies and supporters from Iraqi threats and attacks.[6]
6 Destroy terrorist networks in Iraq. Gather intelligence on global terrorism; detain terrorists and war criminals, and free individuals unjustly detained under the Iraqi regime.

The military level translated these goals into the following objectives:[7]

1 Defeat or compel capitulation of Iraqi forces.
2 Neutralize regime leadership.
3 Neutralize Iraqi TBM/WMD delivery systems.
4 Control WMD infrastructure.
5 Ensure the territorial integrity of Iraq.
6 Deploy and posture CFC forces[8] for post-hostility operations, initiating humanitarian assistance operations for the Iraqi people, within capabilities.
7 Set military conditions for provisional/permanent government to assume power.
8 Maintain international and regional support.
9 Neutralize Iraqi regime's C2 & security forces.
10 Gain and maintain air, maritime and space supremacy.

Planning Stage

American planners apparently debated two basic approaches to an effective method for attaining victory. One, the more brazen approach of Defense Secretary Donald Rumsfeld, held that the technology tested during the last decade (especially in Kosovo and Afghanistan) was sufficiently developed to be relied on. Military victory in Iraq would come about mainly through precision standoff fire (almost exclusively from the air) that would inflict a high level of damage on key Iraqi targets day and night. Termed the *"shock and awe"* approach, this assault would be backed up by small, mobile armored forces (Rapid Decisive Operations) that would follow in the wake of the fire and exploit the psychological shock created by the swift destruction of Iraqi armament. The second approach, advocated by more conservative planners, first and foremost General Tommy Franks, demanded the concentration of a large land force (*"overwhelming force"*) to create the necessary psychological effect for an unqualified victory.

It appears that the final plan reflected a compromise between these two approaches. Victory would be won mainly from the air, but only after the buildup of a relatively large ground force that would attack simultaneously along two axes – from the south (Kuwait) and the north (Turkey).

In practice, the original plan seems to have gone awry due to several factors. First, on the eve of the war the Americans received information regarding the whereabouts of Saddam Hussein and his inner circle of leadership. This led to a deviation from the original plan and an earlier launching of the attack on the night of March 19–20 against targets in Baghdad, while special forces simultaneously penetrated the arena, especially in western Iraq. Second, the faulty political preparations for the campaign resulted in the absence of expected support of the UN and the rest of the world, and the staunch opposition of key Western powers such as France and Germany. Against this backdrop, fear loomed that the massive bombing of targets in Baghdad might trigger another wave of global protest. This may have been why the Americans – apparently bowing to British pressure – avoided implementing the "shock and awe" concept to its full potential in the first days of the war.[9] Third, the surprising refusal of Turkey to approve the launching of an invasion force from their country impinged on the original plan and forced the Americans to redeploy in the south, which caused a loss of costly days.

Despite these exigencies, and perhaps thanks to Rumsfeld's original concept, the Americans set out on March 20 on a rapid drive from Kuwait to Baghdad, bypassing major cities such as Umm Qasr and Basra on the way, leaving them to the British to capture at a slower pace. In a race along the desert axis (figure 6.1) the American forces completed a 400-kilometer drive in one week, stopping to reorganize at the gates of Karbala, less than 100 kilometers from the heart of Baghdad.

In addition to the military lessons detailed below, the flexibility displayed by the Americans in modifying their plans to changing conditions was outstanding. The readjustment of a military operation of so large a scope is no trifling matter, and it bears witness to the US Army's high level of technology, which enabled such

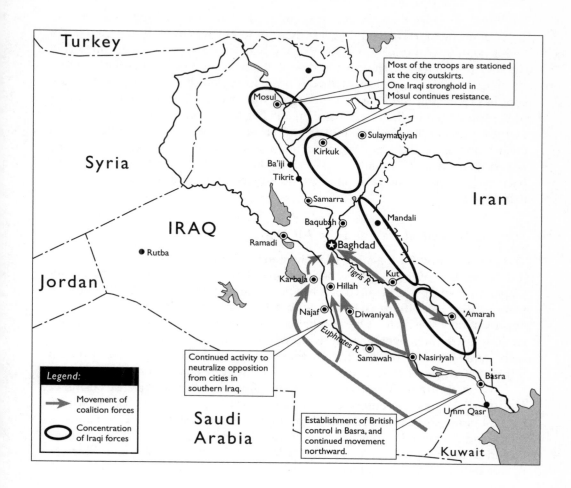

Turkey

Most of the troops are stationed at the city outskirts. One Iraqi stronghold in Mosul continues resistance.

Mosul

Sulaymaniyah

Kirkuk

Syria

Ba'iji

Tikrit

Samarra

Iran

Baqubah

Mandali

IRAQ

Ramadi

Baghdad

• Rutba

Tigris R.

Karbala

Kut

Jordan

Hillah

Najaf

Diwaniyah

Amarah

Euphrates R.

Continued activity to neutralize opposition from cities in southern Iraq.

Samawah

Nasiriyah

Basra

Legend:

Movement of coalition forces

Saudi Arabia

Umm Qasr

Concentration of Iraqi forces

Establishment of British control in Basra, and continued movement northward.

Kuwait

Figure 6.1   Coalition Forces, April 10, 2003

flexibility, and reflects particularly on the quality and professionalism of the commanders.

Stage 1: Kuwait to Karbala (Outskirts of Baghdad)

It took one week for the main American force (the 5th Corps) to reach Karbala and arrive at the outskirts of Baghdad, less than 100 kilometers from the city center. Up to this point the Americans had fought mainly in the desert without encountering significant Iraqi forces. The advance was halted for a number of reasons. The first consideration was logistical, with the need to replenish fuel and ammunition supplies following the long drive. Second, Iraqi troops that had avoided attack were encouraged by their very survival and began sniping at the Americans (and taking a number of prisoners, mostly rear echelon troops). Third, the Republican Guard divisions, the Iraqi regime's main force, were deployed between the American army and the center of Baghdad. Only after they were sufficiently incapacitated, which would take time, would American ground forces engage them directly.

Stage 2: A Tactical Halt and the Air War

The time required for logistical organization was primarily used for the methodical destruction of the Republican Guard mainly from the air, effected by fighter planes and bombers. The main bombs were Laser Guided Bombs (LGB) and Joint Direct Attack Munitions (JDAM)[10] with a Circular Error Probability (CEP)[11] of approximately one meter. One bomber carrying more than twenty such weapons could unleash them over an armored force and each bomb would home in on "its own" tank. Twenty sorties a day by these planes could wipe out 2,000 armored targets in five days (!) regardless of weather or lighting conditions.

While the Iraqi divisions were pounded, Iraqi air fields, air defense positions, radar installations, C^2 centers, and similar targets came under attack. Nearly 30 percent of the sorties were allocated for infrastructure targets, especially government and communications sites, in order to create confusion and strategic blindness among the Iraqi leadership. "Classic" infrastructure objectives, such as power stations, bridges, and dams, were hardly ever targeted out of consideration for the "day after."

A total of 36,000 sorties were carried out during the war: 14,000 attack missions, 5,000 missions to establish air supremacy, and approximately 2,500 intelligence and control missions. Approximately another 14,000 were support missions, such as refueling, transportation, electronic warfare, and so forth.[12] In a war of this sort, however, the effectiveness of air strikes is not measured by the number of sorties but in the number of precision bombs launched and targets destroyed. The American Air Command planned its missions not according to the sorties but according to the number of targets to be attacked. Each aircraft was given an index that represented how many targets it could hit in one sortie, depending on its mission type and weapons capability.[13]

Stage 3: The Capture of Baghdad

Military theory argues that a sufficiently large force – a division, for example – cannot function as an organic unit if 10–20 percent of its weapons and manpower are destroyed. In practice, the Americans began moving their forces into Baghdad only after verification via satellite photographs that over 50 percent of the Republican Guard division tanks, armored vehicles, and artillery defending the city had been eliminated.

The pace of the Republican Guard attrition at this stage was between 5 and 10 percent per day of fighting. Little wonder then that the American forces entering Baghdad encountered almost no resistance. The Iraqi soldiers who survived the onslaught fled in all directions. The Americans' decision of April 1 to expand the list of approved targets in Baghdad and increase bomb weight undoubtedly had a powerful demoralizing effect on the Iraqi forces.[14] As a result of the psychological strain from the air blitz, the possibility of prolonged resistance by compelling house to house fighting à la Stalingrad was at best remote.

On April 3, two weeks after the opening of the ground campaign, US troops seized control of Baghdad's international airport, which is twenty-five kilometers from the city center. The final capture of the city took place the following week, on April 9. Significantly, the image engraved in popular consciousness (including the Iraqis' minds) that epitomized the moment of victory was not when the Iraqi divisions disintegrated, and indeed this occurred beyond the visual range of the ground forces and the media cameras. Rather, to most, the decisive moment occurred when American troops entered Baghdad's main square, and when the statue of Saddam Hussein came crashing down live on TV before the eyes of the world.[15]

Western Iraq

Parallel to the moves just described, the Americans operated in western Iraq, mainly with air power and special forces units. This was a lesson learned from the 1991 Gulf War when the United States failed to prevent missiles attacks against Israel.

To the best of our knowledge a relatively limited number of commandos – at most a few thousand – took part in this theater of operations. They were assisted by heavy air support that patrolled the desert regularly in order to spot and destroy Iraqi potential surface-to-surface missile (SSM) launch sites.

The Americans eventually gained control of observation and fire positions in an enormous area – twice the size of Israel – without recourse to a large number of troops. The story of the campaign in western Iraq requires a comprehensive examination since it appears to refute one of warfare's most basic axioms: territorial control demands a significant ground presence.

The Military Conceptual Approach and Doctrine

The RMA Concept

The concept of the Revolution in Military Affairs was developed after the 1991 Gulf War. As modern technology advanced to what was termed the "information revolution," the need arose to redefine warfare theory. According to the American approach this was based on four pillars: precision strike; space; dominant maneuver; and information warfare.[16]

The term *precision strike* relates to precision guided munitions (PGM) capable of hitting targets within an accuracy of a few meters. Such precision enables a revolution in the fighting effectiveness, especially from the air. No longer are waves of bombers required to drop a massive quantity of explosives over a particular area for carpet bombing. Instead, individual bombs, each guided to a specific objective, can attack the target with a high degree of certainty that it will be killed. Since these bombs are dropped from standoff ranges, that is, beyond the range of enemy counter fire, enemy forces can be demolished with an extraordinarily low number of casualties to the attacker. In a month of combat (until April 20) the Americans and coalition forces lost 159 troops, a very low figure relative to losses in previous wars.[17] The expected attrition on the side utilizing this weaponry, therefore, is minimal, while the attrition impact on the opponent is great. The net effect of these two factors results in attrition ratios entirely different from past experience.

Yet herein lies a mixed blessing. Since standoff PGM technology is employed, usually no visual line exists between the launcher and target, and hence intelligence sensors are mandatory for this kind of attack. These sensors must operate in real time and supply updated target intelligence to the platform that launches the munitions. The intelligence sensor has to be linked to the firing units via a computerized C³I system capable of delivering the relevant information to the right fire unit in the required time.

The key requirement for the realization of this concept is an accurate intelligence picture of enemy targets. Spy satellites can provide this but it demands control of *space*. Such control provides not only intelligence[18] but also communications of unlimited ranges (communications satellites), precision navigation (GPS satellites),[19] early warning of ballistic missile launches (Defense Support Program – DSP – satellites),[20] control of television media, and weather forecasts. The Americans made use of nearly fifty (!) satellites in the course of the war.[21]

The third tenet of RMA is *dominant maneuver*. The control of the battlefield by means of precision fire can create a situation where the enemy is constricted in deploying its armored forces, that is, in maneuvering in the battlefield. Every piece of armament entering the fighting area will be detected and destroyed. In this context, some people began referring to the "empty battlefield."

The notion that reliable target intelligence is one of the indispensable conditions for the success of RMA[22] is a specific case of the more general principle in which information is transformed into a strategic asset. The side that controls information – that can obtain information about the enemy and prevent the access to similar information about itself – has a major advantage on the modern battlefield. According to the American concept, the term *information warfare* refers to a number of different features: cyber-warfare (computers are the main technological means for storing and transmitting information), electronic warfare (waged mainly against radio and communications systems), psychological warfare,[23] and the handling of the media (beginning with press briefings, through journalists attached to fighting units, and culminating in the manipulation of information released to the public).[24] The first feature was almost entirely absent in the recent war, but the other aspects of the information warfare were tested in live situations, generally with great success.

The Main Principle: Victory by Fire instead of by Maneuvering

It is important to understand the fault line dividing the classic concept of warfare and RMA. In the classic concept, victory is won by means of maneuvering; in RMA victory is gained by fire, that is, by a high destruction rate of point targets, from standoff ranges.

It is true that maneuvering also uses firepower, but then the goal of firepower is assisting the maneuver. In other words, maneuver uses firepower to achieve its main goal, which is flanking, capturing territory, and so forth. RMA theory contends that firepower is liberated from its exclusive role of assisting maneuvering, and contributes directly to victory by eliminating the enemy's weapons. Precision fire is also a key element in maneuvering,[25] but in that case its goal is the "classic" one – assisting the maneuvering force, which is distinctly different from precision strike whose goal is decision of the battle.

In the war in Iraq the roles were reversed: precision strike was the main factor that defeated the Iraqis, while maneuvering fulfilled a role of assisting precision fire. The American forces' rapid movement prevented the Iraqis from concentrating on entrenching their positions and on self-survival, and pressured them to move their forces, thus exposing them through movement to air attack.

Precision Guided Munitions

The first major appearance of precision weapons came at the end of the Vietnam War with laser-guided bombs launched from F-4 planes that struck at bridges. The Israeli Air Force was one of the only air forces in the world that understood the significance of this weaponry and began developing it in the early 1970s. The inability to overcome Arab surface-to-air missiles (SAM) in the 1973 Yom Kippur War greatly hastened Israel's PGM R&D. Less than a decade later, in the Peace for the Galilee War, the Israeli Air Force's achievement of air supremacy over Syria in the Lebanon Valley was the first major battle in modern history that was determined by PGM.[26] Today, three focal points of PGM development can be observed internationally: the United States, France, and Israel.[27] These countries are almost alone in working on the development of the PGM system, and their military forces are the only ones significantly equipped with it.[28]

PGM also have an Achilles' heel. The Iraqis, for example, used six GPS jammers supplied to them by Russia. The jammers were only partially successful because they were unable to span the entire range of GPS frequencies, and American armaments were equipped with anti-jamming devices. This illustrates the difficulty in relying solely on PGM and the need to develop and install countermeasures at the same time as PGM development proceeds (this is one of the reasons why the concept of precision strike has not been eagerly embraced by other armies in the world).

America's experience in local wars over the last decade has contributed much to bolstering confidence in these weapons and in developing the doctrine of precision strike (table 6.3).

Table 6.3 PGM in US Wars between 1991 and 2003

	Number of warplanes (US and coalition)	Length of war (days)	Number of sorties	Number of bombs	Percentage of PGM
Gulf War (1991)	1,850	43	120,000	265,000[29]	8
Kosovo (1999)	1,000	78	38,000	23,000	35
Afghanistan (2001)	500 and 30 bombers[30]	60[31]	29,000	22,000	56
War in Iraq (2003)	730 and 40 bombers	20 (until the capture of Baghdad) Total: 30[32]	36,000	29,200[33]	68

PGM launched by the Americans in Iraq were based on a variety of technologies, including GPS, electro-optic guidance,[34] radar guidance, and cruise missiles. Of the 19,950 PGM launched, approximately one-third – 6,642 – were JDAM type (GPS-navigated), and one half – 9,180 – were laser-guided bombs.[35] The total number of these two types came to about 80 percent of the smart munitions used in the war. As stated, the massive use of PGM renders the quantitative measure of sorties irrelevant. The American Air Command translated the war's objectives into a list of missions (gaining air supremacy, destroying ground forces, gathering intelligence, and so forth) and drafted a list of targets according to priority. Table 6.4 illustrates the division of planned targets against the targets actually attacked. Eighty percent of the targets struck were Iraqi ground forces. Given the accuracy of the hits by the munitions employed, one can estimate the number of targets hit to be over 10,000!

The air force's extraordinary effectiveness in demolishing the Iraqi Army's structural framework stemmed in part from the fact that the majority of the airpower operated independently of the ground forces' offense rather than in the

Table 6.4 Attack Objectives in the War in Iraq

Mission	Number of targets planned for attack on list of priorities	Number of targets actually attacked (% of total)	
Attack of ground forces	12,893	15,826	(80)
Command posts and regime operations targets	4,559	1,799	(9)
Air supremacy	2,124	1,441	(7)
Surface-to-surface missiles and non-conventional weapons	1,840	832	(4)
Total	25,240	19,898	(100)

classic mission of close support. Close air support is always problematic and demands exceptional coordination in battlefield conditions.

Mobile Targets

As described above, a dominant component of the PGM used in the war relied on GPS navigation whose principal advantages are its nighttime and all-weather operability.[36] Its drawbacks are apparent in highly fluid battlefield conditions because the time required for photographing a target, calculating its coordinates on the GPS network, and feeding them into the smart bomb is liable to be unduly long. This problem is exacerbated in cases of SSM and Weapons of Mass Destruction (WMD) warfare when destruction of the launchers must not be too late,[37] or in "targeted assassinations" when the target is a moving individual.

To overcome this dilemma, bombers were equipped with synthetic aperture radar (SAR) that allows the target to be "seen" even through clouds. The target's GPS coordinates were automatically delivered into the bombs in the plane's bay, which were then released on the assumption that the target would remain stationary. Since the number of bombers equipped with this technology was small, the Americans developed a system for handling highly mobile targets, or TST (Time Sensitive Targets).[38] This method was based on a formation of planes in which one platform (usually a bomber or unmanned air vehicle) was equipped with SAR radar, while other planes were carrying arms. The planes in the formation were linked via a command and control system that enabled them to stay in contact with the radar and receive real-time coordinates. In the course of the war wider use was made of this method and it proved its effectiveness against mobile targets not connected with the Iraqi leadership or SSMs, for example, tanks.[39]

Most of the American PGM were applied against static targets, such as command posts, radar installations, and airfields. Even when tanks and armored vehicles were attacked, most of the munitions were launched against static targets because of the Iraqis' clear defensive strategy. This means that in a more dynamic war, other types of homing and guidance technologies might be needed against moving targets whose stationary time is short.

Weather and Nighttime Conditions

One of the classic weak points of the concept of precision strike is its dependency on lighting and weather conditions for the identification of targets and guidance of munitions toward them. In thirty days of combat in Iraq (from March 19–20 to April 18) only seventeen days offered good weather.[40] The US solved this problem by employing GPS navigated ordinance. This was the first war in history in which the air forces preferred to operate at night and in inclement weather since these obstructed the Iraqi air defenses more than they influenced the performance of the American planes. Nevertheless, in a more dynamic war, if reliance on the GPS system becomes impossible, the need will arise to devise more generic solutions to the problem of nighttime conditions and cloud covering.

Collateral Damage and Civilian Casualties

Although the PGM system was initially developed as part of a purely military concept to enhance the destruction rate of military targets, a byproduct was its immediate implications for collateral damage, that is, injury to innocent civilians who inadvertently were close to military targets. The PGM concept guarantees damage within the specified targets and greatly reduces damage to adjacent targets. Nevertheless, there is always a possibility of technical error (or operational error – such as selecting the wrong target). In general, the war in Iraq proved that modern technology can significantly reduce collateral damage.[41] Furthermore, added to the precision factor were the great standoff ranges involved that were generally beyond the range of media cameras. These two attributes together not only reduced actual injury to civilians but also the impact on the media. The American media reported little in the way of Iraqi casualties, not because its embedded journalists were censored, but because most of the casualties occurred at distances of dozens or hundreds of kilometers from the moving ground forces, and were not observed by the journalists attached to the units.

The hitch in the PGM technology's undisputed effectiveness stemmed from the fact that it was partially launched from standoff ranges, without being able to identify the targets. This led to an increase in casualties from friendly fire. According to current figures, 10 percent of the battle casualties resulted from friendly fire[42] despite the great effort made by the US Army to provide its troops with means to prevent accidents of this nature.[43]

The End of the Era of Attack Helicopters?

Although the verdict regarding the role of attack helicopters in the war against Iraq is still pending, we can cautiously state at this point that (once again) they proved to be a disappointment. In contrast to previous wars in the last decade, the Americans made a genuine effort this time to put the attack helicopter's enormous firepower to full use. Similar to its performance in Kosovo and the 1991 Gulf War, the helicopter proved capable of dealing only with short-range armored targets, yet in these distances it was highly vulnerable to opposing fire. Of the seven manned aircraft lost by the Americans and British, six were attack helicopters – four Apaches and two Cobras.[44]

Attack helicopters were developed in the Vietnam War for use against guerilla forces, and not specifically for anti-tank missions. Originally the attack helicopter was designed as a kind of "flying tank," with an emphasis on mobility and firepower rather than heavy protection.[45] Following its failure in Kosovo it seemed to recover some of its former glory in Afghanistan, but there too it was not operating against a regular army. In Iraq the situation was entirely different. For example, a force of thirty-four Apache Longbow helicopters completely failed in an assault on the Republican Guard Medina Division on March 24. The helicopters were caught in withering fire from small arms and light anti-aircraft guns and had to withdraw without any successful strikes on the Iraqi tanks. After this encounter American commanders refused to send them on missions beyond the front lines of friendly ground troops.[46]

Excluding a number of minor engagements (the capture of Umm Qasr, for example) no actual use was made of attack helicopters, and a big question mark hovers over their future.[47]

Air Supremacy

The US Air Force went to war believing it was unnecessary to invest valuable time and energy in destroying Iraqi air defenses, especially SAM batteries. Instead, it preferred to develop a number of techniques (munitions as well as electronic warfare measures)[48] for "suppressing" the air defense systems and operating in their presence.[49] This concept is termed SEAD: Suppression of Enemy Air Defense.

In general, the concept passed the test. The fact that the war ended almost without any air losses bears witness to its success. The American effort to maintain SEAD, however, was much greater than what was needed to destroy the original air defense system (via PGM). It is quite possible that in the coming years there will be a reversal from the SEAD orientation to Destruction of Enemy Air Defense (DEAD).

Special Forces

Unprecedented use was made of special forces in the war in Iraq, with the deployment of approximately ten thousand troops in these operations.

The plan to prevent the launching of SSMs from western Iraq was assigned solely to special forces who through observation and firepower succeeded in gaining control of an enormous area. This was made possible thanks to the high professional abilities of the troops and their extremely close contact with air power (helicopters and fixed-wing planes). In future wars the use of special forces can be expected to increase.

The War against Surface-to-Surface Missiles

The US learned a bitter lesson from its failure to counter SSMs in the 1991 War and came prepared this time with answers on two levels: offense and defense. The offense component was based on a system that integrated bombers, fighter planes, and special forces. The defense umbrella was to be provided by Patriot missiles specially adapted to intercept SSMs.[50] In practice, the overall response was not tested, but regarding the defense component a number of serious questions were raised.

According to US Army claims, the Patriot batteries succeeded in intercepting eight or nine[51] of the twelve al-Samoud and Ababil-100 missiles fired at Kuwait. In the previous war the meaning of "interception" had not been clear, and it seems that this time too "interception" was not always a matter of neutralizing or exploding the SSM warhead. Even if the American claim of a 60 percent success rate is accepted, this figure is low considering the relatively slow and short-range missiles employed by the Iraqis.[52] Furthermore, another problem also vexed the allies – the shooting down of friendly planes,[53] a lapse rooted in the defects of the Identification of Friend or Foe (IFF) system.[54]

Non-Conventional Weapons

As of this writing, the effort is underway to uncover WMD facilities in Iraq. No one doubts that Iraq had the capability to develop chemical weapons, though there is far less certainty regarding its biological weapons, and the issue on today's agenda is whether Iraq actually possessed these weapons during the war. Whatever the verdict, their potential use exerted much influence on American moves during the war. In the final tally it seems that the story of Iraq's WMD can support the school of thought claiming that there is a low risk of chemical weapons being used against a force that is equipped with a strategic deterrent.

Force Multiplier

The main force multiplier in the war was, of course, the PGM. Table 6.5, which charts the implications of this force multiplier, shows that the ability of one PGM-equipped plane attacking a point target, such as a tank, can be compared to that of fifteen planes twenty years ago or sixty planes thirty years ago. It comes as no surprise that this technological revolution has had a decisive influence on warfare doctrine.

At the same time, other vital factors should not be dismissed as force multipliers. The majority of American planes took off from bases and carriers located hundreds of nautical miles from Baghdad.[55] In this context, the value of refueling planes cannot be overstated, and indeed, refueling tankers in the Gulf numbered more than two hundred. Added to these were one hundred intelligence and surveillance planes and nearly fifty command and control planes. The successful application of the RMA concept occurred largely thanks to these planes, in conjunction with the satellite system.

Table 6.5   PGM as a Force Multiplier

	Yom Kippur War (1973)	Peace for the Galilee War (1982)	War in Iraq (2003)
Weapon systems	Only some planes were equipped with (analogue) weapon release computers	All planes were equipped with (digital) weapon release computers, and a few with PGM	Nearly all planes equipped with PGM
Average CEP[56]	25–30 meters	12 meters	3–4 meters
Probability of hitting a point target[57]	1–2%	7%	~ 100%
Force's efficiency proportion	1	1:4	1:60

The war in Iraq demonstrated the unequivocal value of an advanced computerized network system (communications, command, and control) in modern combat.

Survival – The Strategy of Despair (Asymmetric War)

One of the great fears of the designers of the RMA concept was the possible development of an asymmetric answer to technological warfare. Three types of responses were hypothesized: (1) in classic warfare scenarios: through survival strategy, heavy use of dummies, camouflage, smoke, and so forth; (2) covert means to unleash force, especially terror; and (3) the development of WMD as a deterrent to classic technological superiority.

From today's vantage point regarding the war in Iraq, such fears turned out to be highly exaggerated. First, against the backdrop of a total war, terror's impact is clearly minimal. By its nature terror is designed to destabilize the life of the ordinary civilian, so its impact is reduced especially when it is pitted against highly trained military forces (a distinction should be made here between terrorism and popular guerilla warfare). Second, terror operations require meticulous planning and preparations, and cannot be implemented as readily as standard weapons, such as planes or tanks. Third, WMD (or more precisely, chemical weapons) clearly failed to pose a sufficient deterrent against an opposing force also armed with similar (and even superior) weaponry. Fourth, and perhaps most significantly, the strategy of survival does not usually lead to victory. At best it is capable of postponing the inevitable, the defeat of the weak. Iraqi behavior demonstrated that in the final count the strategy for survival is a strategy of despair; the aim was not to win the struggle but to postpone defeat. Concealment, camouflage, smoke, and shunning actual combat cannot effectively triumph over PGM.

Implications for Israel

The IDF versus Syria

When the US forces against Iraq are compared with the balance of forces between Israel and Syria an interesting conclusion is reached: Israel is militarily capable of attaining victory against the Syrian army to the same degree (at least) as the American victory over the Iraqi army. Israel has the power, technology, and battlefield conceptualization necessary for this.[58]

In general, Syria's position is similar to Iraq's. Since the collapse of the Soviet empire it has been at a loss to obtain new weapons in any significant quantity, and its existing military equipment continues to deteriorate. In contrast, Israel has succeeded in developing and introducing all the necessary elements of the RMA doctrine. This enterprise, whose conceptual roots date back to the 1973 Yom Kippur War, was tested in the air war with Syria over Lebanon during the Peace for the Galilee War (1982), and forms the main pillar in the IDF's buildup. If the IDF were required to provide an answer to Syria alone, it could, like the Americans, significantly reduce its maneuvering forces, that is, cut back the number of armored divisions and tanks, and compensate for this with precision standoff fire.[59] It should be emphasized that a decrease in size does not imply a comparable decrease in quality of performance; on the contrary, the greater the reduction in numbers, the higher the quality.

IDF Buildup

The removal of Iraq from the circle of states on Israel's eastern front inclined to disrupt peace treaties with Egypt and Jordan, and the influence of the war in Iraq on Syria, gives the IDF a span of several years to complete its precision strike buildup while significantly reducing its maneuvering force. (Note, however, that because of the Palestinian conflict and the terror threat, it is important to maintain a quality infantry.) The resources available after the reduction of armored divisions must be channeled primarily toward strengthening the air force and military intelligence, as well as enhancing R&D with an emphasis on C^3 systems.[60]

Paradigm Shifts

While the IDF must apply the lessons of the war in Iraq, one has to bear in mind that these lessons do not cover all the areas where the IDF has to provide a security response.

The threats that the IDF, or for that matter any modern army, has to face can be roughly outlined on a single axis: the distance of the threat from one's homes and streets. The terror threat lies at the near end of the spectrum – at "zero" distance from private homes and residential neighborhoods. At the far end of the spectrum lie threats such as SSMs that can reach Israel from afar. These include the recent threat from Iraq, the present threat from Iran, and the future threat from Libya. In the center lies the area of classic warfare between national armies (figure 6.2).

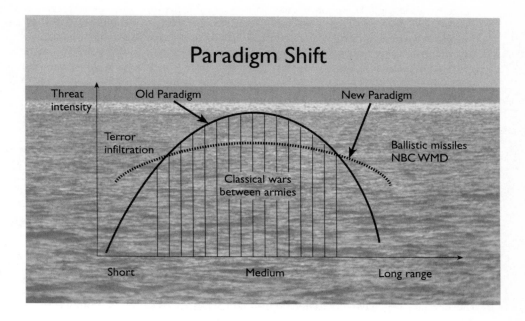

Figure 6.2   Paradigm Shift in Warfare

Until recently the IDF operated according to the classic paradigm: the bulk of its resources were invested for cases of war between armies of states. The main theme of force buildup of this nature (illustrated by the central curve in figure 6.2) was based on the concept of precision strike. The IDF has gained so many assets in this field that today it can allow itself to relax its effort a little in this area.[61]

Fifteen years ago the Israeli military establishment began dealing seriously with long-range threats, and five years ago it began treating with grave concern the threat of guerilla warfare and terrorism. This "awakening" was the result of involvement with the concept of technological warfare, as described above, and the fear of the asymmetric response it might have to face. It was expected that adversaries at present incapable of technologically handling the new concept (adopted by the IDF twenty years ago) would develop two extreme responses in the form of asymmetric answers: terror and guerilla warfare on the one hand, and non-conventional SSMs on the other hand.

Today the IDF must continue its precision strike buildup in the middle area (classic combat between armies), and greatly reinforce its means of dealing with threats at the extremes: terror and distant menaces. Like it or not, Israel is situated, together with the United States and the rest of the free world, in the epicenter of the crystallizing process of a new paradigm.

Notes

1 This chapter is based on a wide variety of sources and data published on the war, most of them unclassified. Three sources were of special value in preparing the essay: Lt. Gen. T. Michael Moseley, "Operation Iraqi Freedom – By the Numbers," USCENTAF, Assessment and Analysis Division, April 30, 2003. This is an excellent source as General Moseley was Commander of the Combined Forces Air Component (CFACC) during the war. His data was collected during operations primarily from the Combined Air Cooperation Center set up in the Prince Sultan Air Force Base in Saudi Arabia. Other principal sources were Anthony H. Cordesman, "The 'Instant Lessons' of the Iraq War," Center for Strategic International Studies (CSIS), May 14, 2003; and Shlomo Brom and Yiftah Shapir (eds.), *The Middle East Military Balance 2001–2002* (Cambridge, Mass.: MIT Press with the Jaffee Center for Strategic Studies, 2002).

2 The following two sets of goals are the formally defined aims of the war, Moseley, "Operation Iraqi Freedom – By the Numbers," p. 4.

3 The wording here is of particular interest since it does not relate specifically to "democracy."

4 Comprised of 275 Apache helicopters of the 101st Airborne Division, 140 Apache helicopters of the 4th Division, and approximately 60 Cobra marine helicopters. These were in addition to helicopters of the American 3rd Division and the British forces.

5 The number is irrelevant since the Iraqi Air Force refrained from any offensive attempts.

6 The broad American operation in western Iraq was generated by this particular goal.

7 Moseley, "Operation Iraqi Freedom – By the Numbers," p. 4.

8 I.e., US and coalition forces.

9 The air attack began two days later, on the night of March 21. Before the outbreak of the war, there were those who demanded an opening of fire similar to the 1991 Gulf War, with continuous aerial bombing for twenty days before the ground operations. This time span was later shortened to ten days, then to five, three, and finally zero. See R. Scarborough, "Decisive Force Now Measured by Speed," *Washington Times*, May 7, 2003.

10 These are heavy aerial bombs (each weighing hundreds of kilograms) equipped with a GPS navigation system. Via electromagnetic signals, the bomb fixes its location relative to the GPS satellites and its place on the GPS network. Target coordinates are delivered to the bomb before launching.

11 CEP is a measure for precision and gives the distance from the center of the target in which 50 percent of the weapons hit.

12 See table 6.4.

13 The F-16's target index was one, and the B-52s had an average fixed index of four targets per sortie.

14 A. Cordesman, "Iraq War Note: The Developing Battle of Baghdad and the Early Lessons of War," CSIS, April 7, 2003.

15 A ceasefire was declared on April 14 after the takeover of northern Iraq.

16 See, for example, Eliot Cohen, "A Revolution in Warfare," *Foreign Affairs* 75, no. 2, 1996. See also Eliot Cohen, "America's View of the Revolution in Military Affairs," *Advanced Technology and the Future Warfare*, BESA Center for Strategic Studies, 1996. Involvement in this subject stemmed from the need to adapt military doctrine to the unipolar era following the collapse of the Soviet Union and the lessons derived from the 1991 Gulf War. See Joseph S. Nye Jr., *Bound to Lead: The Changing Nature of American Power* (New York: Basic Books, 1990). In American military circles the new concept was generally described as "transformation." For the official summary of this concept see *Joint Vision 2020*, Washington DC, GPO, June 2000.

17 The average loss was about five soldiers per fighting day, as compared with 210 dead Americans in World War II or eighteen dead per day of combat in Vietnam.

18 As far as is known, six photo satellites were used during the war; they also supplied important data on battle damage assessment (BDA).

19 Twenty-four GPS satellites were used.

20 The DSP satellites spotted twenty-six (short-range) missile launches during the war.

21 Regarding the different roles of space in modern warfare, see and Martin C. Libicki and Stuart E. Johnson (eds.), *Dominant Battlespace Knowledge: The Winning Edge* (Washington: National Defense University Press, 1995); also see, Lt. Col. P. Hays, *United States Military Space into the 21st Century* (US Air University Press, 2002).

22 Excluding the satellites, the Americans and British operated eighty manned photo reconnaissance planes during the war that carried out 1000 sorties, collecting 42,000 battlefield images, 2,400 hours of SIGINT, and 1,700 hours of radar cover.

23 The Americans dropped 31.8 million fliers (eighty-one different types) on Iraq, which required 124 sorties by fighter aircraft and thirty-four sorties by B-52 bombers. In addition, propaganda was broadcast for 306 hours on radio and 304 hours on television.

24 At the same time, the Iraqis' ability to obtain and distribute information was either electronically jammed or physically attacked – 116 targets were hit, including ten media installations.

25 To this end the Americans employed ATACM (Army Tactical Missile System) artillery rockets extensively.

26 On the special mutual relations, feedback, and war lessons exchange between Israel and the United States, see Isaac Ben-Israel, "Technological Lessons," *Ma'arachot*, 332 September/October 1993 [Hebrew].

27 On Israel's PGM engagement in general, and RMA in particular, see Isaac Ben-Israel, "Security, Technology, and the Future Battlefield," in Haggai Golan (ed.), *Israel's Security Web: Core Issues of Israel's National Security in its Sixth Decade* (Ma'arachot, 2001 [Hebrew]), and Shmuel Gordon, *The Bow of Paris: Technology, Doctrine, and Israel's Security* (Sifriyat Hapo'alim, 1997 [Hebrew]).

28 Presumably the picture will change in the aftermath of the war.

29 This includes 300 Tomahawk cruise missiles launched from ships in the Persian Gulf and Mediterranean Sea.

30 The bombers in Afghanistan carried out approximately 1500 sorties (5 percent of the total), unleashing 65 percent of the total munitions and 50 percent of the PGM.

31 Until the fall of Kabul.

32 The table's data refers to thirty days of fighting from March 19–20 to April 18.

33 This includes approximately 800 sea-launched Tomahawk cruise missiles and 153 bomber-launched cruise missiles.

34 Mainly 918 air-to-surface MAVERICK missiles.

35 This includes 562 helicopter-fired Hellfire missiles.

36 This is because the bomb "doesn't care" if the target is obstructed by clouds. It only needs to be in communication with the satellites circling above it in space.

37 In contrast to Israel and its defensive Arrow system, the American forces lack an effective ballistic missile defense system to oppose Scud-type SSMs and their derivatives.

38 Three categories of targets were defined as TST: Iraqi leaders, weapons of mass destruction (especially SSM launchers), and terrorists. During the war 156 missions were carried out in this framework.

39 These additional targets were termed "Dynamic Targets." A total of 686 missions were carried out against dynamic targets.

40 For only 30 percent of the time was less than 70 percent of Iraq's territory covered by clouds.

41 Even official Iraqi briefings claimed that the number of civilian casualties until the entrance into Baghdad on April 3 stood at 1,252 killed, a relatively low number for a campaign of this nature.

42 Losses from accidents must be added to this figure in order to understand the astonishingly low number of casualties from Iraqi fire.

43 This effort was the direct result of lessons from the 1991 Gulf War, when out of a total of 147 soldiers killed in action, thirty-five were killed by friendly fire.

44 Another plane was the A-10. The Americans also lost thirteen additional aircraft as a result of accidents and friendly fire.

45 From this point of view it stands in contrast to the idea behind the Israeli "Merkava" tank where emphasis is placed on increased protection capability instead of other features.

46 R. Scarborough, "Apache Operations a Lesson in Defeat," *Washington Times*, April 22, 2003.

47 Ironically, heavy battle tanks won praise in the war, and there are now second thoughts about the plan to phase them out. Frank Tiboni, "US Army Rethinks Armor Cuts," *Defense News*, April 7, 2003, p. 22.

48 The air orbat in Iraq included thirty-five EA6B planes for electronic warfare.

49 During the war 408 HARM radar-guided missiles were launched.

50 This was done partly by introducing a change into the original batteries, turning them into the PAC-2 GEM type (Patriot Advanced Capability – Guidance Enhanced Missile). In addition an entirely new type was developed, the PAC-3, which was designed to have an improved capability against SSMs.

51 Only four Patriot missiles were of the PAC-3 type because they were deployed in limited numbers.

52 The Patriot also failed to intercept Soviet-made CSSC-3 and Silkworm guided missiles that were launched on March 20 and 29, respectively.

53 A Patriot battery intercepted a British Tornado on March 22 and an F-18 on April 2. In another incident, on March 24, the battery operators switched to automatic mode and hid in the bunker because of Iraqi artillery. The battery automatically locked onto an F-16, which countered by launching a HARM missile that destroyed the Patriot's radar.

54 W. Goodman, "New Questions Surround Patriot Missile System," *Defense News*, April 7, 2003.

55 The distance from the aircraft carriers to Baghdad is comparable to the distance from Tel Aviv to Baghdad.

56 See note 11.

57 Consider a tank as an example of a point target.

58 Israel has also an inherent advantage because of its permanent bases and the short distance to targets in Syria. See note 57.

59 A reduction in the number of tanks, however, does not necessarily mean that Merkava tanks are no longer required: on the contrary, the fewer the tanks the more the IDF will need better ones.

60 Isaac Ben-Israel, "Relativity Theory of Force Buildup," *Ma'arachot*, 352–353, August 1997 [Hebrew], and Ben-Israel, "The Security Doctrine and the Logic of Force Buildup," *Ma'arachot*, 354, November 1997 [Hebrew].

61 This reflects a partial realization of theories that predicted the diminished frequency of war between armies, a concept developed by Martin Van Creveld, *The Transformation of War* (New York: Free Press, 1991).

The Victory in Iraq and the Global Oil Economy

7

Shmuel Even

Goal of the Offensive *vis-à-vis* the Oil Market

From the standpoint of the oil market, the United States victory in the 2003 Iraq War can be viewed as an achievement in the struggle for control of the Persian Gulf, the world's major energy reserve. The White House strategists did not define the goals of the offensive in terms of oil but rather in terms of removing the growing Iraqi threat to the United States and its allies. They were certainly well acquainted, however, with the global consequences of control over oil resources, in part as a result of their backgrounds. President George W. Bush is a former governor of Texas, the leading American oil state. Vice President Richard Cheney's previous position was chairman of the board and chief executive officer of Halliburton, a company that provides oil services and employs 85,000 workers in various countries. National Security Advisor Condoleezza Rice served on the board of directors of American oil giant ChevronTexaco. Secretary of State Colin Powell was Chief of Staff of the US Armed Forces when it freed Kuwait from Iraqi occupation in 1991 under the leadership of President George Bush Sr.

Before and during the war, the United States displayed caution and sensitivity on the issue of oil. For example, on April 8, 2003, at the height of the battles and after gaining control of a major part of the Iraqi oil fields, President Bush and Prime Minister Tony Blair declared that Iraq's oil was "the exclusive property of the Iraqi people, which would be used solely for its benefit." This declaration was not merely an answer to Saddam Hussein's claim that the US had gone to war in order to gain control over Iraq's oil fields; it was also a message to quite a few parties in the global arena who believed that oil was the main reason behind the US decision to eliminate Saddam Hussein.

Indeed, the US needed neither Iraq's oil, nor the profits from its sale. The American interest was in removing the threat posed by Saddam Hussein to the

Persian Gulf, the world's largest energy reserve. The Persian Gulf oil reserves constitute 65 percent of the world's total proven oil reserves (table 7.1). Currently the Persian Gulf supplies 30 percent of the global oil consumption and 40 percent of the oil traded around the world, and dependence on this region is expected to increase with time (tables 7.2 and 7.3).

Table 7.1   Oil Reserves in the World's Principal Countries[1]

Oil Producing Country	Billions of Barrels	% of Global Oil Reserves	No. of Production Years at Current Annual Production Rate
United States	30.4	2.9	10.7
Venezuela	77.7	7.4	63.5
Russia	48.6	4.6	19.1
Saudi Arabia	261.8	24.9	85
Iran	89.7	8.5	67.4
Iraq	112.5	10.9	—
Kuwait	96.5	9.2	123
United Arab Emirates	97.8	9.3	112
Persian Gulf Total	685	65.3	86.8
Global Total	1,050	100	40.3

Table 7.2   Global Oil Production and Consumption[2]

	% of Global Oil Production	% of Global Oil Consumption	Gap in %
North America	18.3	30.4	−12.1
Europe	9.0	21.7	−12.7
Asia and the Pacific	10.6	27.7	−17.1
Central and South America	9.9	6.2	3.7
Former USSR	11.8	4.8	7.0
Africa	10.3	3.3	7.0
Persian Gulf	30.0	5.9	24.1
Global Total	100	100	0

Table 7.3   Global Oil Consumption and Forecasts (millions of barrels of oil per day)[3]

2001	2002	2003	2004
76.9	77.5	78.6	80.0

Iraq was a radical factor in the oil market even before Saddam Hussein rose to power, and it was Iraq that led the Arab countries in imposing an oil embargo on the West following the 1973 Yom Kippur War. Yet especially in light of the global oil state of affairs, the US administration could not allow a dictator like

Saddam Hussein to acquire nuclear weapons, thereby terrorizing the other oil producers and dictating the world's policy on oil supplies and prices, as he apparently tried to do after occupying Kuwait in 1990. Had he attained such a position of influence he would have used it to pressure oil importers, including France, Germany, Far Eastern countries, and others, who had been highly vulnerable to Iraqi pressure in the past, in contrast to Britain, which had no need of Arab oil. Global susceptibility to Iraqi pressure would clearly have detracted from the status of the United States as a superpower. From this viewpoint, the war was a preemptive attack, following the failed American attempt to subdue or at least restrain Saddam Hussein's regime through an economic siege.

In addition to the global importance of controlling oil, the importance of foreign oil to the US economy has grown as a result of rising American dependence on imported oil (table 7.4). Proven oil reserves in the United States are limited to ten years of production at the current rate. The US increases its oil imports continually while reducing its domestic production, in order to preserve its reserves. While the United States currently obtains most of its oil from outside the Middle East (table 7.5), this is expected to change in the long term, due to the dominant proportion of oil reserves in the Persian Gulf and the limited reserves in the rest of the world. This projected trend bolstered the American interest in eliminating Saddam Hussein's regime in Iraq.

Table 7.4 US Oil Consumption and Imports (millions of oil barrels per day)[4]

	1991	2001	2002	2003	2004
Oil Consumption	19.9	19.65	19.68	20.22	20.61
Oil Imports	7.8	10.9	10.5	11.1	11.5

Table 7.5 Principle Exporters of Oil and Oil Products to the United States, January–October 2002[5]

	Imports (thousands of barrels per day)	% of Total Imports to the United States	% of US Oil Consumption
Canada	1,911	16.9	9.7
Saudi Arabia	1,527	13.5	7.8
Mexico	1,504	13.3	7.7
Venezuela	1,423	12.6	7.3
Nigeria	591	5.2	3.0
Britain	464	4.1	2.4
Iraq	456	4.0	2.3
Norway	391	3.5	2.0
Others	3,051	26.9	15.5
Total	11,318	100	57.7

The Oil Market during the Crisis

The behavior of the oil market during the crisis resembled the pattern of the previous Persian Gulf crisis. After Iraq invaded Kuwait in August 1990, the price of oil skyrocketed to $40 per barrel. Even before the coalition attack in January 1991, prices dropped to $30 per barrel, and sank to $20 per barrel after the war ended. Similarly, the uncertainty over the course of events in 2003 caused oil prices to rise sharply until the beginning of March 2003. American WTI Cushing oil prices neared $40 per barrel, and gasoline prices rose to an average of $1.70 per gallon at the beginning of March, 60 cents higher than in the corresponding period in 2002. Oil consumers around the world assumed that Iraqi oil exports would cease, and also feared that oil exports from the Persian Gulf would be further affected if other oil producers, such as Saudi Arabia, Kuwait, and the United Arab Emirates, reduced their production. The prolonged strike in the Venezuelan oil industry likewise contributed to the tension in the global oil market.

Yet despite the rise in the price of oil, the oil market was not under heavy pressure. The Persian Gulf crisis caused no disruption in the supply of oil. The developed countries kept a reserve of 2.4 billion barrels of oil, which was lower than the five-year average during this period.[6] The uncertainty lessened even before the outbreak of war. After the fighting began, when it became clear that Iraq was incapable of disrupting oil exports by the other producers, and that the Organization of Petroleum Exporting Countries (OPEC) was cooperating with the United States, oil prices began to fall: first to $30 per barrel, and later to $25 per barrel (figure 7.1).

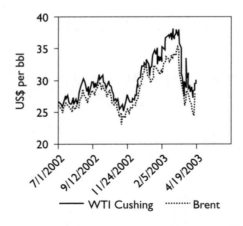

Figure 7.1   Trends in Oil Prices (American WTI Cushing Oil and Brent UK Oil)[7]

The Iraqi Oil Economy: Current and Potential

The oil industry will constitute a growth engine for Iraq, which in the future may become one of the most advanced countries in the Middle East, provided it remains politically stable and affiliated with the West. Iraq's great potential lies in its relatively good balance between capital and human resources. In other words, Iraq is rich in natural resources, such as oil and water, has a medium-sized population of about 25 million, and has relatively good human capital, in contrast to the lightly populated wealthy oil countries, such as Kuwait, and large countries with few resources, such as Egypt. From the time it gained power until it collapsed, Saddam Hussein's regime prevented the wealth of Iraq from being used for the benefit of its people. Iraq was at war during most of Saddam's rule, which severely restricted its oil exporting capacity. There is now an opportunity to use Iraq's economic potential for the benefit of its people.

Most of Iraq's oil wealth lies in its proven oil reserves, which are estimated at 112 billion barrels – 11 percent of the world's total reserves, the world's second largest national reserves, after Saudi Arabia. The Energy Information Administration in the United States Department of Energy (DOE) estimates Iraq's total oil reserves at 220 billion barrels, but the total is likely to be greater, since no oil exploration has taken place in Iraq in recent years. Iraqi sources have declared in the past that Iraq's total oil reserves are likely to amount to 300 billion barrels.

Before the invasion of Kuwait, Iraq produced 3.1 million barrels of oil per day from thirteen major oil fields, and has produced at least 2.6 million barrels per day in recent years. Under the UN-sponsored oil-for-food program, Iraq exported an average of 2.2 million barrels, and also produced 300,000 barrels of oil for domestic consumption, while smuggling a certain amount of oil to other countries. In addition, before the war, Iraq had ambitious plans to expand its oil production. At the end of 2001, the Iraqi Ministry of Oil announced that Iraq's oil production stood at 3.2 million barrels of oil per day, and was scheduled to reach 3.5 million barrels of oil per day in 2003. At the end of 2002, the Iraqi Ministry of Oil announced its intention to increase production to 4 million barrels of oil per day in 2003.

The oil production infrastructure in Iraq has been undermined by sanctions, which have disrupted the supply of equipment, spare parts, and up-to-date technology for over a decade. The infrastructure suffered further damage during the recent war, even though coalition forces gave higher priority to preserving and defending the oil fields and infrastructure than to any other asset in Iraq, with the result that only a few oil wells and facilities were damaged.

Iraq's oil pipelines are now suffering from long-term neglect. The internal pipeline network, which is thirty years old, includes two major pipelines for transporting oil south from the Kirkuk region and north from the Rumaila region. Iraq has two relatively new pipelines for its oil exports, which were laid during the war with Iran. One leads to the port of Ceyhan in Turkey. Its maximum production capacity is 1.6 million barrels of oil per day; before the war its flow was limited by a shortage of spare parts for its six pumping stations. The second export pipeline runs through Saudi Arabia to Yanbu on the Red Sea coast. This pipeline, which has a maximum capacity of 1.7 million barrels of oil per day, was incapacitated completely in the 1991 Gulf War. The third and older major export pipeline leads from Iraq to Syria. The flow in this pipeline was cut off in 1981 by the Iran–Iraq war, but was renewed in recent years after a twenty year hiatus.

Iraq has seven oil refineries, with an aggregate production capacity of 415,000 barrels of oil per day. These refineries were damaged in the 1991 Gulf War, but have since been repaired.

The many years of war and sanctions have also affected Iraq's oil exploration and the development of its oil fields. The sanctions prevented the Iraqi oil industry from using advanced technology, such as three-dimensional seismic surveys, and overall the industry has been unable to obtain foreign capital for exploration and development. According to the EIA (Energy Information Administration), 75 billion out of Iraq's 112 billion barrels of proven oil reserves remain totally undeveloped. Oil market estimates are that Iraq's oil production can be expanded to 3.2 million barrels of oil per day within a year, to 3.5 million barrels of oil per day within two years, and to 5 million barrels of oil per day within five years.

Iraq also has great natural gas potential. The EIA estimates Iraq's proven natural gas potential at 110 trillion cubic feet (2 percent of the world's proven natural gas reserves), even though almost no exploration has been undertaken in Iraq in this field. Most of the gas currently produced in Iraq is a result of oil production. In 1979 this amounted to 700 billion cubic feet, but shrank to only 11 billion cubic feet by 2000. Before the recent war, Iraq estimated it would be able to produce 550 billion cubic feet of gas within two years after sanctions were removed, and 4.2 trillion cubic feet within 10 years.

Foreign oil companies are eager to renew their activity in Iraq. The American and British oil companies are waiting for new tenders to be published for development and exploitation of Iraq's oil fields, while the oil companies that previously operated in Iraq and had signed contracts with the Saddam regime are demanding that their contracts be honored. For example, LUKOIL, the largest oil company in Russia, announced on April 10, 2003 that it would defend its rights to the West Qurna oil field, one of the largest in the world (15 billion barrels of oil) and Russia's most valuable asset in Iraq. The company threatened to intercept Iraqi oil tankers and initiate international arbitration against anyone attempting to cancel the contract it had signed with Saddam's government, despite the fact that in December 2002, Iraq announced that it had canceled an agreement with LUKOIL and signed with a different Russian company instead. Iraq Deputy Prime Minister Tariq Aziz explained that LUKOIL had negotiated with Iraqi opposition groups in order to guarantee that any arrangement to develop the oil field would remain valid even with a change of regime in Iraq, and therefore the Saddam government reneged on the original agreement.

The Iraqi oil industry is in need of reorganization, including the replacement of the managers appointed by Saddam Hussein. The most likely solution is help from foreign experts. Yet the main obstacle to the development of the Iraqi oil industry is financing. The external debt of Iraq is estimated at $100 billion, excluding tens of billions of dollars more in debts for damages resulting from the Iraqi invasion of Kuwait in 1990. Furthermore, Iraq urgently needs financing for essential civilian infrastructures, such as transportation, hospitals, schools, and other basic services. Worthy of note since the beginning of the war is the jump in stock prices of major construction companies such as Fluor and tractor manufacturer Caterpillar, due to the expectation that these companies will win a substantial share of the contracts for the reconstruction of Iraq. The US administration awarded Stevedoring Services of America a $4.8 billion project for rebuilding the Umm Qasr port, to the dismay of the British, who wanted to let Iraqi experts manage the port.

Despite the financing limitations, all parties involved realize that the renewal and development of Iraq's oil fields is the key to the country's reconstruction and without which Iraq will be unable to repay its debts. It can therefore be expected that oil industry development will be awarded top priority. Realization of Iraq's oil potential is also dependent on the political situation in Iraq. Only political stability will make it possible to implement reconstruction plans and to raise the necessary capital.

If Iraq remains a member of OPEC it is likely to have to struggle for its oil production quota. It is clear that Iraq must be allowed to increase its production; the question will be to what extent. Iraq will undoubtedly claim the right to make up for the unused quotas from the years in which it was unable to produce oil, while other OPEC members benefited. Iraq's current interest is in high oil prices, in view of its urgent need for cash, so it will not wish to flood the market.

The American Victory and the Balance of Power in the Oil Market

The American military victory has significantly increased the status of the United States in the global oil market. It removed the Iraqi threat to the Persian Gulf oil producers, and Iraq will gradually increase its own oil production. A reasonable forecast is that Iraq will initially increase production to 3 million barrels of oil per day, to 4 million within a year or two, and afterwards to 5–6 million (table 7.6). If the United States succeeds in installing a friendly regime in Iraq, a bloc of friendly oil producers will be created, with the largest proven oil reserves in OPEC (Iraq has 11% of the world's proven oil reserves, Kuwait 9.2%, and the United Arab Emirates 9.3%).

Fulfillment of this scenario will reduce American dependence on Saudi Arabia, which possesses 25 percent of the world's oil reserves, making it the dominant factor in OPEC. Anti-American feeling in Saudi Arabia has been growing, particularly since the September 11, 2001 terrorist attacks. This is liable to find expression in terrorist strikes against American targets. On May 12, 2003, for example, terrorists attacked a Western residential compound in the Saudi Arabian capital, in advance of a visit there by US Secretary of State Colin Powell. The global price of oil responded by jumping 2.5 percent. It should be noted that the oil region in Saudi Arabia is particularly vulnerable from a demographic standpoint, since its population is composed mostly of Shiite Muslims.

Nevertheless, Saudi Arabia proved its loyalty to the United States during the current crisis, at least where the oil market is concerned, by quickly boosting its production, thereby making up for the shortage in the oil market. It is therefore reasonable to expect that the US will not turn its back now on Saudi Arabia, and will continue to support its status in OPEC.

Table 7.6   The Historical Progress of Oil Production in Iraq[8]

Year	Production in millions of barrels per day	Comments
1928	0.022	
1940	0.055	
1950	0.14	
1960	0.97	
1970	1.54	Continuous increases in production, following oil discoveries in Iraq
1979	3.47	A sharp rise in production, after Iran halted its oil exports following the Islamic revolution
1981	0.90	A steep decline in production, following the Iranian attacks on the Iraq oil export route in the Persian Gulf, as part of the Iran–Iraq war
1987	2.35	A steep rise in production, after oil pipelines to Turkey and Saudi Arabia were laid
1988	2.74	A further rise in production, following the end of the Iran–Iraq war
1991	0.28	A drastic drop in production following a halt in exports, due to the sanctions imposed for the occupation of Kuwait and the ensuing Gulf War
1999	2.7	A rise in production, under the oil exports for food agreement, and as a result of oil smuggling
2000	2.8	
2001	2.6	
2002	2.6	
2003	2.8–3.2	An end of year forecast
2004	3.2–3.8	Forecast
2005	3.8–4.2	Forecast
2006	4.2–4.5	Forecast
2007	4.5–5.0	Forecast

OPEC will try to convince Iraq to limit the pace at which it increases its oil production, while simultaneously convincing other producers to cut their production, in order to maintain oil prices. The chances of succeeding at this task in the long run are not good. Therefore, OPEC's status is likely to be further eroded in the new situation. At the same time, the US may believe its interest lies in propping up OPEC as an integrative framework for influencing the oil market, as it did during the attack on Iraq. It should be kept in mind that low oil prices – although not too low – suit the interests of the countries with large oil reserves, such as Saudi Arabia and Kuwait. It is in the interests of the owners of large oil reserves to maintain prices that do not encourage the development of oil substitutes so that they are able to exploit all their oil reserves over a period of decades.

Implications for the Oil Market

The principal importance of the US victory for the global oil market is that it prevented further attempts by Iraq to gain control of the Persian Gulf oil, the world's main energy source, and convert this control into economic and political power. In addition, the victory significantly boosted the status of the US in the global oil market, and further eroded the status of OPEC. At the same time, the US may consider it in its interest to conserve the OPEC framework as an integral body for influencing the oil market. Preserving the American achievements depends on maintaining internal stability in Iraq and the other major Persian Gulf oil producers.

The United States victory will make a long-term contribution to the economies of nations dependent on the oil market. It is believed that maintaining low energy prices will contribute to world growth. The link between oil prices and economic output is estimated as follows: maintaining a price of $25 per barrel, as opposed to $35 per barrel, means an additional 0.2% increase in the American Gross Domestic Product (GDP), 0.4% in the Japanese GDP, and 0.2%–0.4% in the GDP of European countries, depending on their dependence on oil imports.[9]

The US victory will greatly contribute to the diplomatic freedom of action of the oil importing countries. Under these circumstances the Arabs will be unable to employ, even in milder form, the oil and money weapon they wielded after the Yom Kippur War. At the same time, low oil prices are liable to retard the development of energy substitutes for oil, and create a greater long-term dependence among the oil-consuming nations.

Finally, the oil industry will constitute Iraq's growth engine, which is likely to make it one of the wealthiest and most advanced countries in the Middle East in the distant future, provided it maintains its political stability and affiliation with the West.

Notes

1 British Petroleum Statistical Review of World Energy 2002.
2 *Ibid.*
3 US Energy Information Administration (EIA), May 2003.
4 *Ibid.*
5 Department of Energy Supply Monthly December 2002.
6 EIA.
7 Oil-Gasoline.com, May 2003.
8 OPEC Annual Statistical Bulletin 2001 and the author's forecast.
9 Organization for Economic Cooperation and Development (OECD) Economic Outlook.

Military–Media Relations: Embedding as a Case Study

8

Hirsh Goodman and Jonathan Cummings

One of the most striking features of the 2003 war in Iraq was the extent to which engaging the media in the battle for public opinion became a critical concern of military planners. A carefully crafted media policy was designed in order to win public confidence and capture popular support for the war. As part of the overarching strategic planning of the campaign, the Pentagon invited journalists to be as close as possible to the fighting through a process of "embedding." The move signaled a realization that since there was little chance of precluding media access and something to be lost by trying and failing, there was much to be gained by facilitating access under controlled terms.

The organized effort notwithstanding, implementation of the new policy did not result in the universally positive coverage of the war that planners might have hoped for. In the early stages of the war, particularly week two, the news seemed to be dominated by coalition failures: soldiers falling into Iraqi captivity, long and vulnerable supply lines, generals complaining of insufficient forces, delays in the battle for Baghdad, massive resistance building up in Baghdad and Tikrit, and a "phenomenon" of suicide bombings, though only few actually occurred. These, along with gruesome pictures of civilian casualties, combined initially to cast doubt on the image of unassailable superiority of coalition forces, reflect infighting and disagreement among the Pentagon and the military, and present a distorted picture of the American-led campaign in jeopardy.

Yet as the campaign progressed a more positive picture of the war emerged. The media policy chosen by the coalition began to yield desired dividends, and by the third week the media were reporting a swift coalition victory, minimal Iraqi resistance, and few coalition casualties. The consistent messages in coalition briefings, complementing the reports from embedded journalists within coalition units, successfully positioned the war as "liberating" Iraq from a despotic regime, deflecting attention from both the initial setbacks, and perhaps more importantly from the fact that no weapons of mass destruction were discovered during the campaign, one of the original reasons for the decision to go to war according to both President George W. Bush and Prime Minister Tony Blair.

This chapter will examine the media strategy of the 2003 Iraq War through the prism of media embedding, specifically the policy's rationale, background, and implementation; the most important effects of the policy; some thoughts on the future of "embedding" – if it is a policy that can or will be implemented again; and on the lessons learned in the field of military–media relations.

Ironically, though the war in Iraq attracted more media coverage than any war in history, the media did not and could not cover the real story behind the coalition's quick and successful completion of the military campaign: the use of new generation weapons, instruments of the Revolution in Military Affairs that were invisible to the journalistic eye, which critically weakened Iraqi defenses and Saddam Hussein's ability to communicate with his forces, and whose true capabilities were top secret.

Embedding Media: The Rationale

Today there is an ever-increasing expectation for instant, real-time news.[1] For most people in the developed world, television news and the internet are the predominant sources of information about national and international affairs.[2] Access to rolling news TV channels continues to widen, as does access to a vast number of news sites on the internet. Some 580 million people, 10.8 percent of the world's population, currently have access to the World Wide Web, mostly in North America and Western Europe. That figure is growing annually,[3] with access widening to less developed parts of the world. The nearly universal access to news and the insatiable public desire for real-time news are givens of the twenty-first century, and have perforce created a new dynamic between governments, the military, and the media.

Several countries have implemented a variety of policy measures so as to bring order to this changing relationship. In the UK in the 1980s, the military and the media agreed on a set of ground rules regarding media relations in times of emergency or conflict, "with the aims of ensuring that the background situation and the operational response is understood and that the British public can be properly informed of events." According to the policy – known as the "Green Book" – the military is committed to "provide for the media a range of facilities to enable first hand reporting, in addition to an accurate, objective and timely information service," and to brief journalists "so that a regular and frank flow of information is maintained." In turn, the media is expected to submit all their material for security vetting and to undertake not to publish or divulge any operationally sensitive information.[4]

Much of the same thinking is to be found in the Australian Department of Defense's 2001 "Defence Overarching Organizational Communications Strategy," which attempted to improve the defense establishment's ability to communicate to domestic and international audiences during times of conflict and times of peace.

In the Israel Defense Forces (IDF), military correspondents are required to sign a code of conduct when accompanying troops. All of these measures point to the understanding in Western governments that in order to maintain public support for military operations, they will have to engage with the media rather than wish it away.

The changing relationship between the military and the media is perhaps best illustrated by Donald Rumsfeld's decision to appoint Victoria Clarke, a corporate communications expert, as Assistant Secretary for Public Affairs, rather than someone from within the Pentagon. Similarly, the appointment of Charlotte Beers, a Madison Avenue executive, as Under Secretary of State for Public Diplomacy and Public Affairs, and the creation of a White House Office of Global Communications, point to this new thinking on the public face of policy.[5]

Against this general background the Pentagon drew up a strategy for military–media relations directed at possible operations in the Persian Gulf. On January 17, 2003, the Pentagon issued a ten-page memorandum entitled "Public Affairs Guidance on Embedding Media," which summarized the current thinking on dealing with news media. Key principles of the policy were stated as follows:

- Media will have long-term, minimally restrictive access to US air, ground and naval forces.
- Media coverage of any future operation will, to a large extent, shape public perception of the national security environment now and in the years ahead.
- Opinion can affect the durability of our coalition.
- Perceptions of [publics in countries where we conduct operations] can affect the cost and duration of our involvement.[6]

The policy is tacit recognition that it has become very difficult to keep ever-increasing numbers of journalists, equipped with constantly improving means of communications, away from the war zone, or to exercise any kind of control over their coverage once they are there. With self-contained communications equipment fitted into all-terrain vehicles, reporters can file stories from wherever they are, independent of the kind of technical support that tied them to the military until the last decade.

Aware of this new reality, and cognizant of the critical role played by the media, Pentagon planners decided to treat the media inclusively, making journalists an integral part of the fighting force, but on the military's terms. They hoped that the flood of reportage from the front line would satisfy demands for information while at the same time give an impression of greater openness. It was also assumed that the proximity of reporters to fighting units and exposure with them to the same dangers would create a sense of comradeship and, consequently, positive coverage.

Moreover, because of the controversy surrounding the decision to attack Saddam's regime, the way the war would be broadcast became an especially critical foreign policy consideration for its two principal partners, the US and the UK. Thus, to "shape public perception of the national security environment now and in the years ahead," there was a desire to control the message as well as to provide access through the embedding system.

This was achieved in part by placing absolutely off limits to the media those command centers where a full picture of the war and its progress could be obtained. Instead, official information was limited to formal briefings at CENTCOM HQ in Doha, Qatar, the press center in Kuwait, and the Pentagon, where carefully crafted messages designed to serve coalition interests were disseminated. Thus, while the flood of fragmented news coming from the embedded reporters was such even to satisfy the insatiable demands of the 24-hour news channels, the media overall was not able to provide a full and accurate picture of the war and its progress.

Background to Embedding

Reporters have long accompanied soldiers to the battlefield. Journalists such as William Howard Russell, whose reports on the Crimean War for the *Times* did much to inform Victorian England about war, and Ernie Pyle, whose reports from Europe and the Pacific theater for the *Washington Daily News* were staples of the Second World War, ate and slept with the troops, reported what they saw, and sent their stories back home.[7]

At the outset of the twenty-first century, however, the journalistic environment is far different. Although war has been televised since the 1950s, few people in the US had television sets to watch the Korean War. By a decade later, television ownership in the US had skyrocketed, and concomitantly TV reporting of Vietnam became a critical element in domestic attitudes toward the war. Significantly, television coverage was not tantamount to rousing patriotism or unequivocal support of the military. In fact, it seemed that the journalistic narrative to the Vietnam War heightened the division between soldiers and reporters, who lived apart, worked apart, and performed very different jobs. Indeed, so blatant was the distance between soldier and reporter in Vietnam that there was a perception in the military that hostile television coverage, especially after the 1968 Tet offensive, may have turned American public opinion against the war effort that ended with the only defeat in American military history.

In the 1982 Falklands War, twenty-nine journalists sailed with British troops to the South Atlantic. Sharing cramped conditions on board, the same food, and some of the dangers of war, the journalists bonded with the soldiers and the coverage of the war was generally positive, even when events went awry. However, media access to the ground troops was limited by the fact that the journalists were on Royal Navy ships, and had to be transported to and from the Islands by military transport. Since they had no independent means of filing their stories, particularly given the relatively isolated location of the Falkland Islands, their dependence on the Royal Navy's communications systems was another instrument of control and effective filter for negative coverage.[8] The same was true for many of the small regional wars of the 1980s and 1990s, such as those in Somalia, Grenada, and Panama.

The "pool" system, devised in the 1980s by the Pentagon and employed in the 1991 Gulf War, continued this method. Under the system, Media Reporting Teams of journalists reported on the war and pooled their copy. Access to the troops was strictly controlled, and was supplemented by daily briefings from commanders who attempted to portray a "clean" war with minimal casualties. But the public did not get to see enough of their troops in action. In the words of one commentator, the US military "built the finest army in the world, and they success- fully hid it from the American people."[9] The coverage from within Baghdad, notably by CNN's Peter Arnett, and the reporting of the independent or "unilat- eral" reporters who were frustrated by the limits of the pool, was by far the more compelling viewing.

The Pentagon's handling of the media aspects of the 2003 Iraq War illustrates the increasing refinement of thinking on military–media relations in general and in the US in particular. Not least of the issues was the awareness of the impact the media can have in shaping public opinion, both domestic and foreign. Hence the coalition's drive "to tell the factual story – good or bad – before others seed the media with disinformation and distortions."[10]

Implementing the Policy

Requirements

The first component of the new approach was the launching of week-long military-style courses for journalists in order to familiarize them with the armed forces, and to give field commanders a measure of confidence that journalists would not hinder operations. Since the end of the US draft in 1973, very few American reporters have had any direct military experience. Moreover, apart from the largest networks, very few media outlets can afford to maintain specialist defense corre- spondents, with the result that for many journalists this was their first war.

As the war with Iraq loomed increasingly likely the policy was announced and applications were invited for embedded slots with US ground forces. According to the Public Affairs Guidance, the standard for release of information was "why not release" as opposed to "why release":

- Media will be given access to operational combat missions, including mission preparation and debriefing, wherever possible.
- Media embeds . . . [will] remain with a unit on an extended basis – perhaps a period of weeks or even months.
- Seats aboard vehicles, aircraft and naval ships will be made available to allow maximum coverage of US troops in the field.
- Units should plan lift and logistical support to assist in moving media prod- ucts to and from the battlefield so as to tell our story in a timely manner.
- No communications equipment for use by media in the conduct of their duties will be specifically prohibited.[11]

Later, a more detailed Ground Rules Agreement was issued, in which prospective "embeds" agreed to remain with their military escorts and "follow instructions regarding their activities," and sign a statement releasing the US military from liability for any injuries suffered. There was also a list of limitations on reporting where "publication or broadcast could jeopardize operations and endanger lives," and included specific prohibitions on reporting numerical "information on troop strength, equipment and critical supplies," "specific geographical locations of units," "information regarding future operations, current operations or strikes," "security precautions at military installations or encampments," and "information on intelligence collection . . . or special operations."[12]

The restrictions notwithstanding, over 600 journalists decided to "embed" with the US troops prior to deployment in the Persian Gulf. In order to give access to a wide range of media, the embedded slots were not limited to the national daily newspapers and the network news channels, nor were they restricted to the US media networks. Alongside the twelve embedded reporters of the *New York Times*, the *Fayetteville Observer* received a slot with the Fayetteville, NC-based 82nd Airborne Division.[13] *Rolling Stone* magazine and *Penthouse* also had journalists with the troops.

Journalists welcomed the opportunity to report from the battlefield, despite the inherent dangers. Although it is unlikely that all the reporters involved will ultimately specialize in military or defense affairs, reporters who have experienced war will be better able to analyze military affairs in the future. In his summation of the embedding process, Secretary Rumsfeld noted that "there's now a new generation of journalists who have had a chance to see what kind of people volunteer to put their lives at risk. And that's a good thing."[14]

Compliance

There were concerns among the news organizations that the policy of embedding would result in one-sided coverage of the war. As a result most news organizations decided to dispatch independent correspondents to the field, specifically to areas in which embedded reporters were not operating.

In violation of their commitments, some embedded reporters did fall foul of the regulations once in the field. Within the first days of the ground fighting, Phil Smucker of the *Christian Science Monitor* was expelled from Iraq for disclosing operational details regarding the location and the intentions of the unit he was traveling with. In a similar incident, Fox News reporter Geraldo Rivera was removed from the unit in which he was embedded for revealing operational details by drawing in the sand a map with his unit's location. Their expulsion may have encouraged other reporters to take the rules more seriously.

Compliance, however, often evolved into partisan coverage. The proximity of reporters to the soldiers, and their dependence on them for their safety and the ability to report, seems to have led some journalists to adopt a more patriotic tone in their coverage. The tendency was reinforced for many who had never experienced war, and who felt the vulnerability of the battlefield. As one UK correspondent later wrote, "my objectivity was shot to bits. All I wanted was for the Americans to win quickly: for my own safety, rather than any political reasons."[15]

Of particular note was Fox News' coverage and its decision to send former senior military officers such as Oliver North as embedded reporters, which obfuscated the lines between military jingoism and reportage. The network, whose current TV slogan is "Real Journalism. Fair and Balanced," adopted an unmistakably pro-war stance, describing MSNBC journalist Peter Arnett as "an American citizen who is making treasonous statements," and regularly referring to allied troops as "us" and "we."[16]

Other networks too fell easily into the trap of patriotic coverage. In the UK, the BBC's use of the term "liberation" to describe the fall of Umm Qasr, and the description of the death of two servicemen as "the worst possible news for the armed forces," did little to reassure the public, particularly those opposed to the war, that journalists were maintaining a professional distance from the soldiers they were living alongside.[17] Interestingly, the American public strongly – at least ostensibly – rejected "pro-American" coverage, with 67 percent preferring neutrality in news coverage, although four in ten did say that there was too much coverage of anti-war protests.[18]

Yet while the program of embedding journalists was designed, at least in part, to encourage compliance and generate positive news, coverage of the war did remain reasonably balanced, and was largely restricted to factual reporting of what was witnessed, rather than analysis or interpretation of the events. According to one survey, 94 percent of the reports from embeds were factual in nature.[19] And in some cases embedded reporters even managed to uncover "negative" stories, such as William Branigin's report on the roadblock incident at an-Najaf in which 10 civilians were killed by panicked soldiers.[20]

Safety

"Commanders will ensure the media are provided with every opportunity to observe actual combat operations. The personal safety of correspondents is not a reason to exclude them from combat areas."[21] And yet, safety was clearly an issue of the war. Embedded reporters, three of whom were killed during the fighting, were made aware of the dangers of covering wars in the Ground Rules Agreement, which stated: "covering combat and other military operations carries with it certain inherent risks," and that the US military in no way guaranteed their safety. They agreed to "assume any and all risks," and to "release, indemnify and hold harmless" the US government for any injuries sustained.

The 2003 Iraq War was particularly dangerous for journalists. During the month of fighting fourteen journalists lost their lives, including four in accidents and natural causes.[22] In comparison, only four journalists lost their lives in the 1991 Gulf War, and in the 21 years from 1954 to 1975, including the Vietnam War, 63 journalists were killed.[23] Even taking into account that an estimated 3,000 journalists – the majority of whom were independent – covered the 2003 Iraq War, their loss of life was out of all proportion to casualty rates of allied forces – approximately ten times higher. Significantly, it was the independent, non-embedded journalists who proved most vulnerable in the war, or who, in the words of one senior reporter, "took a hammering."[24] A few examples:

- On March 22, a television crew from the UK's ITN came under fire from allied troops at Imam Anas, near Basra. The reporter Terry Lloyd was killed and other members of the crew were injured.
- Also on March 22, Paul Moran, a free-lance cameraman on assignment for the Australian Broadcasting Corporation (ABC), was killed in an apparent suicide bombing when a man detonated a car at a checkpoint in northeastern Iraq. Another Australian journalist, ABC correspondent Eric Campbell, was injured in the incident.
- On April 8 the Baghdad offices of al-Jazeera and of Abu Dhabi television were bombed by US planes, killing reporter Tareq Ayyoub and injuring another. This despite having given the Pentagon the coordinates of its office two months earlier. On the same day, a US tank fired a shell at the Hotel Palestine, the base for most of the foreign media reporting on the war from the Iraqi capital. Two journalists were killed in this attack. The question of whether the journalists were deliberately targeted remains open.

Results of the Media Strategy

Over-exposure, Under-analysis

In addition to the live news from the front, the daily briefings from military commanders remained a significant source of information for journalists, although none of the briefers developed the "star" profile that General Schwarzkopf had in the 1991 war. Yet while the Hollywood-designed Central Command media center in Doha provided a more comprehensive picture than could be put together from the dozens of local reports from the field, there were criticisms that the briefings were short on detail. These briefings encouraged skeptical journalists to question the progress of the war, while providing those running the war with a controlled environment in which to impart particular messages. Hence the sense that the Pentagon was furthering its manipulation of the media by complementing the policy of embedding with controlled briefings and military statements.

The sheer number of journalists in the field resulted in a flood of real-time reportage, feeding networks who suspended all other programming to provide round the clock news coverage of the war. There were times when the news channels employed a "split-screen" technique in order to try and track developments simultaneously on a number of different fronts. Interestingly, despite the demand for news, the saturation coverage was overwhelming for viewers. A poll conducted during the war revealed that 42 percent of US viewers agreed or strongly agreed that watching the war on TV was tiring, and 58 percent found the coverage frightening.[25]

Moreover, the wealth of coverage did not result in more accurate coverage, nor was it matched with an ability to analyze and contextualize the developments in real time. Indeed, one noticeable result of the torrent of unchecked information was that a number of stories were reported which later, notwithstanding attempts at accuracy, were proved to be false, inviting claims of allied attempts to sow disinformation.[26]

- In the first days of the war the successful capture of the port of Umm Qasr seemed to be a significant breakthrough by allied troops. First reports about its fall were broadcast on March 20 and were confirmed by the British commanders in the field and by Secretary Rumsfeld, despite the fact that reporters on the ground were still transmitting pictures showing fighting until five days later.
- On March 24, the *Jerusalem Post* and Fox News, both of whom had journalists embedded with the troops, filed a potentially critical story about the discovery of a facility at an-Najaf, quoting unnamed Pentagon sources that it was a chemical weapons factory. Such a discovery would have been of significant value to the US administration's justification for the war. Four days later, General Franks was forced to concede that he "wasn't entirely sure" that it was used for manufacturing chemical weapons.
- On April 8, Sky News reported that US troops had shelled the Palestine Hotel, deliberately killing two journalists. The Pentagon accepted responsibility, claiming the fire was in response to Iraqi sniping from the building. This version was supported by numerous commanders, including General Brooks. The next day, an Israeli website reported that the explosion had been rigged and planted by Iraqi military intelligence, but that the US had preferred to admit responsibility to defuse tensions with irate members of the press.[27] It is not clear which of these narratives is correct.[28]

Similar stories surfaced and vanished regarding an uprising in Basra, the capture of Ali Hassan al-Majid, more chemical weapons plants, and the death of Saddam Hussein in an April 8 air strike.

Public Opinion

US polling figures on the war revealed an unwavering commitment to the war (figure 8.1). Approval ratings remained above 70 percent throughout the conflict, which is typical for a nation at war,[29] but there was a significant dip in the perceived success of the campaign during the first week of fighting. Having been promised a war with minimal casualties and with troops expected to face only nominal resistance from Iraqi forces, the initial reality appeared somewhat different. As US troops engaged with the Iraqis, news of military casualties, POWs, and civilian casualties filtered through. The number of Americans who thought that the war was going "very well" fell from 71% on March 22 to 38% on March 24.[30]

The early sense of disappointment felt by the American public was due to unrealistic expectations and a poor grasp of the facts. Pre-war polling data shows that 44% of Americans believed that most or all of the hijackers in the September 11 attacks were Iraqi, and 41% thought that Saddam Hussein possessed nuclear weapons.[31] Some of these views may have been deliberately encouraged by misinformation in order to bolster support for the war.

In Britain, whose troops made the only other numerically significant contribution to the allied force, 62% felt that "we should be proud of Britain's role in the war with Iraq," although six in ten Britons also believed that Britain should not have gone to war.[32]

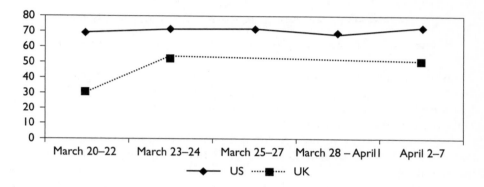

Figure 8.1 Public Support for the War in the US and the UK[33]

However, news of casualties and the pause in the progress of troops on the way to Baghdad coincided with reports that senior war planners were unhappy with Secretary Rumsfeld's handling of the operation aspects of the war.[34] A number of retired officers who had held senior command positions in 1991 attacked the policy in public. The criticism centered on the decision to reduce force size, based on assessments that Iraqi forces would offer little resistance, but reflected deeper disagreements regarding the 1991 Gulf War. They addressed the perception that Rumsfeld and his advisors were using the opportunity of renewed conflict with Iraq to "reposition" the US after the previous Bush administration had failed to remove Saddam's regime. No matter what prompted the criticism of the former generals, some of whom were employed as military analysts by the news networks, as the advance on Baghdad halted amid concerns about the lengthy supply lines, public confidence in the prospects for a quick and decisive victory ebbed.

The rescue of Jessica Lynch, the nineteen year old soldier who was dramatically released from Iraqi hands in a Nasariyah hospital on April 1, marked a decisive watershed. Described as "the woman who changed the face of this war," the story captured public attention and confidence in the outcome of the war rose again.[35] Although considerable doubt has been placed on the story as reported,[36] its value in restoring crumbling support for the war was critical. The story refocused attention on the successes, rather than the perceived failure of the allied campaign (figure 8.2).

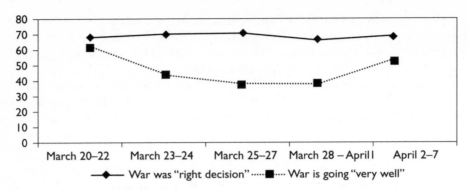

Figure 8.2 American Public Perceptions of War's Success Improving after April 1[37]

Another significant element in changing attitudes to the progress of the war was the increasingly eccentric appearances by Iraqi Information Minister Mohammed Saeed al-Sahaf. His claims of Iraqi invincibility – "Cruise missiles do not frighten anyone. We are catching them like fish in a river. I mean here that over the past two days, we managed to shoot down 196 missiles before they hit their target," and "There are no American infidels in Baghdad. Never!"[38] shown on split screens with shots of allied soldiers in the Presidential palaces, provided iconic moments of coverage, and added to public confidence in the success of the war.

Despite the mass of information available there was very little editorial disagreement across the networks. With little divergence in coverage one story dominated the media at any one time, creating a national "mood." In this environment it was more important than ever for government media managers to promote "positive" narratives, such as the Jessica Lynch story, and to relegate confidence-sapping reports of military delays to less prominence. This proved to be remarkably effective, particularly since public perception had to be transformed from pre-war expectations of rapid and decisive victory to a more realistic scenario that would include the inevitable deaths and delays of war.

Assessment

The media policy adopted in the 2003 Iraq War, particularly the embedding of correspondents with coalition troops, resulted in both overwhelmingly positive coverage of the war and an almost unlimited flow of real-time reportage. It appeared to be a policy with which both military planners and news networks could be satisfied.

Yet in the aftermath of the war a number of points of difference did arise, often suggesting doubts over the policy. "I don't know how we launched into this without any form of skepticism . . . I think the whole principle is intrinsically dangerous," reflects one embedded reporter. "I don't think we should be attached to military forces. There's no way you wouldn't become an adjunct to those forces."[39]

Many of the reporters who were assigned to Central Command in Qatar complained that the media operation did not do enough to put the events of the Iraq war in context. According to one reporter, "we did get a lot of spin and odd little stories, but didn't get a very good overview from the military high command."[40] Interestingly, this assessment was shared by senior British officials. According to a senior British source, "Central Command in Qatar was clearly an American-led operation. We admit there are issues arising out of Qatar. That's what we're looking at the moment. If we'd been a UK command we would have given context-setting briefings."[41]

Embedding, then, is not the ultimate refinement in military–media relations. The US has shown a flexible approach to media management in crisis or combat situations, and will continue to tailor policy to circumstances. In the 2002 Afghanistan campaign journalists were far more restricted in their ability to report independently, both because of the difficult terrain and because of the dangers of reporting on a war waged primarily from the skies. It appears that the fear that adverse coverage can turn public opinion against wars remains,[42] and explains the tendency of defense establishments to instinctively restrict access to the press whenever possible. The Pentagon's response was to give briefings, and allow limited access to the troops. It appears that greater access will be granted to the media only in cases when they could cover the story without the military's help.

Conversely, media organizations know that in today's world they have the means and resources available to accept the principle of embedded reporters, but the freedom to deploy independents as well. If news organizations are to choose an "enemy" in their relations with the Pentagon in the future it should not be over the policy of embedding, but rather ensuring the right of independent reporters to work outside of the "system," a right that was threatened in Iraq in the 2003 war.[43]

Notes

1   "What the World Thinks in 2002," Pew Research Center Report, December 4, 2002.
2   *Ibid.*: "In the 44 nations surveyed, nearly everyone cited television news as their predominant source of information about national and international affairs."
3   "Global Internet Population Grows An Average of Four Percent Year-Over-Year," report from Nielsen Netratings, February 20, 2003, www.nielsen-netratings.com /pr/pr_030220.pdf
4   United Kingdom Ministry of Defence Green Book.
5   Ms. Beers resigned from the State Department in May 2003.
6   "Public Affairs Guidance on Embedding Media during possible future operations/deployments in the US Central Command area of responsibility," US Department of Defense, January 17, 2003, p. 1.
7   For a fuller historical account of war correspondents, see Miles Hudson and John Stanier, *War and the Media* (Stroud: Sutton Publishing, 1997).
8   See, for example, Max Hastings, *Going to the Wars* (London: Macmillan, 2000).
9   Joseph Galloway, quoted in "Pentagon Gambles on Open-War Policy; Media Wary of Access Pledge," James Janega and Tim Jones, *Chicago Tribune*, January 26, 2003.
10 Public Affairs Guidance, January 17, 2003, Article 2(A).
11 Public Affairs Guidance, January 17, 2003, Article 2(C).

12 Coalition Forces Land Component Command (CFLCC) Ground Rules Agreement, Article 8.

13 Rogel Alpher, "How the Media Warriors Invaded Iraq with Satellite Phones," *Ha'aretz*, March 30, 2003.

14 Rumsfeld at a briefing at the Pentagon on April 18, 2003.

15 Jason Deans, "'I didn't want to die' says *Times* Man," *The Guardian*, April 11, 2003.

16 Paul Farhi, "The Gung-Ho Morning Gang," *Washington Post*, April 4, 2003.

17 Jason Deans "BBC Boss Admits 'Daily' Mistakes in Iraq," *The Guardian*, March 28, 2003.

18 "War Coverage Praised, but Public Hungry for Other News," Pew Research Center Report, April 9, 2003.

19 "Embedded Reporters: What Are Americans Getting?" Program for Excellence in Journalism report, April 3, 2003.

20 William Branigin, "A Gruesome Scene on Route 9," *Washington Post*, April 1, 2003.

21 Public Affairs Guidance, January 17, 2003. Article 3(G).

22 Committee for the Protection of Journalists report, "Media Casualties in Iraq," www.cpj.org/Briefings/2003/gulf03/gulf03casualties.html.

23 Tim Rutten, "Covering Conflict Exacts a Price," *Los Angeles Times*, April 9, 2003.

24 Jason Deans, "Simpson: Journalists 'Taking a Hammering,'" *The Guardian*, April 9, 2003.

25 "TV Combat Fatigue on the Rise," Pew Research Center Report, March 28, 2003.

26 Annie Lawson, Lisa O'Carroll, Chris Tryhorn, Jason Deans, "War Watch: Claims and Counter Claims Made During the Media War over Iraq," *The Guardian*, April 11, 2003.

27 "Is the War of Words Over?" www.debka.com, April 9, 2003.

28 Joel Campagna and Rhonda Roumani, "Permission to Fire: CPJ Investigates the Attack on the Palestine Hotel," May 27, 2003, www.cpj.org/Briefings/2003/palestine_hotel/palestine_hotel.html.

29 Philip Taylor, "Credibility: Can't Win Hearts and Minds Without It," *Washington Post*, March 30, 2003.

30 "Public Confidence in War Effort Falters," Pew Research Center Report, March 25, 2003.

31 *Ibid.*

32 Populus Poll, *The Times*, April 1, 2003.

33 US results collated from Pew Research Center reports; UK figures from Guardian/ICM war tracker polls.

34 Seymour M. Hersh, "Offense and Defense," *The New Yorker*, March 31, 2003.

35 Lawrence Donegan, "How Private Jessica Became America's Icon," *The Observer*, April 6, 2003.

36 John Kampfer, "The Truth Behind Jessica," *The Guardian*, May 15, 2003.

37 "War Coverage Praised, But Public Hungry for Other News," Pew Research Center Report, April 9, 2003.

38 See, for example, www.welovetheiraqiinformationminister.com

39 Michael Wolff of *New York Magazine*, talking at a MediaGuardian forum on war coverage on June 25, 2003.

40 Nick Pollard, Head of Sky News, talking at a MediaGuardian forum on war coverage on June 25, 2003.

41 David Howard, the UK Ministry of Defense's Head of Communication Planning, talking at a MediaGuardian forum on war coverage on June 25, 2003.

42 See Philip M. Taylor, "Conflict and Conflicting Cultures: The Military and the Media," Paper delivered at the Geneva Center for the Democratic Control of Armed Forces conference "The Role of the Media in Public Scrutiny and the Democratic Oversight of the Security Sector," February 2003.

43 On March 25 a group of four independents, including two Israelis, were detained by US troops for "the worst 48 hours of our life," despite the fact that they were carrying press

accreditation. See "Coalition accused of showing 'contempt' for journalists covering war in Iraq," Reporters without Borders press release, March 31, 2003.

The Middle East Dimensions

PART

II

The War in Iraq: Regional Implications

9

Ephraim Kam

The war in Iraq demonstrated once again that the Gulf region has been the main focus of instability in the Middle East for a generation, even more so than the Arab–Israeli conflict. No major war has erupted between Israel and the Arab states since 1973, while since 1980 the Gulf has been shaken by a series of three major wars. The Gulf's instability began in the late 1970s and stemmed largely from the seizure of power in the two principal and powerful rival countries, Iraq and Iran, by radical regimes that have posed serious threats to the region and triggered an accelerated military buildup. One of these regimes, Saddam Hussein's, remained undeterred from employing massive military force against its neighbors. The imbalance created in the Gulf compelled the American superpower to intervene with unprecedented military power on two occasions in an effort to stabilize the region. US involvement stemmed from a commitment to its allies' security and the need to counter the threat to its other interests, especially the flow of oil from the Gulf.

The 2003 war had a traumatic impact on other countries in the region, most notably the Arab states, as a consequence of the total subjugation of an Arab country by a great power for the first time since the beginning of Arab independence; the first overthrow of an Arab regime by a foreign military power; and the astonishing demonstration of American military strength that has undoubtedly brought the Arab world to reconsider its own military weakness. At the same time the traumatic effect of the war also stemmed from the rapid capitulation, for a second time in little over a decade, of the Arabs' largest military machine; the shattered expectations of a heroic, drawn-out, house-to-house struggle in Iraqi cities; the humiliating capture of a major Arab state and its capital city; the fear of US plans for control of Iraqi oil; and the images of human suffering in the country.

The war in Iraq and its outcome are likely to have far-reaching implications in the Gulf region and the entire Middle East. The significance of these implications

101

stems from two reasons. One, Iraq has been a key player in the Middle East due to its military and economic potential and political weight. It has been part of the main developments in the Middle East and has striven to influence them. Together with Iran, Iraq is the link between instability in the Gulf and the Arab–Israeli conflict, as expressed in Iraqi missile attacks on Israel during the Gulf War. Iraq's foreign and security policy and internal developments have influenced the strategic environment, as was felt especially in the regional shockwaves that resonated during and following the 1991 Gulf War. Iraq, more than any other Arab state, has been involved in the Middle East's wars: it participated in all of the major wars between Israel and the Arab states, and in the last 23 years has drawn the Gulf area into three major conflicts.

Two, the American military campaign that was launched despite widespread international and regional reservations was so impressive in performance and result that it can be expected to impact on the conduct of other countries in the region. Moreover, the Bush administration has made it clear that the war in Iraq is not an isolated campaign, and that it plans to build on the war's outcome to influence other aspects of the Middle East arena, above all the war on terror, the development of Weapons of Mass Destruction (WMD), and the deadlocked political process between Israel and the Palestinians.

This essay examines the implications of the war in Iraq for the Middle East in general and for the leading states in the region in particular.

Constructing a New Regime and the Future of Iraq

An analysis of the recent and impending developments in the region begins with the future of Iraq itself, especially the shaping of a new regime and the US policy regarding Iraq. The American government has openly sought to establish a stable, moderate, democratic regime in Iraq that is linked to the United States. However, stabilizing such a regime will require dealing with an array of difficult and complex challenges, and Iraq presently lacks a basis strong enough for establishing this type of government. The former political system, based on the Ba'ath party, the Iraqi army, and the security organizations, has disintegrated. Saddam Hussein's generation-long rule in Iraq relied on brute force, atrocity, and fear, and during this period he suppressed the growth of any real opposition to his regime. The new government will have to be established at the ground level with foundations the American administration is trying to create from various constituents: a coalition of the main power centers in Iraq, including representatives of the leading population sectors, along with opposition elements who returned from exile at the culmination of the war, as well as perhaps elements from the Iraqi army.

Moreover, Iraq's population is divided between Shiites, who make up over half the population, Sunnis, and Kurds, as well as other small minorities. Further subdivisions define the main ethnic groups, while the interests of the three major groups clash. The Sunni minority held the top government positions in Saddam Hussein's regime, and it is now waging a rearguard battle to retain at least some of its status. In the wake of the 1991 Gulf War the Kurds gained autonomy under the protection of the United States and Britain in northern Iraq's Kurdish region (Kurdistan), and are now seeking to exploit the results of the latest war in order to expand their autonomous territory, move toward independence, or at the very least have Kurdistan integrated within the framework of a federated Iraqi state. The Shiites see the vacuum created in Iraq as an historic opportunity to obtain their rightful share in the government, and in addition certain elements hope to foment a Shiite religious awakening in Iraq with the aim of establishing an Islamic–Shiite regime. The conflicting interests among the three groups could lead to violent power struggles that would frustrate American efforts to set up a stable, Western-oriented regime in the country.

These incongruent trends have aroused fear in Iraq, its neighbors, and the American government of the possibility of two ominous developments. One is the possibility that the governmental vacuum will result in the partition of Iraq and secession of certain areas – especially the Kurdish north and Shiite south. This fear is particularly acute regarding the Kurdish region. Iraqi Kurdistan is a defined territorial unit populated by the majority of Kurds who possess a military organ-ization and who have already attained a large degree of autonomy. If the Kurds try to exploit the vacuum and strike for independence, they are liable to spark a violent internal struggle in Iraq that might invite military intervention by Iran, and even more so by Turkey, because of the fear that Kurdish independence in Iraq would encourage a similar inclination among the large Kurdish populations in their countries.

This scenario still remains only a possibility, and the likelihood that the Kurdish region would break away seems low, though it should not be completely discounted. The Kurds were quick to exploit the shock of the war by trying to gain control of additional territories in Kurdistan, including the large cities of Mosul and Kirkuk. American pressure and the threat of Turkish military intervention, however, aborted their expansionist trends, and the Kurds evacuated Kirkuk. In light of the Turkish threat and the US commitment to Iraq's territorial integrity, it seems that the Kurdish leaders would opt not to strive for independence lest they endanger their gains. At the same time they are now politically active not only in their enclave in the north, but also in Baghdad, trying to affect the shape of the future regime in Iraq. They will also probably endeavor to preserve their status in the framework of an Iraqi federated state, if it is created.

The second concern is the establishment of an Islamic–Shiite regime in Iraq. Unlike the Kurds, the Shiites do not seek autonomy. During the war between Iraq and Iran, for example, they demonstrated loyalty to the Iraqi state and displayed no sign of wishing to separate from it; instead, they struggled for equality and greater participation in government. The vacuum created in Iraq in the wake of the fall of Saddam Hussein's regime could provide the Shiites with the opportunity to lead the future regime on an Islamic–Shiite platform, while exploiting a number of factors: their majority in the population; the emotional postwar outburst among Shiites who had been oppressed under the previous regime; the weakness of the Sunni population that was identified with Saddam Hussein's regime; and the Shiite religious assets of special importance that are located in Iraq, led by two holy cities,

Najaf and Karbala, whose sanctity is superior to the Shiite sites in Iran. Unlike the Kurds, the Shiites do not enjoy American cooperation and protection. A Shiite regime in Iraq could undermine American plans to establish a moderate regime and ignite a struggle to oust American forces. A Shiite-dominated Iraq could also ally itself to the Islamic–Shiite regime in Iran and create a consolidated stronghold of Shiite power in the Gulf, although it would probably choose to preserve its Iraqi Shiite uniqueness. For these reasons, the United States is working to avert the creation of a Shiite regime in Iraq, but the Americans have expressed concern that the Shiites are better organized than was previously thought and that blocking Shiite aspirations will be a difficult task.

The Bush administration's declared interest in building a democratic regime in place of Saddam Hussein's dictatorship coincides with the American campaign to promote democracy in the Muslim and Arab world. The institution of democratic reconstruction, however, will invariably confront enormous obstacles. In addition to the absence of any genuine organized opposition to the former regime that might form the core of a new government, Iraq has no basis of even the most rudimentary democratic processes. It lacks any semblance of democratic mechanisms and norms, or any tradition of open political activity that could be restored. In this respect it lags behind other Middle East states, such as Egypt, Jordan, and Iran. The collapse of the former one-party system has led to the mushrooming of many old and new political parties and organizations, but the emergence of these parties increases the difficulties for the Americans to control Iraq and build a new regime with broad appeal. Thus, the process of building democratic institutions in Iraq could take years, and particularly since democracy cannot be imposed from without, no one can guarantee its success. Moreover, if the main goal of the American government is the foundation of a stable regime, then a discrepancy might easily develop between a stable regime and a democratic one. Regime stability might depend on a strong leader, rather than be based on shaky democratic foundations. The introduction of democratic processes is apt to hasten the establishment of an Islamic–Shiite regime in Iraq, since Shiites constitute the majority of the population. Furthermore, the effort to build a democracy will disturb several of America's Arab allies that regard the leap to democratic rule as a threat to the character and stability of their regimes. For these reasons, the American government might have to abandon its plans to institute a democratic regime in Iraq, at least until the new regime stabilizes.

Three months after the end of the war, the United States has not made much progress in regime building, nor does it seem to have come sufficiently prepared for the task. Most of Saddam's government mechanisms disintegrated during the war, and the Americans have been only partially successful in setting up new ones that can guarantee a return to normalcy and an end to anarchy. The coalition of representatives from the main Iraqi sectors and the opposition members recently returned from exile that the American administration is trying to build as a nucleus for the new government has not yet proven itself effective or even functional, and the Americans have been repeatedly forced to postpone the installment of a provisional government. In the meantime, management of the routine in Iraq is executed in part by the Americans themselves, with assistance of remnants from the previous government. The country's rehabilitation has also encountered setbacks because of the severe economic situation, and therefore in southern Iraq the Americans have restored oil production, paralyzed because of the war, in an attempt to jumpstart economic activity.

On the other hand, since the end of the fighting there have been no widespread displays of violence or clashes among the ethnic groups. While some manifestations of opposition to the United States as an occupying force have appeared – few Iraqis look forward to a prolonged American presence in their country – none of these incidents have translated into a massive terror wave against American and British forces. In the Arab and Muslim world too there have been no signs of wide anti-American turbulence or actual unrest against regimes linked to the United States.

In view of the hurdles on the path to regime stabilization, the United States has left a large military force in the country that could remain there for several years, with an eye to turn it into a multi-national force under its leadership. Such a peace force would be the surest guarantee for establishing a moderate, stable regime in Iraq. Its deployment, however, is liable to have distinct disadvantages. It could serve as a focus for heightened resistance to the American occupation, and become a target for wider terror attacks – both by Iraqi elements and terrorist organizations of the al-Qaeda type. The American administration would find it difficult to maintain the force in Iraq over a long period if it suffered heavy losses of the type sustained by the American and French troops in Beirut in 1983. The deployment of such a force could also fan the flames of anti-American unrest in Arab and Muslim countries and reinforce the impression that American intervention stems from imperialist interests, such as the desire to control Iraq's oil reserves.

Despite these obstacles, the United States has a good chance of setting up a moderate regime, linked to Washington and free from the strategic ambitions that characterized Saddam Hussein's rule. The future leaders of Iraq will likely be more balanced and careful, less aggressive and adventurous than Saddam, and, unlike Saddam, will not have control of a vast military power. The removal of sanctions and the restoration of oil production will enable the country to rebuild its economy. Later, the army could gradually be reconstructed, under close supervision, and serve as a reduced force for defensive missions, one that posed no danger to regional stability.

However, even if the American administration succeeds in establishing a moderate regime in the near future, the long-term problem remains after it withdraws its troops, especially if conditions of instability emerge in the country. The open question is: will the next regime focus on Iraq's long-term rehabilitation by reducing internal suppression, increasing personal and political liberties, and breaking free of its international isolation, or will it revert to its radical character and resume the quest for regional hegemony on the basis of a military buildup? Part of the answer lies in the willingness of the main power groups in the country to concentrate on rebuilding the nation rather than on fostering ethnic and religious interests that could lead to confrontations.

If the American supervision over the stabilizing process in Iraq slackens or disappears, the Iraqi regime could revert to a radical path in the distant future. This possibility merits serious attention, since Iraq's policy under Saddam Hussein did not originate exclusively from his personality and political outlook but from deeper roots and Iraq's geo-strategic reality. Iraq's perception of the Iranian threat, which was a principal factor in Baghdad's decision to develop WMD and invade Iran in 1980, will no doubt continue to serve as the key component of its security concept for the next Iraqi regime as well. Even if a moderate regime evolves in Iraq, it will be committed to providing a response to the Iranian threat and its ever-increasing WMD stockpile. The acquisition of ballistic missiles, non-conventional weapons, and especially nuclear weapons by Iran is likely to motivate the next Iraqi regime to seek similar weapons, as much as conditions will allow. It will be forced to abandon its WMD development as long as the United States demands it, but would probably return to its development program if American supervision tapers off (and provided Iraq has no alternative answer to the Iranian threat).

At this point it is still unclear if the challenges to stabilizing a moderate regime in Iraq are birth pains or reflections of structural problems inherent in the Iraqi system. The long-term trend in Iraq's reconstruction will hinge on several factors: the continuation and nature of American involvement; Iraq's ability to meet the challenge of complex problems; the degree of stability attained; the ability to strengthen cooperation between power elements in the country; the degree of success in introducing a basic transformation of the Iraqi elite, and perhaps in the state's structure, without merely being satisfied with personality change at the top of the government. This test of the reconstruction lies on a time axis; that is, the sooner the new regime stabilizes and the American presence departs, the more the American administration's victory will be enhanced and the easier for the United States to enlist support for its moves. Conversely, the longer it takes for these goals to be realized, the greater the threat to US interests and US achievements from the war.

The War's Impact on the Region

The regional impact of the collapse of Saddam's regime will largely depend on whether a moderate, stable government replaces it, or Iraq enters a prolonged period of instability requiring US involvement, which will affect the region negatively. If despite the obstacles the United States succeeds in establishing a moderate, stable regime with reasonable speed, it will achieve a strategic gain that will validate its military victory and assist it in shaping other elements in the Middle East. Yet if the Iraqi system fails to stabilize and the United States becomes a target of terrorist attacks in the wake of anti-American turbulence in Muslim and Arab countries, then the American military victory will be overshadowed by widespread unrest and its anticipated regional gains limited.

Whatever happens in Iraq, certain basic implications for the region are already apparent, though their intensity will become clear only in the future. First, a radical regime with an offensive security concept that menaced its neighbors was toppled. Of its own initiative Iraq participated in all the major wars between Israel and the Arabs, and even prior to Saddam Hussein's rise to power strove for regional hegemony. Saddam, however, gave extremist belligerent expression to Iraqi strategy that was reflected in its unparalleled military power and the initiated invasion of two of its neighbors. The fall of Saddam's regime and Iraq's strategic decline have also weakened to a great extent the group of radical countries in the Middle East – leaving only Iran, Syria, and Libya, as well as the extremist organizations – and are likely to buttress the region's moderate states.

Second, Iraq has been stripped of all its military power, at least for a number of years. This includes not only the complete obstruction of its WMD programs, but also the destruction of its conventional capabilities. At present Iraq cannot effectively wield any form of military force against its neighbors, though this situation will probably change in the coming years when Iraq will commence rearming. If Iraq develops a moderate, stable regime, the United States might have an interest in supplying it with military hardware to strengthen it domestically, and enable it to thwart foreign intervention and counterbalance radical elements in the region. But even when Iraq begins to rebuild its military power, it will probably take place gradually and under control in order to prevent a return to WMD development and any renewed threat to regional stability. For this reason it can be assumed that even if a radical or fundamentalist Shiite regime rises to power, Iraq will not have recourse, at least for several years, to a vast military arsenal that could intimidate its neighbors.

The destruction of Iraq's military capability has several ramifications for the region's power balance. Obviously the elimination of Iraq's military might, coupled with the downfall of Saddam Hussein's regime, will restrict Iraq from threatening its immediate neighbors or Israel. Essentially, the only way that Iraq could endanger the region is through terror, whose net effect is limited. Iraq's military weakness renders it susceptible to threats from its neighbors and may induce some of them, chiefly Iran and Turkey, to make attempts at interfering in its territory. Iraq's weakness will also allow domestic elements – the Kurds in the north and Shiites in the center and south – to weaken the central government, and join with corresponding elements across the border. This powerlessness has further significance for the region: it leaves Iran the main force in the Gulf arena, with no other regional player capable of providing a counterweight to Iranian military power, which will continue to grow in the coming years. This change will require the United States to invest greater input in containing the Iranian threat.

The collapse of Iraq's military strength has an additional positive consequence for the region: it can serve as a key factor in slowing down the Middle East arms race. Iraq was a major catalyst for this accelerated race, at both the conventional and non-conventional levels. Its invasion of Iran in 1980 was the main reason for Iran's military buildup during the Iran–Iraq War and its projects for development of ballistic missiles and non-conventional weapons. Iraq's 1990 invasion of Kuwait went far to encourage military stockpiling in Saudi Arabia and the smaller Gulf States throughout the 1990s. Iraq's involvement in the Arab–Israeli wars affected Israel's threat perception, and the need to deal with the Iraqi menace was a constant factor driving the IDF's military buildup. In turn Israel's buildup convinced its Arab neighbors, such as Egypt and Syria, to revitalize their military forces. It seems, then, that if the main power elements in the Middle East, such as Iran or Israel, decide to slow the pace of military strengthening in the coming years because of the absence of the Iraqi threat, then the arms race in the entire region might be reduced. Signs of such a reduction have been visible in recent years for budgetary and other reasons, and would receive further backing from increased American pressure on Iran and Syria to cut back their WMD programs.

Third, instability in Iraq may overflow onto the greater strategic environment, in the form of military intervention or political subversive activity in Iraq by other states; the spillover of Iraq's Kurdish problem into Turkey or Iran; and terror attacks against American, Western, and Israeli targets because of American involvement in Iraq. Although such attacks have occurred outside the Iraqi context, the American military presence is likely to help radical Islamic movements recruit activists and supporters to unite against the hated enemy who occupies a Muslim state and degrades the Arab people. If American military involvement in Iraq extends over a long period, it could contribute to anti-American unrest in the Middle East and backlash against regimes tied to the United States. Viewed from a different perspective, the vacuum created in Iraq invites competition on two levels: among the United States and other powers for economic assets and political leverage; and among countries in the region – mainly Iran and Turkey, and to lesser degree Saudi Arabia and Syria – for political, religious, and economic influence.

Fourth, the Iraqi crisis again illustrated the weakness of the Arab world and its schisms. Even though the crisis involved a key Arab state, the Arab countries failed to resolve the crisis and stave off the war. They also failed to consolidate a joint position, remaining split in their approach to the American military campaign. Most of the Arab states displayed signs of staunch opposition to the invasion of an Arab country aimed at toppling an Arab regime, but in practice several Arab states assisted the US war effort. All told, regardless of assistance given to the American forces by some of Iraq's Arab neighbors before and during the war, the Arab world had no actual influence on the war or in the postwar shaping of the country and its regime.

Finally, the war in Iraq significantly increased the US military, political, and economic involvement in the region. The American involvement impacts first and foremost on Iraq, where it will likely continue until a regime acceptable to the United States stabilizes. But it has also had an impact on other states in Iraq's strategic environment – especially Iran, Syria, Turkey, and the Gulf States. The involvement was expressed by the war itself when the United States demonstrated its determination and ability to amass a large force to protect its vital interests, even in defiance of large-scale international opposition. It also underscored the Bush administration's intention to use the military campaign in Iraq and the new strategic conditions created in the region to pressure other radical Arab states in the area, mainly Iran and Syria, to repudiate basic elements in their policies that in American eyes are counterproductive to regional stability, especially WMD development and involvement in terror.

The United States' increased intervention in the region will strengthen its ability to pressure and deter radical regimes. The campaign in Iraq serves as a severe warning to radical regimes and organizations of the Hizbollah type that the United States will not be deterred from operating against them, by force when necessary, when its vital interests are in danger. Thus, while the administration claims that it has no intention of going this far, and it is hard to imagine it would resort to a major military operation of similar proportions as the one employed in Iraq against another state, the possibility of an American military move against them remains on the agenda. The radical states understand that they have to take into account more than in the past the possibility of a small-scale American military operation against them – for example, against targets linked to WMD development or against Hizbollah – if the American government's demands are rejected. The US commitment to widen the ramifications of the campaign in Iraq could also be expressed along non-military lines, for example, support for increased democratization in the region's countries, a renewal of the Arab–Israeli peace process, and the creation of a free trade zone in the Middle East. These intentions would place new challenges before the region's states and force them to deal with them in the coming years.

The War's Impact on Neighboring States

The toppling of Saddam Hussein's regime, especially if replaced by a moderate, stable one, will contribute to the security of the moderate Arab states. Saddam's downfall has removed a serious threat from them, and a stable regime in Iraq can join the moderate Arab camp as a major ally. The removal of the Iraqi threat will have a particular impact on Saudi Arabia and Kuwait, which were in the regime's line of focus for many years. Regime change could also assure Iraq's integration in the creation of a Gulf security network. In addition, the fact that the United States, which forms one of the cornerstones in the national security of the Gulf States, launched a large-scale military campaign against a radical state for a second time will contribute to the deterrence of their rivals. These developments also apply to Jordan, which would like to see a moderate government in Iraq. Over the years Saddam forced Jordan, whose economy depended on Iraq, to toe the Iraqi line. Jordanian support of Iraq during the Gulf War impaired its relationship with the United States and Gulf States. The Iraqi hold also threatened to fashion Jordan as an arena of military confrontation between Iraq and Israel. The desire to be free of this manipulation contributed to Jordan's support of the recent campaign in Iraq and gained it American economic aid. The Egyptians too view Iraq's integration into the moderate Arab bloc in a positive light, although further along, after Iraq recovers its strength, it might challenge Egypt again for leadership in the Arab world.

On the other hand, the developments in Iraq also harbor risks for the moderate states. Prolonged instability would likely spill over to Iraq's neighbors, especially regarding all aspects of the Kurdish challenge and the possible partition of Iraq. The moderate Arab states equally fear a Shiite awakening and the Sunni loss of control. In their view, a charged Shiite center of power will hinder the establishment of a moderate regime, alter the balance of forces in the Gulf, and possibly create a fundamentalist link between Iraq and Iran. Furthermore, Iraq's weakness will inhibit its ability to deter Iran or allow it to serve as a counterweight to the Iranian threat in the Gulf. And again, the rise of anti-American unrest in the Middle East, and a wave of terrorist attacks against American targets, could unhinge the stability of the moderate regimes and make it hard for them to cooperate with the United States.

Iran will probably be the state most influenced, for better and worse, by the war in Iraq and its aftermath. The collapse of Saddam Hussein's regime almost completely neutralizes the Iraqi threat for the near future, especially regarding its WMD program. In the wake of the war, Iran remains the main regional military power in the Gulf, and the vacuum in Iraq can create new opportunities for Iran. At the same time, however, the American military presence in Iraq completes Iran's encirclement by countries tied to the United States (on most of which American troops are stationed). American's unprecedented military campaign in Iraq, executed despite massive international opposition, should serve as a warning sign to Iran – a member of the "axis of evil" and already engaged in WMD development and the promotion of terrorism – that its turn could arrive. The Iranian regime cannot ignore the fact that the United States attacked Iraq for the same infractions Iran is now accused of to an even greater degree than Iraq, and that voices in Washington are calling for American intervention to effect regime change in Iran. Thus, the United States has increased its leverage to pressure Iran to halt its WMD program and involvement in terrorism. The American government's diplomatic and media blitz since the beginning of 2003 against Iran's accelerated nuclear development and its contacts with al-Qaeda should thus be regarded with concern by Tehran's leadership. Iran is also worried that the Bush administration has marked Hizbollah, joined at the hip to Iran, as one of its next objectives, and has been pressuring Syria to disarm the Lebanese organization and remove it as a military force on Israel's northern border.

After the American government attains its objective in Iraq, will it decide to tackle the threat emanating from Iran, especially its nuclear weapons program? In recent months, even before the war in Iraq, the Bush administration increasingly took note of Iran's intensified nuclear project. It is doubtful whether the administration will take large-scale military action against Iran since this would be a far more complex and costly operation than the campaign in Iraq, and would be void of international legitimacy. The administration, therefore, has pinned its hopes on internal developments in Iran to lessen the nature of the threat, and for the time being it gives priority to diplomatic efforts aimed at containing Iran. But if the administration assesses that Iran is coming very close to obtaining a nuclear weapon, it might consider a pinpoint military operation against WMD sites inside the country. This decision will depend not only on regional circumstances, but also on the estimate of internal developments in Iran, especially regarding the ability of moderate elements to attain power and the prospects of engaging in a genuine dialogue with the Iranian regime.

Furthermore, in the aftermath of the war there are new reasons, at least in theory, for Iran to support an enhanced dialogue with the United States. The elimination of the Iraqi military machine has removed Iran's prime motivation for a strategic buildup, including the development of WMD, and could encourage Tehran to reconsider its armament program. The exacerbation of the American threat and the deployment of American forces in Iraq and Afghanistan could persuade Iran to display an interest in bilateral dialogue with the United States. Prior to the American action in Afghanistan and the war in Iraq, a limited dialogue at the working group level took place between the two countries, and this could be expanded in the future. Iranian leaders have recently been signaling such a possibility though the country's spiritual leader, Khameini, continues to decry compromise with the United States.

The results of the war in Iraq have also influenced Iran in the religious sphere. The Shiite awakening in Iraq raises the possibility that a revitalized Shiite center will be created. The return of the Shiites' holy cities Najaf and Karbala to their religious prominence following the demise of Saddam's regime poses a threat to the primacy of Iran's Shiite legacy. Thousands of religious Shiites from Iraq have gathered in Iranian religious seminaries, especially in the city of Qom, after fleeing Saddam Hussein's regime, and many are likely to return to the holy cities in Iraq whose religious importance is considered far greater than those in Iran. The awakening of a Shiite center in Iraq might strengthen the separatist identity of Arab Shiism, as distinct from Iranian Shiism, and create a rivalry between Najaf and Qom for the leadership of the Shiite world. Under these circumstances Iran is likely to try to encourage the development of an Iranian–Iraqi Shiite alignment and, whatever the outcome, increase its involvement in Iraq, especially among the Shiite population in order to influence the shape of the future regime.

Syria's strategic position too has suffered from the war in Iraq. The loss of Iraq's military strength eliminated the last chance – already small since the 1991 Gulf War – for Iraq to exert military pressure on Israel, and thus reestablish an eastern front against it. The possibility of Iraq joining the moderate Arab camp has wounded the radical group, of which Syria is a member. The deployment of American troops for the first time across Syria's eastern border – with Israel to the south and Turkey to the north – reinforces Syria's sense of encirclement and its vulnerability to pressure. If instability continues in Iraq for a long period, it might spill over into Syria, which has its own problem with a Kurdish minority.

More important, Syria has increasingly come under American pressure to adapt its foreign policy to the new strategic situation created by the war in Iraq. The Bush administration has severely criticized Syria because of the military assistance, albeit limited, that it extended to Iraq during the war, dispatching volunteers and offering refuge to senior figures in Saddam's regime. The American government has therefore begun to make explicit demands on Syria: namely, end the chemical weapons program; cease military assistance to Hizbollah and distance it from Lebanon's border with Israel; and disband the Palestinian organizations' military headquarters in Damascus. In the wake of growing criticism in the American Congress of Bashar Assad's policy, the Bush administration is likely to demand that Syria withdraw its troops from Lebanon. Faced with these pressures, and with no ally excluding Iran, Syria is trying to present a positive image by improving its monitoring along the Iraqi border; displaying willingness to cooperate with the United States in the war on terror; signaling its readiness to shut down the offices of the Palestinian organizations and lower Hizbollah's profile, though without disarming it; and showing an interest in renewing the political process with Israel.

For Turkey the significance of the war in Iraq has been ambivalent. On the one hand, the government supported the war's aims as defined by the American administration since they serve Turkish interests: the replacement of Saddam's regime by a moderate, pro-American one, and the elimination of Iraq's WMD capability. On the other hand, more than any of Iraq's other neighbors, Turkey was apprehensive over the turmoil in Iraq and its implications for Turkish security. Turkey was particularly disturbed over the possibility of Kurdish autonomy transforming into an independent entity, or the possible creation of a federal structure in Iraq that would provide greater independence for the Kurds. From Turkey's point of view, such a development could quickly trigger unrest among its own large Kurdish minority that would demand similar gains. Turkey's opposition to the Iraqi Kurds' takeover of Mosul and Kirkuk or the northern oil fields stemmed from the fear that their economic independence would enable them to push for political independence. The Bush administration understood Turkish sensitivities and pledged to stop the Kurds from seizing control of Kirkuk.

Yet continued instability in Iraq will have an influence on Turkey in the coming period and leave open the possibility of Turkish military intervention in northern Iraq. In practice, Turkey military forces have exploited Iraq's weakness and repeatedly penetrated into northern Iraq since the mid-1990s, with thousands of Turkish troops deployed there since 1997 to counter the activity of Kurdish PKK fighters concealed in the area. Turkey has threatened to increase its involvement in northern Iraq if certain conditions develop, such as terrorist attacks inside Turkey that emanate from Iraq; a threat to Turkish forces in Iraq; growing confrontation on the border between the Kurds and Iraq's Turcoman minority that Turkey is committed to supporting; or a flood of Iraqi refugees into Turkey.

Added to this is the rupture in Turkey's relationship with the United States. Since the 1990s, and following Turkish assistance to the United States in the Gulf War, the strategic partnership between the two countries has deepened. This partnership is what contributed to the Turkish government's decision to aid the United States in the war in Iraq, permitting the use of Turkey's territory and bases for launching the military campaign into northern Iraq. The Turkish decision was also influenced by Ankara's interest in regime change in Iraq and the American promise of generous financial aid to ease Turkey's current economic crisis. But the recently installed Turkish parliament, comprised of an Islamic-oriented ruling party with an absolute majority, vetoed the government's approval to grant US forces deployment rights in Turkey. This volte-face suddenly became a major stumbling block in American–Turkish strategic cooperation. Turkey's negative reply to its ally in an hour of urgency forced the Americans to make major revisions in their operational plans, and added unnecessary complications to their diplomatic campaign. The seriousness of this blow was highlighted even more by Turkey's alacrity in renouncing most of the economic aid promised to it and reneging on its commitment for deeper involvement in shaping Iraq after the war, in exchange for cooperation with the United States.

Turkey and the United States will probably resolve their main differences since the continuation of strategic cooperation is important to both sides. The American government promised Turkey nearly one billion dollars in aid for the use of Turkish air space during the war, although there were those in Congress who wanted to stipulate that the sum be partially dependent on economic reform in Turkey. The entire Iraq war chapter, however, could leave a bitter residue in American–Turkish relations with lingering questions over the boundaries of cooperation. In the coming period a list of key issues between the two countries will have to be drafted. These include: the shaping of Iraq's future; the future of American forces in Turkey; Turkey's ties with the Europe Union, NATO, and the United States; the link between internal changes in Turkey, following the last elections that brought a party with Islamic roots to power, and its foreign policy and ties to the United States; and the management of Turkey's economic crisis.

The Ramifications for Israel

The war's ramifications for Israel will also depend on America's degree of success in stabilizing a moderate regime in Iraq. If Iraq becomes the focus of instability, if a Shiite center of Islamic fundamentalism is created, or if a rising wave of terror and anti-American fervor sweep the region, then this will have a negative impact on Israel. Terrorist threats against American objectives might be joined by attacks on Israeli and Jewish targets. Unrest in moderate Arab regimes and the threat to their stability would harm Israel's ties with these countries and detract from Israel's regional status.

Yet despite these potential dangers, the war in Iraq and its results have given Israel a number of strategic gains. The elimination of Iraq's potential for WMD and conventional weapons has removed Iraq from the ring of confrontational states around Israel, thus lessening one of Israel's major strategic threats for many years. If the region's arms race declines, it will also have an important implication for Israel. Additional gains include the increased American pressure on Iran that, if continued, is likely to diminish the Iranian threat to Israel. The impression left by the military campaign in Iraq will probably strengthen America's deterrent capability *vis-à-vis* Iran. It seems that the United States will take advantage of the upheaval in Iraq for dealing with the Iranian nuclear threat, especially since Iran is now the only major military power in the Gulf area. American pressure on Syria is also likely to bear fruit by reducing Hizbollah's military capability and operational freedom, and constricting the activity of Palestinian organizations located in Damascus.

Israel will gain additional vital assets through the successful installment of a moderate regime in Iraq, the improvement of the US position in the Middle East, and the strengthening of the moderate Arab camp. The removal of the Iraqi imperative from Jordan's foreign policy will contribute to a stronger regime in Amman. The campaign's results will also assist the United States in advancing the Israeli–Palestinian political process, especially since Washington will have more time to devote to it, and also because of the potentially positive influence of a moderate Iraq on the process. These benefits notwithstanding, however, it is difficult to foresee that an Iraqi regime friendly to Israel will arise in the near future since the hostility toward Israel has deep roots that predate Saddam's regime, and a reversal is not dependent on his ouster alone. Nevertheless, it can be assumed that the next regime may adopt a position toward Israel similar to that of the moderate Arab regimes, and will reduce or cease its material assistance to the Palestinian organizations. In the longer run, an Iraqi–Israeli dialogue might develop, one that could radiate a positive light onto the entire moderate Arab camp.

Israeli–Palestinian Peacemaking After the War

10

Shai Feldman

The war in Iraq was followed by a series of important developments in Israeli–Palestinian peacemaking. The most dramatic among these were the official announcement on April 30, 2003 of the Quartet's roadmap for Palestinian–Israeli peace, the June summits orchestrated by President Bush in Sharm el-Sheik and Aqaba, and the meetings held between Israeli Prime Minister Ariel Sharon and Palestinian Prime Minister Mahmoud Abbas, especially their highly publicized meeting in early July. These developments may mark the beginning of the first serious attempt by Palestinians and Israelis to reverse the tense, violent course of their relations since late September 2000.

In comparison to other factors that preceded the war, it is impossible to ascertain the relative weight that the war in Iraq exerted on these dramatic events. Most likely, the war affected the matrix of incentives of the principal players in the Palestinian–Israeli conflict, boosting the impact of other developments in the conflict that began to surface at least a year prior to the war in Iraq and have evolved over time. This chapter attempts to identify these developments and to assess how the war in Iraq has accelerated their impact to produce the first signs of hope that Palestinians and Israelis might again substitute diplomacy for violence as the preferred venue for resolving their dispute.

Pre-War Developments

On the Palestinian side, three related issues appear to have increased the prospects of renewed negotiations. The first is that during 2002 many among the mainstream Palestinian elite concluded that the violence that had escalated since September 2000 had become a strategic disaster, and that the rampant terrorism must be stopped to allow the resumption of peacemaking efforts. Several important ramifications of the violence seem to have informed this conclusion, not least of which was the pain incurred by Palestinians throughout the West Bank and Gaza as a result of Israel's response to the ongoing violence. This relates not only to the many Palestinian dead and wounded but also to the massive damage to the Palestinian economy and the hardships caused by the many curfews, closures, checkpoints, and Israeli incursions into Palestinian population centers. In addition, there was a complete paralysis of Palestinian state-building efforts, as much of the Palestinian governmental institutions were either destroyed or lost their efficacy as a result of the escalating violence. The violence also had a disastrous impact on US–Palestinian relations after two decades of Palestinian investment in building these ties. And finally, Israel's peace camp suffered a dramatic loss of credibility, since it appeared, at least to the population at large, to have banked too heavily on Arafat's good intentions. Thus, a domestic constituency favoring Israeli concessions to the Palestinians essentially disappeared.

The second development was the impetus to improve governance within the Palestinian Authority (PA). The first sign of progress in this context involved making the PA's finances transparent. In large part this was prompted by the insistence of donors to the PA that funds no longer be diverted to terrorist activities and organizations. At the same time it had the effect of lessening Yassir Arafat's hold over Palestinian activity, as his ability to use "the power of the purse" at will was somewhat curtailed.

Herein follows the third important development experienced on the Palestinian side: Arafat's gradual weakening. Internationally, the position of the US and Israel – that Arafat has become an obstacle to a negotiated resolution of the conflict and that he must therefore be superseded if not replaced by a leadership not tainted by blood and violence – became increasingly widespread. This view also gathered support among mainstream Palestinians, although it was tempered by continued popular allegiance to Arafat as the father of modern Palestinian nationalism and by resentment of outsiders who were perceived as dictating the composition of the Palestinian leadership.

On the Israeli side the most positive development of the past few years was the growing awareness of the demographic dimensions of the conflict, namely, of the fact that among those residing between the Mediterranean Sea and the Jordan Valley, Jews already comprise only 53 percent of the population. An even more indicative statistic is that among those under the age of fifteen, Palestinians comprise a significant majority. Sensitivity to this problem has led an increasing number of Israelis to conclude that if their country's future as a Jewish and democratic state is to be secured, Israel will have to disengage from the areas where most Palestinians reside: the West Bank, Gaza, and East Jerusalem.

In the Middle East at large, the most important development prior to the war in Iraq was the conclusion reached in 2001–2002 by a number of key Arab states, notably Saudi Arabia and Egypt, that they erred in mid-2000 by failing to foster a regional environment conducive to a successful conclusion of Palestinian–Israeli negotiations. As a result, by early 2002 these states adopted a more proactive approach to these efforts. Primarily, this was manifested in the launching of the "Saudi Initiative" and its subsequent adoption by the Arab League in March 2002.

For Egypt this translated into growing involvement "on the ground," in an effort to persuade the Palestinians to end the violence, especially against Israeli civilians inside the 1967 lines. These efforts, directed primarily at the Islamic opposition groups Hamas and Islamic Jihad, were spearheaded by General Omar Suliman, head of Egypt's General Intelligence Service.

While these developments were underway well before the war in Iraq, they were far from sufficient to produce an effective return to the negotiating table. Instead, the two parties remained locked in an evolving cycle of violence, while Israelis also grew increasingly pessimistic about the prospects of renewed negotiations as long as Arafat remained at the Palestinian helm. Continued Palestinian terrorism and Arafat's refusal to counter the violence led Israelis twice to elect a government headed by Ariel Sharon and to back any measure taken by the government to stem the violence. Thus, latent support for disengagement from the Palestinians remained coupled on the Israeli side with wide support for a prime minister who vowed not to bow to the violence with concessions and to resort to harsh measures if necessary. Wide distrust of Arafat and the Palestinians restrained Israel from taking conciliatory measures that might have given the PA greater incentives to reverse its violent course.

Instead, general anger at the punitive measures applied by Israel made it very difficult for Palestinians who favored a cessation of hostilities to argue their case. Moreover, as their casualties and hardships accumulated, Palestinians obstinately refused to end the violence without tangible gains. In practice, they rejected the various conflict resolutions proposed during 2000–2002 on the grounds that they had no assurances that implementation of these plans would not be frozen once violence was halted and Israel's security requirements were met. Finally, growing criticism of the violent path chosen by Arafat in September 2000 did not result in his removal or in any national decision to change course. Arafat repeatedly proved his capacity within the Palestinian domestic arena to ward off any attempt at opposition by threatening his opponents to the point of their near-paralysis.

In the US, the latent positive strategic developments in the Middle East did not persuade a skeptical Bush administration that it should engage itself in diplomatic efforts to resolve the conflict. Against the advice of some in the State Department, the White House remained steadfastly opposed to active involvement in the conflict, largely based on the conviction that as long as the Palestinians did not have a leadership comprised of individuals committed to combating terrorism, there was little chance of creating an environment conducive to successful negotiations. Indeed every US proposal drafted since the violence began in September 2000 failed: from the Sharm el-Sheik summit in late 2000 through the respective Mitchell, Tenet, and Zinni plans presented in 2001 and 2002. Moreover, Arafat's behavior when the attempted smuggling into the Palestinian territories of large quantities of weapons and ammunition aboard the *Karine-A* ship was aborted in January 2002 – primarily his blatantly false denial of any knowledge or personal involvement in the attempt – led President Bush to conclude that he was "a liar and a cheat" and that, therefore, he could not be considered a partner to a viable peacemaking effort. As a result, the president's national security team and his political advisors concurred that any new effort to restart the peace process was not worth the domestic risks that such an endeavor was likely to entail.

This skepticism, if not outright hostility, towards official Palestinian political efforts complemented the impact of the September 11 attacks on the Pentagon and the World Trade Center. The al-Qaeda attacks prompted increased US sympathy for Israel's efforts to combat terrorism and laid the basis for a growing convergence of views between President Bush and Prime Minister Sharon. Central to both leaders' post-9/11 approach was the conviction that terrorism should not be rewarded in any way. While the US did not go so far as to equate Arafat with Osama Bin Laden, President Bush seems to have accepted Sharon's argument that the PA leader should be regarded as part of the problem, not part of the solution to the Palestinian–Israeli predicament.

To be sure, these predispositions did not lead the US to disengage completely from peacemaking efforts. Through visits by mid-level officials as well as participation in the attempts of UN, European, and Russian representatives (the so-called Quartet) to define a "roadmap" for Israeli–Palestinian peace, the Bush administration indicated that it was not indifferent to the importance of diplomatic efforts to end the conflict. However, the White House gave reason to believe that President Bush was not deeply involved in these efforts and that he was not about to clash with Prime Minister Sharon over a futile effort to implement the plan.

Prior to the war in Iraq, therefore, the positive changes in the Middle East regional environment appeared inconclusive. After the Saudi initiative was adopted by the Arab League in March 2002, not a single serious effort to implement the initiative could be detected. And while Egypt remained active in efforts to corral the Palestinians into a strategic decision to end terrorist attacks against Israeli civilian targets, all its efforts to broker an agreement between Fatah, Hamas, and Islamic Jihad failed miserably.

The Impact of the War

While the deposal of Saddam Hussein's regime and the decisive military victory of the war in Iraq became apparent immediately, the struggle over Iraq's political future is far less defined, even three months after the war. Consequently, any assessment of the long-term political consequences of the war should be considered tentative at best. Nevertheless, a number of observations about the impact of the war on the Palestinian–Israeli arena can already be ventured with some confidence.

On the positive side of the ledger, senior Bush administration officials were persuaded that the war created an opportunity as well as a necessity for Washington to persuade Middle East states that the administration was not anti-Arab or anti-Muslim. The administration also seems to have concluded that this could be best achieved by forging a breakthrough in Palestinian–Israeli peacemaking that would end Israel's occupation of Palestinian land. This conclusion led the administration to allow the publication of the Quartet's roadmap to Middle East peace just after the war. Moreover, Bush administration officials took steps to signal that the Quartet's document enjoyed the backing of the White House and should not be regarded as the result of a State Department rogue operation. In order to reduce the document's exposure to conflicting pressures, National Security Advisor Condoleezza Rice also made clear that the roadmap formula was not open to amendments or adjustments proposed by Israelis and Palestinians.

In the Middle East at large the immediate outcome of the war seems to have altered the balance of forces against continued Palestinian–Israeli violence. First, it removed an Iraqi regime that encouraged Palestinian terrorism through the financial rewards it granted to families of suicide bombers. More important, the war's outcome removed Iraq from the camp of radical Arab states that are adamantly opposed to Israel's existence. If so, then Iraq, once stabilized, might resemble Egypt – a country willing to accept Israel's role in the Middle East under specified conditions and not actively associated with terrorist operations in Israel.

Second, there are some tentative signs that in the impressive demonstration of US willingness and ability to obliterate a member of the "axis of evil," the war may produce greater caution in Damascus and Tehran. The most important test is how this will translate into reduced support for Hizbollah in South Lebanon and for Palestinian organizations that are committed to opposing Israel's existence violently, primarily Hamas and Islamic Jihad. While Syria's President Bashar Assad initially demonstrated confusion about the war's necessary impact on Syria's behavior, unequivocal statements by President Bush and Secretaries Rumsfeld and Powell seem to have had a clarifying effect. Assad appears to have subsequently grasped the message and has taken some steps to accommodate Washington priorities.

Third, the war established America's hegemony in the region, for not only was the US able to act unilaterally in Iraq, but even the timing of the publication of the Quartet's roadmap was determined by Washington. This seems to have persuaded the Palestinian leadership that it had no choice but to meet the Bush administration's preconditions for re-involvement in peacemaking efforts. Consequently, the PA finally moved to implement at least some of Washington's demands for political reform by naming Mahmoud Abbas, better known as Abu Mazen, as prime minister, and by beginning to restructure the PA's security services in a manner congruent with US demands.

Sensitivity to America's new regional standing was also demonstrated by Hizbollah. While initially encouraging if not directing some of its foot soldiers to help Saddam's beleaguered regime during the war, the Lebanese Shiite organization refrained from any activity during and immediately after the war that might have provided the Bush administration with added motivation to make it a high priority target in its ongoing War on Terrorism. At the same time, it is too early to tell whether the long-term effect of the war in Iraq on Hizbollah will impact positively on the prospects for peace. Quite possibly, the new constraints on the Shiite organization's freedom to mount overt operations against Israel might lead it to become more involved in assisting Palestinian opposition groups in planning and executing terrorist activities.

A much clearer manifestation of the new regional environment was Egypt's deeper involvement in brokering a Palestinian decision to implement internal reforms. Without massive pressures from Cairo, Arafat could not be persuaded to accept the minimum demands presented by Abu Mazen as preconditions for his nomination as prime minister.

In Israel, too, there were signs of growing acknowledgment of America's new role and of the need to satisfy the Bush administration's minimal post-war requirements. At least in part, this tendency was fueled by the wide-ranging support provided by the United States to Israel prior, during, and immediately after the war. This included the stationing of Patriot air defense units, the quiet but detailed understanding reached between the two governments regarding the manner in which Israel might react in case it was attacked by Iraq, and the provision of $1 billion in direct economic assistance and $9 billion in US government loan guarantees.

Consequently, Prime Minister Sharon decided to avoid a direct confrontation with the Bush administration over the publication and content of the roadmap. Instead, Israel's reservations were scaled back in number and scope, and a decision was made to enter a quiet dialogue with the White House on the manner in which the roadmap might be implemented in the aftermath of its publication. In parallel, Prime Minster Sharon gave a number of interviews in April 2003 in which he pledged his determination to use his final years as prime minister to make every effort to reach a permanent peace with the Palestinians. In this context, he expanded upon statements he has made previously, recognizing the inevitability of establishing a Palestinian state and of the need to make "painful concessions" in the framework of a peace agreement. Yet at this point he went much further, declaring that in his view continuing to control a large Palestinian population against its will was not a tenable proposition. In addition, he specified various locations in the West Bank that he considers cradles of Israeli history from which Israel might have to withdraw in the framework of a peace agreement with the Palestinians.

Constraints on the Road to Peace

While the war in Iraq may have created more favorable conditions for restarting Israeli–Palestinian negotiations than any time since the beginning of the violence in September 2000, in May and early June 2003 the road from violence to peace continued to be replete with obstacles and question marks.

First, it was not clear whether the PA's new prime minister would be able to overcome the main internal obstacles to his bringing about a reduction of the violence: Arafat's interest in allowing violence as a means of undermining Abu Mazen's chances of establishing himself as an effective successor; the determination of Hamas and Islamic Jihad to circumvent any effort to reach an accommodation with Israel; and the young Fatah fighters (the so-called "Tanzim") who rose to prominence with the escalation of the violence that began in 2000 and whose image is inexorably linked to the armed conflict. While Hamas and Islamic Jihad threatened to reject any decision to lay down their arms, the principal risk with regard to Tanzim was that given its amorphous structure no decision on a ceasefire would be observed, and that various loosely affiliated groups and individuals would continue fighting regardless of the decision that the Fatah leadership would adopt. Thus, the effort to move from violence to the negotiations table remained exposed to the capacity of the Palestinian opposition groups to launch terrorist attacks that invite harsh Israeli responses, in effect guaranteeing that the parties remain chained to a cycle of terrorism and counter-responses.

Second, just as many questions surrounded the true intentions of Israel's Prime Minister Sharon. Indeed, Sharon has given significant evidence of his understanding that controlling millions of Palestinians against their will is untenable and that the creation of a Palestinian state should be acceptable to Israel. But it remained far from clear whether Sharon was truly prepared to implement the far-reaching measures that ending Israel's control of the Palestinians and establishing a viable Palestinian state would require. Thus in May Sharon continued to prove unyielding on the issue of Israeli outposts and settlements in the West Bank, and he has displayed little understanding that the Palestinians have come to regard Israel's settlement policy as a test of Israel's true intentions. In fact, the statements made by Israel's prime minister that Israel was prepared to make painful concessions in the framework of a peace agreement with the Palestinians were followed by others that sent the opposite message: namely, that no concessions would be made in Israel's settlements policy as an incentive for the Palestinians to abandon violence in favor of negotiations. Thus, while serious question marks continued to surround the capacity of the PA's new leadership to overcome the opposition within and outside the mainstream Fatah movement, the odds that he might be supported by an Israeli policy appeared bleak.

The reluctance of Israeli leaders to take measures that might improve Abu Mazen's internal standing seemed to be matched by doubts within Israel's defense community about the wisdom of an armistice. Primarily, they worried that an internal Palestinian decision to halt Hamas and Islamic Jihad terrorism would prove temporary, merely affording them time to regroup and improve their infrastructure. Should this prove to be the case these organizations, which Israel has successfully opposed since Operation Defensive Shield in April 2002, would pose a far greater threat once violence is resumed.

Overall, Israel's litmus test for assessing the true intentions and effectiveness of the new Palestinian leadership continued to be as demanding as the Palestinian tests of Israel's intentions: not merely a cessation of hostilities but a willingness to completely disarm the Palestinian opposition groups in a manner that would prevent them from using any hiatus in violent activity to their long-term advantage. This in turn would require a much more decisive change than that implied by the Egyptian-orchestrated attempt to broker an end to Palestinian terrorist attacks against Israeli civilians.

Beyond these challenges lie additional difficulties in Israel's position over basic issues at the heart of the Palestinian–Israeli dispute. Israel's concerns about the magnitude of the demographic threat may encourage some flexibility in order to achieve an effective separation between the two communities. Yet these same fears foster rigidity elsewhere, primarily regarding the "right of return" for Palestinian refugees. The combination of increased sensitivity to demography and the loss of any measure of trust with respect to the Palestinians' true intentions have made Israelis even less willing than before to entertain the idea of any return of Palestinian refugees to locations inside the 1967 lines, even if the numbers are symbolic only. The result has been a growing Israeli call – as a condition for progress in implementing any roadmap to peace – that the Palestinians publicly renege on their demand for the "right of return."

These obstacles on the Palestinian and Israeli sides simply compounded the doubts that remained regarding Washington's true willingness to involve itself in a meaningful peacemaking effort. While the wartime and immediate post-war desire to counter the accusation that the US was anti-Arab and anti-Muslim – as well as the wish to accommodate the political imperatives of Britain's Prime Minister Tony Blair – led the Bush administration to permit the publication of the Quartet's roadmap, there was considerable reason to doubt that the US was prepared to do what it takes to pressure Israel and the Palestinians into implementing the plan.

First, the administration had to be convinced that the changes that have taken place in the PA were more than cosmetic and that Abu Mazen has a real chance of success. Arafat's continued efforts to undermine Abu Mazen and the questions surrounding what has been presented as the restructuring of the Palestinian security services left considerable doubt whether a meaningful change has indeed occurred. These doubts were further fueled by the creation of the Palestinian National Security Council – a transparent attempt by Arafat to exert influence over the locus of Palestinian power.

Second, the administration wanted assurance that the Israeli government would be willing to take some risks to ensure Abu Mazen's chances of overcoming his domestic rivals. In the absence of such signs, a meaningful US involvement required that pressure be exerted on both parties so that the atmosphere in their relations would improve to a point permitting some hope that renewed negotiations might succeed. But clashing with the Israeli government requires that the Bush administration be willing to risk not only a confrontation with the organized parts of the US Jewish community but also with the Christian Right. Indeed, it was not clear whether the political advisors of President Bush would suggest that he can risk such a confrontation given the results of the 2000 elections, even if his immediate post-war standing in the polls appeared impressively robust.

Current Prospects for Peace

While the impact of the war in Iraq on the prospects for Palestinian–Israeli peacemaking as yet remains uncertain, there is reason to believe that the war has accelerated previous developments advancing an end to the violence that began in late 2000. What at first appeared as a set of tactical considerations propelling US re-involvement in Middle East peacemaking – the desire to balance America's image in the Arab world and the wish to be sensitive to the political requirements of Prime

Minister Blair – has evolved into a strategic decision by the Bush White House to reverse its previous reluctance to micro-manage Palestinian–Israeli negotiations. In Sharm el-Sheik and Aqaba, President Bush signaled that he has come to regard the attempt to bring peace to the Holy Land as a personal mission and that to this end he was prepared to place his presidential prestige on the line.

The White House turnaround seems to reflect not only a response to the opportunities and imperatives created by the outcome of the war in Iraq but also a change in its assessment of the possible domestic ramifications of such an effort. Thus a course of action that previously seemed too politically risky was now judged as having few internal downsides. Prime Minister Sharon's stated willingness to make painful concessions and his decision to refrain from mounting a serious opposition to the roadmap made it highly unlikely that the American Jewish community would launch an organized campaign against the White House.

In addition, given the Bush administration's proven commitment to implementing much of the Christian Right's domestic agenda, it also seemed unlikely that the Christian Right would break with the White House over the attempt to achieve Palestinian–Israeli peace. These factors combined with the president's popularity in the immediate aftermath of the war to lessen the internal considerations previously inhibiting deep US involvement in the peace process.

In turn, the highly publicized summits in Sharm, Aqaba, and Jerusalem seem to have galvanized an outpouring of hope if not optimism among the mainstream Palestinian and Israeli publics. The cumulative fatigue experienced by the two communities seems to have resulted in a deep desire "to give peace a chance." Thus, the decision of the Palestinian opposition groups to accept an armistice seems to reflect the aspirations of the Palestinian street no less than it was a response to the military pressures exerted by Israel and the political and financial leverage exercised by Egypt and Saudi Arabia.

The course charted by the roadmap is likely to prove very bumpy, and Palestinian and Israeli travelers attempting its path remain vulnerable to the certain efforts by extremists on both sides to derail them. Yet the early aftermath of the war in Iraq signals positive developments in this arena and enhanced prospects for diverting Palestinian–Israeli relations from violence toward a negotiated resolution of the conflict.

The Case of Iraq's Weapons of Mass Destruction

Ephraim Asculai

Even before the 1991 Gulf War there was substantial evidence that Iraq was developing an extensive Weapons of Mass Destruction (WMD) capability. Iraq had already used chemical weapons against Iran and against its own people, and it claimed it had since increased this potential. There was proof that Iraq was pursuing a program to enrich uranium for use in nuclear weapons, and it was also developing more advanced versions of its Scud missiles.

Following the Gulf War in 1991, the UN and International Atomic Energy Agency (IAEA) inspection teams uncovered significant evidence that indicated Iraq had greater ambitions and was far more advanced than had been previously assessed in the development of WMD. The verification work was a sophisticated cat-and-mouse game, the international teams trying to peel the "infinite onion," as some would put it, with the Iraqi concealment teams making intensive efforts to hinder the work of the inspection teams. Yet had Saddam Hussein convincingly come clean about the WMD situation in his country at any stage from 1991 and until the onset of the 2003 war, there can be no doubt that his regime would not have suffered the defeat it eventually did.

This essay will review the status of WMD in Iraq prior to the 1991 war, and as uncovered by the international inspection teams in the years following and up to the 2003 war. It will assess the WMD-related activities of the Iraqi regime in preparation for the recent war and the WMD situation in the war's aftermath, based on the findings of the coalition forces to date. The review is based primarily on published UN and IAEA reports, and on published reviews of this documentation.

The Iraqi Development Program

The Quest for Nuclear Weapons

According to the available evidence, until 1981 Iraq pursued the development of nuclear weapons by the production of plutonium in the Osiraq research reactor, purchased from and erected by France. Israel's destruction of this reactor in June 1981 put an end, at least for the time being, to the project. In addition to the reactor, Iraq purchased (mainly from Italy) and constructed a set of laboratories, including hot-cell facilities for the separation of plutonium from irradiated targets, and auxiliary facilities.

With the plutonium route to the acquisition of a nuclear weapons capability both difficult and easily detectable, Iraq decided that rather than reconstitute its plutonium production project it would pursue the uranium enrichment route, which is less obvious to the outside observer. This drive assumed several directions, the most prominent being the electromagnetic isotope separation (EMIS) and the gas centrifuge enrichment technologies. In addition, Iraq also conducted research into other enrichment technologies such as the gas-barrier, laser, and chemical enrichment methods. In doing so Iraq depended both on published and declassified material, and on clandestinely acquired expertise and equipment, most notoriously from German experts. The extensive amount of materiel needed for these elaborate techniques was acquired from many sources, and some construction work on the huge and sometimes duplicate facilities was done by foreign companies.

Another source for the fissile material needed for the core of the nuclear explosive device was the high-enriched uranium (HEU) contained in the nuclear fuel rods that were to be inserted into the Osiraq reactor core and which were still in Iraq's possession in 1990, although they were of no further use for their original purpose once the reactor was destroyed. Following the August 1990 invasion of Kuwait, Iraq embarked on a "crash program" to extract the HEU from the unused fuel rods and combine it with additional Russian-originated HEU to be utilized in a single explosive device, but the project did not materialize before the 1991 war. Moreover, on top of the large amounts of natural uranium – the raw material needed for the enrichment process – purchased from external sources, Iraq had an indigenous uranium production project, which tapped the large phosphate mines in the northwest of the country.

Thus, professional assessments are quite convincing that had the 1991 war not taken place, Iraq would have had at its disposal a first nuclear weapon in or around 1993.

Uncovering the extent of the Iraqi nuclear weapons development program was no easy task for the IAEA Action Team, set up in 1991 for this purpose. At the beginning, Iraq admitted nothing that was not known before the war. Three factors combined to demonstrate Iraq's capabilities and the extent of its ambitious program: the discovery of gram quantities of plutonium clandestinely produced and separated; the discovery of the EMIS machinery, which came as a huge surprise; and the discovery of the "smoking gun" document, which revealed the plans for the construction of a nuclear weapon itself. In spite of these discoveries, Iraq persisted in concealing many facets of its nuclear program that came to light only in 1995, following the defection of a senior Iraqi official. Even today, it cannot be said with certainty that all has been uncovered.

The Vast Quantities of Chemical Weapons

If the interest in the nuclear program lay in Iraq's many undisclosed activities, focus on the chemical program was mainly on quantities and not on activities, since while the activities were known even if not disclosed, it was the unaccounted-for quantities of agents and precursors (substances from which the chemical warfare agents are produced) that remained a mystery. Iraq's chemical weapons program began in the 1970s and managed to develop and produce both a large variety and vast quantities of chemical warfare agents, some of which were used in the Iran–Iraq war and against the Iraqi people themselves.

Iraq produced many of the publicly known chemical warfare agents: tear, mustard (blistering), and a variety of nerve gases. It also managed to weaponize them, that is, to include them in munitions in a variety of deployable warheads. Furthermore, in April 1990 Saddam Hussein announced that Iraq had mastered the technology of producing a binary chemical weapon, that is, the technology of mixing two basic precursors into the nerve gas just prior to or during the launch of chemical weapons. This gives these weapons a long shelf-life, endowing them with a large advantage over the production of the final product, which deteriorates more quickly with time.

Iraq weaponized its chemical warfare agents in a variety of warheads – from artillery shells to rockets to missile nosecones – and declared it had over 120,000 chemical warheads of all varieties at the onset of the 1991 Gulf War. It claimed that about a third of these were destroyed by the war, and then averred that it had unilaterally destroyed another quarter of the amount (in direct contravention of UN resolutions that were accepted by Iraq), so that in the end nearly half of the warheads produced remained unaccounted for. In addition, according to the UN Monitoring, Verification and Inspection Commission (UNMOVIC) report to the Security Council, about a thousand tons of chemical warfare agents were still unaccounted for at the outset of the 2003 war. According to another report, approximately the same amount of precursor material was likewise at large.

The Large Variety of Biological Warfare Agents

Iraq's biological weapons program came to light only in 1995, following the defection of Iraq's Lt.-Gen. Hussein Kamel. Even then, Iraq acknowledged the existence of only certain parts of the program, and its full extent is still not clear. Iraq's biological warfare development began already by 1973. According to a UN inspection team report to the Security Council, Iraq managed to produce anthrax, botulinum toxin (the most poisonous substance known), gas gangrene, ricin (a toxin produced from plants), wheat smut, and other agents. Iraq was also known to be working on cholera, mycotoxins (a moderately poisonous substance), shigellosis (a bacteria that produces diarrhea), and several viruses. Some of the biological agents such as anthrax were acquired legally under the pretext of research, while Iraq was still a "member in good standing" of the international community. In 1995 Iraq admitted that it had produced 19,000 liters of botulinum toxin and 8500 liters of anthrax, and had experimented with gases that produced gangrene. While it claimed to have unilaterally destroyed these substances, according to a 2003 report presented to the Security Council, "There are strong indications that Iraq produced more anthrax than it declared and that at least some of this was retained over the declared destruction date. It might still exist."[1] There are additional suspicions, based on circumstantial evidence, that Iraq was working on smallpox as well.

Iraq acknowledged that it had tested some forms of biological agents. Even more disturbing was its admission that it had weaponized biological agents between December 1990 and January 1991, just prior to the Gulf War. The types of munitions under development for use with biological weapons included al-Hussein missile warheads, aerial bombs, aircraft drop tanks, pilotless aircraft, helicopter-borne spraying systems, rockets, and fragmentation weapons. Surprisingly, Iraq later admitted that it continued with its biological weapons development until July 1991, months after it had acceded to the Security Council resolutions demanding that all production of WMD be stopped and all programs be dismantled. There are many who believe, in the absence of evidence to the contrary, that Iraq's biological weapons development program was never fully dismantled.

It is very difficult to detect biological weapons development in the research stages, since it is not much different from other, legitimate, biological research activities. Unlike chemical weapons, volume is not a function of biological weaponry, and a small volume or weight of biological warfare agents is sufficient to cause major damage to a large population. Therefore, it will always be possible that even if and when a large cache of these agents is uncovered, some residual quantities will remain somewhere, posing a potential danger should they become available to subversive elements in and outside Iraq.

Missiles

Although missiles are not weapons of mass destruction in the strict sense of the term, they were included in the disarmament requirements of Iraq, and included in the mandate of the UN Special Commission on Iraq (UNSCOM) and its successor, UNMOVIC. Iraq had acquired a significant capability in missiles with a range of up to 650 kilometers, and deployed the missiles heavily in the Iran–Iraq war and against Saudi Arabia and Israel in the Gulf War. Following extensive research, UNSCOM claimed that only two Scud-B missiles with a range of 300 kilometers remained unaccounted for. Some reports have suggested that of the al-Hussein missiles with the range of 650 kilometers, seven remained unaccounted for. However, these figures are not definitive.

Iraqi Preparations for Renewed Inspections and the 2003 War

Since at this stage little is known of the actual residual quantities and the fate of WMD production facilities in Iraq, some assumptions should be made regarding Iraq's preparations for the renewed inspections, which began in late 2002. Two divergent scenarios will be proposed. One (the "concealment" scenario) is that Iraq did, in fact, retain significant quantities of WMD materials and possibly WMD production capability, and the other (the "destruction" scenario) is that Iraq destroyed all hardware – materials, weapons and production facilities – before the start of the renewed inspections, leaving no significant residual capabilities.

The Concealment Scenario

In this scenario Saddam Hussein assessed that the renewed inspections could again be stymied by clever concealment, using the old tactics of procrastination and the submission of only partial information. While not believing that official Iraqi statements were entirely correct, the inspectors would not be able to disprove them conclusively. From studying the mood at the Security Council, Saddam probably hoped that time would be on his side, and the world would soon tire of the American accusations and lift all sanctions, which was his ultimate aim.

Preparations for the renewed inspections would likely have assumed the following dimensions:

- Only essential capabilities and material quantities were kept and stored; the rest were unilaterally destroyed.
- No sites previously known or used for WMD production or storage were chosen for storage.
- The sites chosen for storage were not inside known military installations or government sites.
- Very few senior officials were part of this activity. Thus, the main body of senior officials could safely disavow any knowledge of WMD in Iraq.
- Little or no documentation existed concerning these sites and the quantities stored therein.

On top of this were rumors of storage of WMD agents in Syria, which lent credence to the fact that no WMD storage sites were discovered in Iraq and helped dissuade those looking for material from intensive searches in Iraq.

The Destruction Scenario

In this scenario Saddam assessed that this time the game was up: the possibility of renewed inspections quashed any hope of reviving his ambitious WMD programs. He then decided that the best route would be the destruction of all materials and facilities, keeping only the considerable know-how, blueprints, and data he would need to resurrect the programs, if and when renewed opportunity came. However, he would retain the behavior he exhibited throughout the years, thereby "proving" to the world that he had been truthful all along. This would accelerate his country's return to a normal status among the nations of the world.

The Short and Unhappy Period of Inspections

The renewed UNMOVIC and IAEA inspections lasted less than four months, and did not uncover anything significant. By their own admission, the inspectors needed much more time for reaching any conclusion as to the status of WMD and missile development in Iraq. The reports of these teams to the Security Council did show that Iraq did not fully cooperate with the inspectors, in contravention of the Council's resolutions, but the reports ran short of an outright condemnation.

The inspectors did what the Iraqis expected them to: they behaved in a non-confrontational way. That is, they behaved as inspectors and not as detectives, the role in fact assigned to them. They went to the sites they were expected to visit. They did not press with any intensity for free access to scientists. They did not search thoroughly for documents, bank records, and personnel files unless outside tips and information came to them. In short, they did not employ all prerogatives accorded to them by the various Security Council resolutions. Moreover, after the first report, subsequent reports to the Security Council were masterworks of ambiguity, which allowed everyone to read into them whatever they wanted. While the reports did not exonerate Iraq, neither would they give anyone a substantial pretext for condemning Iraq. Ironically, or perhaps predictably, this should not have surprised anyone familiar with the ways of UN bodies not actively involved in peacekeeping missions.

Either consciously planned this way or not, the inspectors were necessarily to emerge from the inspections in a positive light, whatever the outcome. If a "smoking gun" had been found, i.e., if the Iraqi concealment plans had failed, the inspectors would have scored a victory. If nothing were found following prolonged and intensive searches, this too would have been to their credit. The one measure they strongly resisted was to confront Iraq without strong evidence in hand and reach early conclusions, as the inspectors did not wish to be the direct cause of a war. In this they succeeded.

However, as such, they also failed. Had they carried out intensive, confrontational inspections using all prerogatives, no matter what the outcome would have been, they would have been appreciated as having done their job. Had they done so, could the war have been averted?

Iraq's Preparations for the 2003 War

In either scenario, Iraq did not have to make additional significant preparations for the oncoming war. Most of the previous preparations sufficed to take care of any eventuality. Saddam Hussein probably understood that the coalition forces would occupy at least parts of Iraq, including any obvious WMD production and storage facilities. It can also be concluded that he never intended to use WMD against the invading forces, since the retaliatory actions would probably have been so severe as to preclude any possibility of his remaining in or returning to power.

If the concealment scenario is correct, the only extra task would have been to ensure that none of his storage sites would be located within clearly military targets. This would be additional insurance against an inadvertent hit. The destruction scenario, of course, needed no further preparation.

It is still unknown which scenario was chosen. Given Iraq's past history and patterns of behavior, the concealment scenario would probably be the best guess. Doing away with all WMD capability and then not presenting convincing evidence and testimony to this effect would have been irrational, though not completely out of character.

The US Search for WMD in Iraq

Not much is known about the US search for WMD in Iraq following the 2003 war. However, from the little that is known the US probably repeated some of the mistakes made by the UN inspectors.

The key to any search would be people and documentation, either to locate storage sites or to confirm destruction. Site searches alone, unless based on quality information, would not yield much no matter which scenario Saddam had chosen. The people wanted for questioning were not only the top-level officials who could provide clues and information on policy decisions, but the medium level scientists and technicians who were involved. In many respects, their information would be the most useful to those conducting the search. By some reports, the Iraqis were still afraid of disclosing the secrets for fear they could be held responsible for war crimes; alternatively, they feared retaliatory action by Saddam or his supporters who were still in hiding. Yet these were the very individuals most important to the US, especially the mid-level professionals, and therefore it was incumbent on the US to promise them protection.

Documentary evidence would have been more difficult to find, since rampant looting took place and many documents were either destroyed or removed. Still, much probably remained in private hands, and could be located if the owners were found and persuaded to cooperate.

As reported in the media, the first target of US activities in searching for WMD in Iraq were the sites (1,000 in number) known or thought to have housed WMD development and storage. When searching these sites, nothing could be taken at face value. The 1991 story of how an Iraqi showed inspectors at a nuclear site that they had missed a double floor, below the one they were standing on, carries with it a strong lesson. One should not forget that Saddam was a master of concealment and deceit, and used these skills to the fullest extent.

The approach of assigning people and documentation top priority in the search for WMD in Iraq was proven to be correct, when US officials found significant documentation alongside gas centrifuge components in a nuclear scientist's garden. These were buried there under the orders of Uday Hussein. The scientist who provided the information was taken with his family out of Iraq, providing them with a safe haven. It is to be hoped that this approach will lead in the future to the complete disclosure of the history of WMD in Iraq.

Residual Capabilities and Lessons for the Future

Barring a breakthrough, it will likely be a long time before the true picture of WMD in Iraq is fully uncovered.

Most dangerous is the possibility that some residual quantities of biological and chemical agents remained in the hands of Saddam's followers or in the hands of others, including terrorist supporters. In the case of biological weapons this could present a substantial threat that will be hard to dismiss.

There should be no doubt that Iraq's infrastructure for the production of nuclear materials and the production of a large quantity of chemical warfare agents is all but gone and cannot be resurrected for a long time. The production of small quantities of chemical and biological agents will always be possible, as is the case for all semi-industrialized and industrialized countries. The know-how is there. The Iraqis still have a large R&D force, and although the scientific leadership may have suffered, the accumulated knowledge will be available for a long time.

The real issue then is not the destruction of whatever remains but convincing the Iraqi people and Iraq's future regime that nothing is to be gained by the reconstitution of its WMD programs. This will largely be dependent on its national threat perception, which is essentially no different from the situation regarding any country. In Iraq's case, the main external cause for worry is the formidable neighbor in the east. No other state but Iran should give the new Iraqi regime a cause for worry. This potential threat could be neutralized by the establishment of good neighborly relations, based on evolving confidence-building measures gradually leading to a peace treaty beneficial to both parties.

There are significant lessons to be learned from the way the inspections were conducted, from 1991 until 1998, for the short period before the 2003 war, and by the US forces at its conclusion. These lessons concern not only the inspectors in their enforcement role in Iraq, but the role of inspectors in the verification of multilateral non-proliferation treaties. Some of the lapses in the methodologies employed in Iraq were noted above. However, NPT verification had failed in Iraq prior to the 1991 Gulf War. The IAEA's "93+2 Program," which resulted in the "Additional Protocol," attempted to remedy the failings of the "Full Scope" verification scheme yet remains to be tested in an actual case where proliferation is suspected. Primarily, however, it is the will of the international organizations that has to be tested, since it also seems to have failed notoriously in Iran.

Although it is a matter of prestige to the US, it is almost irrelevant to the disarmament of Iraq whether any evidence comes to light concerning Iraq's WMD capabilities just prior to the 2003 war. It certainly possessed these capabilities in the past, then lost most of them, and probably developed them anew in the period after the inspections came to a halt in 1998. When the renewed inspections were about to begin in late 2002, Iraq decided on the scenario it would employ, and took precautionary measures accordingly. In either scenario, not much remained of its previous capabilities. Thus, Iraq was effectively disarmed, and no longer constitutes a strategic threat.

However, this does not mean that the task is finished. What remains of WMD in Iraq now and the willingness to use it is still of vital importance. Work should not cease on locating the residual capabilities, on the one hand, since at the present time it cannot be ruled out that the concealment scenario was used. On the other hand, the new regime in Iraq must not be given any reason for the reconstitution of a WMD program. This is the great task and challenge for the future.

Note

1   Hans Blix, "UN Security Council Update On Inspection by the Executive Chairman of the United Nations Monitoring and Verification Commission (UNMOVIC)," January 27, 2003.

The Post-War Strategic Balance in the Middle East

12

Shlomo Brom

In the course of the 2003 war the Iraqi army disintegrated to the point of oblivion, and the war ended with the country under the control of American and British military forces. In the months since the end of the war, the new rulers have been at the critical stage of transforming their military triumph into the realization of political objectives, which in contrast to the lightning victory will be a long and hazardous process. To secure these objectives the coalition forces will first have to set up a stable regime in Iraq, a formidable challenge in a country ethnically divided and steeped in a violent, autocratic political culture. Second, they will have to restructure the regime into an open, pro-Western one that will ensure that Iraq does not revert into a rogue state that threatens its neighbors. The degree and difficulty of the challenge will depend on how ambitious are the goals set by the United States. If the main goal is the sweeping transformation of Iraq into a democracy, then enormous obstacles can be expected. If the objective is more modest, namely, to establish an "enlightened" open regime yet not necessarily democratic by Western standards, then it may be attained much more smoothly. The full strategic implication of the Iraqi campaign depends to a great extent on America's realization of these goals.

Nevertheless, the war's impact on the strategic balance in the Middle East in the near future may already be detected. The implications relate to two "realities": the actual reality, that is, the "real" power relations among the main Middle East players, and the perceived reality of power relations. The first level must be analyzed, as it permits us to evaluate the expected results of a possible military clash between the players. An analysis of the second level is equally important, however, because the decisions made by regimes and leaders are not based on the true power relations but on the decision-makers' perceptions of them.

Implications for the Actual Balance of Power

The dissolution of Iraq's armed forces has an influence on the balance of forces in two critical spheres: the Gulf States and the Arab–Israeli conflict. In the Gulf, the balance between Iraq and Iran has been rendered null and void, and Iran is left without any formidable rivals in the region. It faces only the military forces of the Arab Gulf States: Saudi Arabia and the sheikdoms, all of which have acquired advanced air and naval forces, but whose ground forces are extremely limited in comparison with Iran's, and who suffer from a deep lack of confidence in their ability to stand up to Iran alone, without foreign assistance. United States forces will have to remain in the Gulf for the coming years, and will serve, together with America's allies – mainly Britain – as a counterweight to Iran.

In the long run, if the United States succeeds in establishing a stable regime in Iraq, it might permit the buildup of an Iraqi military force capable of redressing the balance with Iran. Iraq's military rehabilitation will probably be a slow and lengthy process because it requires the use of part of the country's oil income. That will be difficult, as most of the oil-derived financial resources will be needed to repair the massive damage inflicted on the Iraq infrastructure in two decades that included the Iran–Iraq War, the 1991 Gulf War, international sanctions, and the 2003 Iraq War. In addition, the US and the UN will undoubtedly continue to place limitations on various areas of Iraq's military reconstruction for a long time. Iraq will also have a different strategic role in the Gulf since it will be part of the American circle of influence, participating in an alliance with the United States and other Arab states in the Gulf facing Iran. This prognosis assumes Iraq will require a military buildup because Iran remains an ayatollah-based regime threatening its neighbors.

The war has eliminated a key player among states confronting Israel. While it is doubtful that given the present climate in the Middle East Israel will attain a formal peace treaty with the new regime in Baghdad in the near future, nevertheless, US influence will neutralize Iraq from playing an active role in the struggle against Israel. Israel may even be able to develop healthy, informal relations with the new regime. In any event, many years will be required for Iraq to rebuild a substantial conventional military capability that can threaten Israel again. It can also be assumed that a vigilant monitoring system will be installed to prevent Iraq from developing strategic weapon systems such as ballistic missiles and Weapons of Mass Destruction (WMD). This too will contribute to eradicating the Iraqi threat for many years.

The question arises whether these conditions significantly alter the balance of forces between Israel and its potential enemies, and here a distinction should be made between two time scales. In the short run the change is not great. Already after the 1991 Gulf War, Iraq's capacity to contribute to the Arab struggle against Israel was seriously reduced. Although it still retained a large military force, its ability to wield power over long distances was irreparably damaged. Its missile system and WMD project were almost completely destroyed (which may explain why the United States has been finding it so difficult to uncover evidence of these capabilities). The Iraqi air force was left with only a fraction of its overall capacity to attack long-range targets, including Israel. Iraq still possessed large ground forces but their ability to travel great distances under an effective protective umbrella in order to confront Israel was crippled. On top of that Iraq was restricted by ongoing US surveillance.

For the long term Iraq continued to be a major threat to Israel because it retained its capability to develop and produce ballistic missiles and WMD, and enjoyed the basic advantages of immense oil reserves and a relatively educated population. These two factors could have contributed to a full-scale renewal of the country's military might in the conventional and non-conventional spheres if and when the international sanctions were removed. Prior to the 2003 Iraq War, two assumptions could be made regarding Iraq: one, sooner or later the sanctions would have been cancelled, and indeed, there was already political progress in this direction in the international arena; two, as long as Saddam Hussein's regime remained in power it would persist in seeking the requisite military capability for regional hegemony and would then proceed to intimidate its enemies. These two factors combined would pose a considerable threat to Israel. One major result of the war, therefore, has been the removal of this potential threat.

Implications for the Perceived Balance of Power

The more profound impact of the 2003 war has been on the perceptual level, that is, on the Middle East players' perceptions of the Arab–Israeli balance of forces. It has strengthened the view that the Israeli military enjoys a profound advantage over its neighbors.

During the three-week war, a coalition of relatively few American and British forces, consisting of approximately 750 fighter planes and bombers, three armored-mechanized divisions, and one airborne division defeated a huge Middle East army numbering twenty-three ground divisions of various types and 280 warplanes, overcoming a dense surface-to-air missile system, and gaining control of a country of almost half a million square kilometers. All of this was accomplished at a very low casualty rate – fewer than 200 killed. It was the dazzling victory of a compact, "smart" army over the large formations of a traditionally conceived army.

Of course it may be claimed that these were unique circumstances: Iraq lost the 1991 Gulf War and its military forces were reduced to half their original strength, and in the twelve-year interim between the two wars the regime came under UN sanctions that blocked it from restoring its military strength. However, faced with these obstacles Iraq managed to set up a small-scale smuggling operation for weaponry replacements and the procurement of new arms such as anti-tank missiles (although not main weapon systems such as planes, tanks, artillery, and so on). This limited refurbishment enabled it to preserve the serviceability of its military forces, at least in some measure. During the war the Iraqis did not encounter particular difficulties in transferring armored and mechanized divisions positioned north of Baghdad to south of the capital, an indication of the relatively high maintenance level of the armored vehicles' automotive systems. The Iraqi ground forces remained the largest military force in the Middle East, excluding Turkey, and its force was about equal to the current armies of Iran and Syria. It resembled many other Middle East armies that are also hard pressed to maintain and build up their military forces because of financial limitations or international sanctions. Leading examples of this are Syria (financial difficulties and obstacles barring weapons procurement from the West), Jordan (financial difficulties), Iran (financial difficulties and sanctions), and Libya (sanctions).

The coalition's victory in Iraq can be clearly attributed to the American and British armies' qualitative advantages, in which two factors played a key role. The first is the Western forces' air and naval superiority over an Arab military force built mainly on outdated East bloc weapon systems and military doctrine, such as dependence on land-based air and naval defense systems. The second and more decisive factor is the Revolution in Military Affairs (RMA) that has transformed the American army. Based on state-of-the-art technology, RMA enables the United States Armed Forces, especially its air force, to render any battlefield transparent in daytime, nighttime, and all kinds of weather, to locate the important targets, hit them with precision guided munitions (PGM) at distances that offer protection to the attacker, and receive Battle Damage Assessment (BDA) in real time. RMA allows small, highly mobile ground units to overwhelm large land enemy armies comprised of traditional tank, armored personnel carrier (APC), and artillery formations that enter the battle after having been exhausted and severely damaged by PGM.

There are good indications that some "traditional" armies, which are built on massive battle formations and traditional fighting doctrines, reacted with great surprise and anxiety to the results of the war in Iraq. For example, Russia's civilian and military leadership expressed shock and concern at the war's outcome. According to various reports, on the eve of hostilities Russian security experts estimated that the United States would become bogged down in a lengthy war and suffer heavy casualties as Russia did in Chechnya. The war's aftermath made the Russians aware for the first time of the enormous gap separating the American and Russian armies – especially as reflected in the results of combat in Chechnya versus those in Iraq.

Although the Arab leaders and security establishments have not reacted to these aspects of the war publicly, indications suggest that they experienced a similar shock. The Arabs' problem is twofold. The war's outcome reflected their weakness – if not impotence – *vis-à-vis* the hegemonic superpower, the United States, and generated their accompanying sense of humiliation at the sudden collapse of a mighty Arab army. In addition, it dramatized their deficiencies with respect to Israel. Since Israel is counted among the few countries that have successfully adopted RMA concepts and practices, the Arab world would likely view the campaign in Iraq as an indication of what could happen in the event of a war between Israel and Syria. The Syrian army is smaller than the Iraqi army was on the eve of the 2003 war. Although Syria has more tanks and planes than Iraq had, its equipment is outdated and its operational doctrine outmoded, as were the Iraqi army's. Israel enjoys undisputed air superiority against Syria, and has RMA capabilities similar to the American army's.

In the event of a war between Israel and its neighboring countries, Israel would have an even greater advantage than the US had over Iraq since it would be operating at shorter ranges than the US air force and could activate its airpower with greater intensity. The Arab problem grows even more acute because of the Middle East states' sense of despair over an improvement in the foreseeable future. The Arab world's military establishments realize that the technological gap will not be bridged anytime soon and that astronomic sums will be required to introduce basic modifications in the Arab armies. Much of the Arab world is experiencing an economic crisis and is presently incapable of investing the necessary sums for a military transformation; furthermore, it is doubtful whether the United States would assist the Arab countries in developing RMA capabilities since it wishes to preserve its own decided superiority. In effect it seems that even sufficient funding and accessibility to state-of-the-art technologies would still be insufficient to advance the Arab armies to a level that equals the IDF. The real transformation demands an infrastructure of technically-trained, qualified manpower and a technologically-based culture – a sine qua non that probably does not exist in the Arab states.

Likely Arab Inferences

It appears, then, that the 2003 Iraq War hammered the last nail into the Arabs' coffin of illusions that their regular armies could be upgraded in the foreseeable future to counterbalance Israel's military capability. Under these circumstances the Arab states and Iran will probably tend to develop asymmetric responses to the conventional superiority of Israel and America. There is indeed nothing new in this, and the last decade has been characterized by this trend, along with the Arab states' increasing awareness of their weakness *vis-à-vis* Israel and even more so *vis-à-vis* the United States. At the current strategic level, two basic asymmetric responses challenge conventional superiority. One is the development of strategic capabilities such as long-range surface-to-surface missiles (SSM) and WMD; the second is the implementation of methods of Low-Intensity Conflict (LIC), that is, guerilla warfare and terrorism.

The results of the war in Iraq will strengthen the motivation in the Arab states and Iran to continue seeking SSM and WMD, but will also increase their awareness that a punitive American reaction can be expected if they pursue this course. Events in Iraq and Washington's attitude to North Korea when it reneged on its obligation as a party to the Treaty on the Non-Proliferation of Nuclear Weapons (NPT) and openly acknowledged its nuclear project for military purposes will probably confirm the view in Middle East authoritarian regimes that nuclear weapons capability along with an effective delivery system are the only means of protecting them and deterring the United States and Israel from wielding their military superiority as an existential threat. This perception was especially reinforced when the United States demonstrated it was not deterred from launching a war even when it was convinced that Iraq possessed chemical and biological weapons and was poised to use them. Moreover, Israel and the United States have developed effective coun-termeasures to the threat of ballistic missiles and chemical and biological weapons, and are in the advanced stage of producing even better defense systems. Only nuclear weapons have no countermeasures.

The obstacle that bars the Middle East states from pursuing this course quickly and productively is the difficulty in bridging the time gap between their present limited deterrent options and their possible future strategic capabilities. According to the US point of view manifested in the Bush administration's new strategic doctrine, the presence of a nuclear project for military purposes in a rogue state suspected of supporting terror organizations is reason enough to initiate a preemptive strike against it. This means that projects intended to deter the United States from an attack could end up inviting an American military operation as long as the rogue state possesses no nuclear weapons. The manner in which Middle East states deal with this dilemma depends on the regimes' propensity to caution versus risk, and to a large degree on the US response to the "day after" after the war in Iraq. If Washington will use its victory as a springboard for exerting unrelenting pressure on states involved in these projects, especially Iran, and will not be loath to using military threats, the greater the likelihood that the decisive factor in the rogue state's decision-making will be fear of an American military response. But if the Americans squander the credibility they gained in the war in Iraq, and the United States is perceived as lacking the stomach for further military engagements, then these regimes will probably have a stronger motivation to accelerate their WMD and SSM projects. In any case, it seems unlikely that Iran, Syria, Libya, or even Egypt, would forgo what surely appears to them the most effective deterrent against Israel, and perhaps the United States as well. More probable is that they will proceed with their projects albeit more gingerly, lest they be detected too early on.

While the strategic asymmetric response described above is designed to deter a political player from exercising its military superiority, the second asymmetric response, LIC, is intended to produce the necessary strategic balance by changing the rules of the game in the tactical and operational arenas. It is assumed that guerilla warfare and terrorism blur a regular army's qualitative advantages, especially its technological superiority, when it is up against highly motivated irregular forces prepared to make supreme sacrifices. Events such as Israel's unilat-eral withdrawal from South Lebanon and Israel's dilemma in struggling against Palestinian irregulars in the al-Aqsa Intifada have strengthened the view that LIC is an effective asymmetric response to Israeli and even American superiority. Yet careful observation of the war in Iraq and Israel's handling of Palestinian violence shows that the efficacy of this asymmetric response against irregular forces is by no means absolute. In both cases the regular army succeeded in dealing with irreg-ular forces while fully utilizing its technological and often RMA-based superiority.

If the United States learned the lessons of the first war in Iraq, then so did the Iraqis who, in the following years, tried to develop asymmetric responses to meet the American challenges. For example, surface-to-air missile units that were constantly under US attack in this period, within the framework of Operations Northern Watch and Southern Watch (for maintaining no-fly zones), developed camouflage and concealment measures and quick redeployment maneuvers in order to lessen damage to them. During the long months preceding the recent hostilities, when it became clear that war was almost inevitable, the Iraqis adopted the asymmetric operational concept of luring American troops into urban areas where irregular forces – Saddam fedayeen – would be waiting to ambush them. The Iraqi High Command assumed that it could embroil the US army in a drawn out war and inflict heavy casualties. According to this concept, when irregulars are deployed in a built-up area, the regular army's technological superiority loses its value. What actually happened was that the United States overcame the Iraqis' asymmetric response relatively easily by making full use of its technological advantages. Two outstanding RMA capabilities in particular contributed to this success: the ability to obtain precise information on the enemy's location, even in urban areas, via a range of sensors; and the ability to make pinpoint strikes against specific targets without causing excessive collateral damage. In comparison to previous wars, Iraqi irregulars were dealt a severe blow, at a low cost to civilian bystanders.

A similar picture comes into focus in the IDF's two and a half year struggle against Palestinian violence. The IDF has waged an effective campaign against the Palestinians by employing a wide variety of sensors and PGM. Although Israel has incurred heavy losses from this type of fighting relative to the American casualty rate in Iraq, the vast majority of Israel's losses have been civilians caught up in the thorny reality that entangles the Israeli and Palestinian populations. Israel's military experience in the territories shows that even when faced with the harrowing challenge of suicide bombers, the IDF has been able to defend itself and confront the difficulty successfully. On the other hand, the job of protecting the country's entire civilian population from suicide attacks has proven far more demanding.

There are those who urge caution before drawing conclusions about the war in Iraq, arguing that the Iraqis fought without motivation. Two counter-arguments may be presented. First, the lack of motivation cannot be separated from the capability gap between the two sides. A major cause of the Iraqi army's low motivation seems to have been the premonition of the High Command and the troops that the war was over before it began. Second, war commentators and observers stressed the fact that Iraqi irregulars displayed a high degree of motivation, although to no avail. The conclusion is that both the intifada and the war in Iraq should raise doubts in the Arab world whether their LIC asymmetric response against Israeli military superiority is an effective one.

The conclusion is that for the elements in the Arab world that still wish to disrupt the status quo, the two asymmetric solutions are not satisfactory. Although nuclear weapons (and to a large extent chemical and biological ones) have an important weight in the strategic balance, they cannot be employed against an adversary armed with like weapons and are useful therefore only as a deterrent, while LIC effectiveness remains of dubious value in many situations. These doubts increase the perception of strategic imbalance between the Arab world and Israel.

Furthermore, the war in Iraq illustrated the tight strategic bond between

Israel and the United States. The close coordination prior to and during the war, the deployment of American Patriot batteries on Israel soil, and the impressive effort made by the US forces to thwart an Iraqi missile attack against Israel all serve as proof of the degree of intimacy and understanding that exists between the two countries. This is another key factor in the regional perception of Israel's strategic superiority.

The Strategic Implications After the War

The post-war reality yields a number of strategic implications, both political and military. First, from the military point of view it is now clear that the window of opportunity for political initiatives in the Arab–Israeli sphere will probably remain open in the coming years. Israel's military superiority enables it to risk taking security initiatives because of its capability of dealing with the ensuing security implications. This is particularly true regarding all aspects of the Israeli–Syrian track where the balance of forces between the two regular armies has a great influence on the ability to work out credible, bilateral security arrangements conducive to a signed peace treaty. At the same time, the Arab side, especially the ruling elites, are far more aware that their inability to counter Israel's power means that their national goals *vis-à-vis* Israel can be realized only through a political process and negotiations.

The second implication is the irrefutable disappearance of the "eastern front." Already after the 1991 Gulf War and the signing of the Israeli–Jordanian peace treaty in 1994, "the threat from the eastern front," which had long dominated Israeli political thinking, was actually an anachronism, even though the disappearance of the threat was still not widely accepted in Israel. Today it is clear that the scenario of an eastern military front united against Israel is not realistic. We may even posit that the removal of Iraq's threat to Jordan will strengthen Israeli–Jordanian ties, stabilize the peace on Israel's eastern sector, and perhaps lead towards a future Israeli–Jordanian–Iraqi strategic alignment under American auspices in which Jordan serves as the link between Israel and Iraq. One of the political ramifications of this scenario is that there is no "eastern front threat" to consider when the time comes for Israel and the Palestinians to agree on security arrangements for a permanent settlement. In light of this the Jordan Valley no longer functions as a security asset for the defense of Israel's eastern front.

The third implication is Israel's improved ability for dealing with the Hizbollah threat on the northern border. Syria's acute awareness of its military weakness *vis-à-vis* Israel, and its need to take into account the American position that accuses it of abetting terror, means that more effective pressure will be applied on Syria to halt, or at least cut back, its support for Hizbollah and Hizbollah operations against Israel. This same is basically true regarding Iranian support of the organization. Hizbollah seems to understand the new strategic reality and is acting more cautiously. Nevertheless it will probably find it difficult to cease its operations completely and at some point may decide to test the limits of its freedom in the new strategic reality by initiating relatively low-level provocations to check the reactions of Israel, the international community, and the regional players. In this event, the new strategic situation provides Israel with greater freedom of action to respond emphatically to Syria and Hizbollah and send a clear-cut message to Hizbollah and its supporters.

The fourth implication is Israel's improved political position, thanks mainly to the United States for exerting pressure on Middle East regimes involved in the spread of ballistic missiles and WMD to cease or deescalate these programs. A good example of this is the US attempt to have the International Atomic Energy Agency (IAEA) declare that Iran is violating the agreement it signed regarding the non-proliferation of nuclear weapons. The source of America's action in this case was an Israeli initiative. In the aftermath of the war it has been easier for Israel to convince the US government to act on this particular initiative.

The fifth implication relates to Israel's need to adapt to the change in the Middle East's balance of threats whereby the regular armies' relative strengths have weakened in comparison to strategic and LIC threats. This change should have an impact on decisions regarding the composition of the IDF and the allocation of resources to capabilities. The change in balance should also influence the total size of the investment in security and undoubtedly point to a need for budget cuts, especially in the current reality of economic crisis. The dominant concept in Israel's security establishment has been to be capable of answering all threats simultaneously. Now it seems that a serious threat by large regular Arab armies could occur only after a fundamental transformation of the region's military forces, one that altered their proportional strengths. This could come about only in a long term and readily observable process. In the meantime the IDF would be able significantly to reduce its preparedness and alert levels against such threats, thereby saving precious resources.

In conclusion, this discussion has outlined the implications of the war in Iraq under the present conditions of flux and instability. A high level of uncertainty surrounds developments in Iraq and may also influence the implications just presented, but it seems that the variable will be the intensity of the implications and not their very existence.

13

The Israeli Public and the War

Anat Kurz and Tamar Malz

During the countdown to the attack in Iraq and throughout the war itself, no substantive and prolonged disruptions were evident in the Israeli routine. The public kept to its established patterns, notwithstanding the fears expressed by generals and politicians that during the course of the military campaign and perhaps even before the actual declaration of war the Israeli home front would form a target for Iraqi missiles. This maintenance of routine life in the face of potential threats to Israel invites an attempt to understand how the Israeli public interpreted security threats associated with Iraq in general and with the war in particular as presented by the decision-makers and formulators of public opinion, and the way in which this interpretation influenced general behavior.

The essay opens with a description of the public's behavior both in the weeks preceding the outbreak of the war and during the war itself. Most indications point to the clear determination to maintain the routine. The discussion will then address the strong support for the war within the Israeli public, support that dwelled on the likely benefits of the war to Israel yet was expressed at the expense of a more balanced discussion of the possible negative aspects that might emerge in the long term. Finally, the analysis will consider the difficult task of drawing conclusions regarding the behavior of the Israeli public during the war, the public's general potential for endurance, and the capacity to adjust to life under conditions of a real alert.[1]

National Consensus and Routine

The public responded to the call of the military authorities to prepare for the possible launching of conventional and non-conventional missiles at population centers with the increased (but certainly not panic-stricken) purchase and preparation of means of domestic protection. Otherwise, however, no extreme changes took place in day-to-day behavior. There were some citizens who on the eve of the war searched for places of refuge outside the range of the Iraqi missiles, where they intended to retreat if a missile attack on Israel seemed imminent. However, this phenomenon was not a widespread one. Even after the war commenced the public did not remain at home near sealed rooms or air raid shelters.[2] In the first two days of the war a significant number of students were absent from school, but otherwise schools functioned normally during the entire period of fighting in Iraq.

The maintenance of the routine was also reflected by the failure to carry the gas masks that were intended to provide protection in the event of an attack with chemical weapons. The public had been told clearly that the probability of such an attack was low, but the directive given by the military authorities to adopt this safety precaution should the unlikely scenario materialize was unequivocal.[3] The public largely ignored the instructions of the Home Front Command already during the first days of the war, and this phenomenon became increasingly widespread as time passed. On April 13, 2003, a few days after Baghdad fell to the coalition forces, the defense ministry decided to release the public from the burden of carrying gas masks, an official decision that in essence merely confirmed the existing situation.

The public's persistence in maintaining its routine against the backdrop of the uncertainty and fears that accompanied the campaign in Iraq may be associated with another phenomenon: the national consensus, specifically, the broad support by the Israeli public for the aims of the campaign and the methods adopted by the US-led coalition forces to achieve them.[4] The extensive support for the war also accounted for the absence in Israel of spectacles such as those observed in many capitals throughout the world in the weeks preceding the war's outbreak, the mass demonstrations intended to dissuade governments from directly or indirectly supporting the US military action in Iraq.[5] In Western Europe the mass demonstrations against the war expressed the powerful, extensive opposition of the public to the war.[6] True, the vocal nature of popular demonstrations does not always reflect the extent of public criticism or protest. Alternatively, the absence of protest does not necessarily indicate full agreement by the public with the policy of its government. However, the routine behavior of the Israeli public during the war was consistent with the limited protest against the war, and indeed reflected the widespread support by the Israeli public.

It is possible to discern the national consensus in support of the war not only from the results of opinion polls and the lack of organized mass protests, but also from the limited public debate on the issue – limited not in the sense of the volume of debate, but rather in the limited range of subjects addressed. Over the course of several weeks the electronic and written media in Israel, as in other countries, devoted most of their time to the events taking place in the political and military arenas surrounding the war in Iraq. The extensive preoccupation with all aspects of the war inevitably detracted from the attention paid to other current issues. However, the Israeli media's fixation with the war was of a clear and uniform nature. The vast majority of the references to the war in Iraq centered on the question of "how," i.e., factual descriptions of developments and moves. Less attention was devoted to the question of "why," i.e., was the planned war the optimal way to create the kind of shockwaves in the Middle East that were supposed to improve Israel's strategic surroundings.

Even during the rather limited debate regarding the question of "why," it was possible to discern an emphasis on the advantages that were supposed to emerge from the war in Iraq. This focus in the media reflected the estimation, shared by military and civilian authorities, that in addition to the low level of risk to Israel posed by the war, including a development that might lead to Israel's direct involvement, one of the major results of the war would be the elimination of a formidable element on the eastern front that Israel would likely confront in the event of comprehensive regional escalation. In fact, maintaining the existing situation, rather than undertaking a war that would oust Saddam Hussein's regime and dismantle Iraq's military capabilities in general and its non-conventional ones in particular, was deemed more dangerous to Israel than the complications that might arise from the war.[7]

Also debated in addition to the threat of missile attacks against Israel were the challenges posed by the war to the Israeli government. Such challenges included the possible escalation of terrorism against Western and pro-Western targets in general and Israeli ones in particular, in response to an attack against Iraq; and shockwaves to the regimes in the Middle East as a result of popular protest against their powerlessness to prevent the attack against Iraq, which would also strengthen the voices of those opposing a negotiated settlement with the Palestinians. Even the American administration's intention – in parallel with efforts towards stabilization in Iraq – to advance the peace process between Israel and the Palestinians did not necessarily portend an easy political future for Israel. The general understanding of this intention was that demands for sweeping concessions on Israel's part would be some of the means adopted by the administration to reduce the tension between it and governments in Western Europe and the Middle East created by the attack on Iraq. Yet Israeli concern regarding this pressure was eased by evidence of the struggle within the American administration against terrorism and countries supporting terrorism. The undermining of the bargaining position of Arab countries, as demonstrated by their political weakness regarding the war in Iraq, would also award the Israeli government a better bargaining position when called upon to meet the challenge.

Thus, emphasis of the public debate was placed on the expectations of an improvement in Israel's strategic surroundings, and the possible risks were marginalized. Only a relatively limited debate took place regarding the range of dangers that might develop during the war and in the long-term aftermath. In general, the references and analyses that conflicted with optimistic evaluations were the exception that proved the rule. Correspondingly, public attention focused on assessments that maintained there was a low probability of such risks,[8] which had a clear and practical result – the continuation of routine life in the country.

It appears that a certain degree of change occurred in one sense only, and that of a narrow, short-term nature. In the first two weeks of the war there was a sharp increase in viewing of TV news programs.[9] Given the other aspects of the public attitude to the war it may be estimated that this increased viewing did not reflect fears for personal safety and for the future of Israel, but was mainly due to interest in the progress of the thrilling military campaign. Indeed, during the course of the battles the Israeli and foreign media supplied the Israeli public (and the rest of the world) with a war film in installments. This action series, which did not lack human drama, reached its expected conclusion with a sweeping military victory of the good guys over the bad ones. The outcome, apart from confirming the optimistic predictions, strengthened the feeling of low-risk interested involvement in the war that characterized the vast majority of the Israeli public. The war in Iraq was presented by the decision-makers, and accepted by Israeli public opinion, as a serious event that on the one hand did not demand a high price from Israel, but on the other hand was likely to yield beneficial changes to the region and reduce the gravity of the challenges facing Israel.

The limited number of issues in the public debate on the war in Iraq may be regarded as an expression of the broad agreement that characterized the public's attitude to the subject. At the same time the possibility cannot be ignored that this attitude was not a unique phenomenon that resulted from the fundamental support for this war, its aims, and the benefits that were likely to accrue from it, but was rather an expression of the more general trend of minimizing the public debate regarding security issues, specifically, in the limited variety of contents and range of viewpoints.

Indeed, no consistent trend has emerged within the Israeli public to challenging the government's security policies. If in fact a protest developed, the process of its institutionalization and integration in the established political system was in most cases a rapid one.[10] The culture that does not encourage the questioning of policy in security matters was reflected in an address by Knesset Member (and then government minister) Michael Eitan at the conference "The Security Zone in Lebanon: A Reconsideration": "I am a minister in the government, but I lack the courage or the full degree of conviction to say that I have a categorical position that is opposed to that of the defense establishment. I am not a professional military man, and I cannot assume such responsibility. But as a citizen I have the right, and perhaps also the obligation, to ask the questions."[11] Yet if a cabinet minister does not regard himself capable of challenging the defense establishment, can the broad public be expected to exercise its right to do so?

Furthermore, it may be estimated that the nature of the public debate itself strengthened the support for the war by pushing aside remarks that were liable to reduce the extent of the national consensus. In other words, the emphasis placed on the advantages of the war, compared to the limited debate about the possible negative consequences of the war, encouraged the public to address selectively the messages given to it by the media. On the other hand, this selective attitude to the threats and the assessments based on softer, less threatening factors discouraged the development of a thoughtful debate of the negative messages liable to erode the concept of the war as a high-yield, low-cost operation.

This notion of high-yield and low-cost challenges the validity of the war as a test case of Israeli society's capacity to adjusting to life in the shadow of a threat.

The War in Iraq as a Test of Endurance

The Israeli public, which supported the war as a way to bring about a change in the Iraqi regime and the removal of Iraq's non-conventional military capabilities, accepted the estimates that attached a low probability to the dangers of the war to Israel. These assessments were confirmed by the events of the war, and consequently the need did not arise to reexamine assumptions and change the routine. The question, therefore, is whether the behavior of the public during the war in Iraq indicates a capability of adjustment to life in the shadow of a real threat. What conclusion, independent of the war in Iraq, may be drawn regarding the expected behavior of the public when confronted with other security threats?

Perhaps, indeed, the continuation of routine life during the war in Iraq is not a good example of rapid adjustment to life under threat, and should not be regarded as a clear demonstration of endurance capabilities, rather as a reflection of the fact that conditions did not materialize to obligate a reappraisal of the situation. In addition, it is not possible to extract from all the possible explanations of the behavior of the public during the war in Iraq any principle regarding long-term confrontation with security threats in general and with terrorist threats in particular.[12] Furthermore, the feeling of security demonstrated by the public regarding the war in Iraq almost certainly reflected an increase in the acceptance threshold of security threats, and the acquisition of a capability of distinguishing between an immediate, real threat, and one perceived to be of low probability.

Before the commencement of the fighting in Iraq, and even before the speed of achieving military victory over Saddam Hussein's forces become apparent, the public in Israel expressed a more serious fear of the terrorist attacks perpetrated by extremist Palestinian organizations.[13] It may be assumed that this approach to the relative danger of the different threats was maintained and even strengthened, parallel to the advance of the coalition forces on Iraqi soil and the realization of the military victory.[14]

In the course of the war no developments occurred that called into question the optimistic evaluations regarding the advantages of the war to Israel, or raised the price of advancing Israel's strategic objectives through the anticipated results of the war. Hence the continued limited public debate over the ratio of war risks to benefits. Yet had any portion of the war threat materialized, for example, if missiles had fallen on Israeli territory, even if they were not armed with non-conventional warheads, a more thoughtful public debate with awareness of the complex significance of the war for Israel would no doubt have emerged. Furthermore, it may be assumed that in such circumstances the routine would have been unrecognizably disrupted. Would it then have been possible to draw the conclusion that the Israeli public lacked the capability of coping with a state of emergency to an extent permitting adjustment to life in the shadow of a threat? Not necessarily. The capability of endurance refers, among other criteria, to the process of adjustment, i.e., to the capability of adjusting behavior to given conditions and in the event of changing conditions, to changing the behavior.

It therefore follows that adjustment is meant to involve the disruption of routine living while under the shadow of a real threat, in order to provide a foundation for renewed organization and the creation of a new routine appropriate to the state of emergency. The capacity for resistance in the presence of a threat should not be judged by the effort required to adjust routine living to the state of emergency, but on the contrary, by the degree to which the public hastens to adjust its patterns of life to the changing requirements of the situation. A necessary, if not sufficient, condition for the active recruitment of the public to confront the threat successfully is assumed to be national consensus regarding the necessity of the unnatural situation and the readiness to pay its price and bear the difficulties it encumbers. Without such agreement it will be difficult for the government and the other national institutions to function appropriately and efficiently in the face of the challenge.

It may be assumed that in the event of a missile attack against the home front and Israel's direct involvement in the Iraq war, the need would have arisen to cope with fears, casualties, and damage to property and infrastructures. In such circumstances the disruption of ordinary life would represent an appropriate response. In fact, the adjustment of ordinary life to a direct and immediate threat took place during the Gulf War in 1991, during the course of which the threat of an attack against the home front materialized.[15] In the face of real threat, therefore, it would be possible to judge the public endurance in light of its capacity to adjust to changing circumstances. An indication of endurance in this case would be the capacity of formal and informal institutions to channel available resources and infrastructures to the new demands, with the aim of overcoming the challenge and preserving the basis for a return to normal life once the danger has passed.

Notes

1   In this context one should recall the term "national strength" that from time to time appears on the Israeli public agenda. In this chapter use of the term "national strength" has been avoided because of the problematic nature both of its definition and of calculating the various criteria used to attempt to evaluate national strength. These criteria are not only quantitative but also, and primarily, qualitative. For this reason they are subject to various kinds of interpretation. Furthermore, it should be noted that the ability of the public to live its life in an organized, controlled manner in the shadow of security uncertainty and, in particular, in the presence of a real threat, does not result only from wishes and intentions. A situation is frequently likely to be produced in which external pressure leads to a collapse of the system. An event of this nature will cause any preliminary estimation regarding national strength to lose its meaning and significance. The term thus connotes more complexity, which is liable to make clear conclusions regarding national strength more difficult. The intensity of "the national strength" may be actually estimated only after the event. We have consequently chosen to engage in a general evaluation of the public's capability of coping with the situation of the war that was waged in Iraq, while focusing on the expressions of behavior that could be observed and monitored.
2   According to a poll conducted by the Dialog Institute before the start of the war and published in Ha'aretz on February 13, 2003, 71% of those questioned had checked and upgraded their gas masks. Ten percent of residents in the center of the country, and 6% of residents overall, declared their intention of moving from their homes to a safer place

in the event of a missile attack. Only about 5% said they would leave the country if Israel were attacked. According to a poll conducted during the fighting and published in *Maariv* on March 28, 2003, 96% of the Jews and 85% of the Arabs questioned reported that they possessed gas masks. Seventy-three percent said they did not take their gas masks everywhere they went; only 27% reported that they did so.

3 For the estimation by the military authorities of the low probability that Israel would suffer a missile attack, see Amir Oren, "Complete Preparation for the Last War," *Ha'aretz*, April 11, 2003.

4 The data regarding the public support for the offensive in Iraq is not uniform, and also indicates the changes in the percentage of support for the offensive over the course of time. According to a poll conducted in early 2002 (in other words, about a year before the beginning of the countdown to the war), 58% of those questioned thought that Israel should encourage the US to attack Iraq. See Asher Arian, *Israeli Public Opinion on National Security 2002*, Memorandum No. 61, Jaffe Center for Strategic Studies, Tel Aviv University, July 2002. According to the Peace Index conducted in February 2003 by Prof. Ephraim Yaar and Dr. Tamar Hermann of the Tami Steinmetz Center for Peace Research, Tel Aviv University, more than 77% of those questioned, while preparations for the war were in full swing, supported the American offensive against Iraq. This agreement crossed different sectors of Israeli society. According to the Peace Index compiled the following month, the level of support for the war did not change. The results of the poll conducted by the Dialog Institute, published in *Ha'aretz* on February 13, 2003, indicated that only 46% of those questioned expressed unequivocal support for the offensive in Iraq, while 23% expressed support for the European position, with reservations regarding the war and supporting efforts at mediation and inspection. A poll in *Maariv*, published on March 28, 2003, reported 64% support for the war compared to 26% opposition.

5 The Peace Index of February 2003 explains the limited protest against the war by the extensive support for the war among the Israeli public, which in turn was explained by the gravity of the Iraqi threat to Israel – in the long term and particularly in the non-conventional sense, ratther than in the immediate context of the American attack – as perceived by a significant percentage of the persons questioned.

6 The mass demonstrations seen in Europe in the months preceding the start of the fighting were phenomena that had not been experienced there for many years. With the outbreak of war the demonstrations continued, but on a smaller scale. On the extent of the opposition to the war in public opinion see, for example, "Antiwar Protest Largest Since '60s," *Washington Post*, October 27, 2002; Fareed Zakaria, "The Arrogant Empire" *Newsweek*, March 24, 2003; "The Strongest in the World, the Most Isolated in the World (apart perhaps from Iraq)," *Ha'aretz*, March 19, 2003; "Hundreds of Thousands Demonstrate in US Cities Against the Offensive," *Ha'aretz*, March 21, 2003.

7 See Ze'ev Schiff, "The Israeli Interest in Baghdad," *Ha'aretz*, August 16, 2002.

8 According to the findings of the February 2003 Peace Index, in the months preceding the outbreak of fighting in Iraq, there was a decrease in the number of those who esti-mated that Saddam Hussein would try to attack Israel during the war. In December 2002, 55% estimated that Israel would be attacked in response to an American offensive, while in February this figure was only 40%. (Fifty-two percent estimated that the prob-ability of an offensive against Israel was low or extremely low.) This trend also continued after the war started. According to the findings of the Peace Index for March 2003, 80% estimated there was a low or fairly low probability that Israel would be attacked, and 11% thought that the probability was high or very high. According to the Dialog Institute poll, many people estimated that the probability of Israel being harmed by an Iraqi missile offensive was high – in contrast to the estimate of a low probability

of this development provided by official sources, and in contrast to other data. According to this poll, which was conducted about a month prior to the initiation of the attack, only 37% of the people estimated that an Iraqi missile attack would not take place, while 43% estimated that missiles would fall on Israeli territory. However, this data, which indicated a relatively high level of fear, was not echoed in public behavior or in other surveys. Indeed, according to the *Maariv* poll of March 28, 2003 – that is: during the war itself – 21% of those questioned estimated that Iraq would attack Israel, and 68% estimated that Israel would not be attacked. According to yet another poll, conducted by Globes Smith and published in *Globes* on April 2, 2003, 77% of those questioned reported that they did not sense a threat of chemical missiles from Iraq.

9   Data from a poll conducted by the head of the Chaim Herzog Institute for Media, Society, and Politics, Dr. Yoram Perry, and Dr. Yariv Zefati, a colleague at the Institute, was announced at a conference on April 14, 2003 on the Israeli and international media during the war in Iraq, held in cooperation with the Jaffe Center for Strategic Studies and the Herzog Institute. The findings of the poll indicated a significant increase in the exposure of the Israeli public to the media. In January 2003 only 22% reported a daily exposure of more than an hour to news broadcasts and other current affairs programs. This percentage increased to 48% at the end of March, with the war in Iraq as the background to this statistic. An additional finding was the positive correlation between the level of belief in the media and the level of fears of war: those who feared the results of the war tended to believe the news more than those who didn't.

10 The protest against the Labor government following the Yom Kippur War was channeled to institutionalized expression in the form of the support for the Likud, which assumed power in 1977. This development strengthened the estimate that the tendency of protest is to be rapidly institutionalized. The wave of doubts regarding the path chosen by the Israeli government to combat the threat to the Galilee arose because of the trauma of the massacre at Sabra and Shatila in September 1982, and not because of basic questioning of the Israeli invasion of Lebanon. Furthermore, many years elapsed before a popular protest was created that encouraged the government decision to withdraw from the security zone in southern Lebanon. Even the public protest against the effects of the Oslo Accords on Israeli security became institutionalized relatively rapidly, as can be seen from the victory of the Likud in the 1996 Knesset elections.

11 The conference was organized by the Davis Institute at the Hebrew University in Jerusalem, September 1997. The title of Eitan's presentation was "The Right to Ask Questions."

12 The subject was debated in depth in Asher Arian, *Security Threatened: Surveying Israeli Public Opinion on Peace and War* (Tel Aviv: Jaffee Center for Strategic Studies and Papyrus Press, Tel Aviv University, 1999), Chapter 1. See also D. Horowitz and M. Lissak, *Trouble in Utopia: The Overburdened Polity of Israel* (Tel Aviv: Am Oved, 1990); and Doron Rosenblum, "Security," *Ha'aretz*, March 21, 2003.

13 According to the Dialog Institute poll published in *Ha'aretz* on February 13, 2003, only 12.4% of those questioned indicated Iraqi missiles as the major cause of anxiety, compared to 43% who indicated suicide bombers as the major cause of anxiety. According to a poll conducted in May 2002, the feeling of personal security among many Israelis (60%) was hurt as a result of living in the shadow of the threat of terrorism, even if only a much smaller proportion (only 16%) had actually been exposed to terrorist attacks. The vast majority of those asked (68%) felt that the lives of their dear ones were in danger. See A. Bleich, "Israeli Society in the Trap of Terror," NATAL (Israel Trauma Center for Victims of Terror and War), No. 5, May 2003.

14 During the war, before the military victory of the coalition became apparent, public opinion adopted a skeptical approach to the capability of overcoming the military and

civilian Iraqi resistance. According to a *Maariv* poll on March 23, 2003, only 22% of those questioned expected the American victory, compared to 68% who expected complications to arise in the war. It should be noted that this data reflects a short-term position against the background of a certain degree of uncertainty that for several days accompanied the reports from the battlefield.

15   On the Israeli public and the 1991 Gulf War see Arian, *Security Threatened*, pp. 85–86. Interestingly, a lively public debate on "national strength" took place following the missile attacks on Israel in 1991. Questions arose at that time regarding the degree to which the public displayed a capability of endurance, or as the term was sometimes used, "national strength." The debate mainly centered on the exodus of citizens from their places of residence in the center of the country, which constituted the main target for the Iraqi missiles, and their search for refuge in other regions of the country.

Israel's Home Front Defense Policy

14

David Klein

During the 1991 Gulf War, Israel was attacked by approximately 40 al-Hussein surface-to-surface missiles, which were fired from western Iraq with the intention of targeting population centers in Israel. The attacks in 1991 constituted a turning point in Israel's concept of civil defense on the home front: defense systems were built to reduce the number of missiles that could strike the home front; the Home Front Command was established; the construction of Apartment Protected Spaces (APS) was approved; it was decided to replace the protective kits and leave them in the possession of the population; and other civil defense measures were adopted to accompany these initiatives.

On the evening of March 19–20, 2003, the Americans and British launched Operation Iraqi Freedom with the intention of destroying Saddam Hussein's regime, and by mid-April 2003 fighting for the takeover of Iraq was completed. In advance of the war the defense establishment in Israel decided that despite the low probability of an attack on the home front, the public would be required to prepare sealed rooms, prepare their gas masks, and keep the masks with them at all times.[1]

The Israeli home front was not attacked even once during Operation Iraqi Freedom. However, all necessary preparatory steps in the sphere of population defense, without actual use of the measures, were taken. This experience, joined with the subsequent removal of Saddam Hussein's regime and the resulting strategic–political change in the Middle East, invites a reexamination of the components of population defense, and in particular the scope of measures and resource allocation to passive defense of the home front against a non-conventional weapons attack.

The purpose of this essay is to review the components of population defense and their implementation in Israel. The discussion will focus primarily on whether there has been a change in the threat to the population on the home front, and on issues regarding protection from chemical and biological agents: how outfitting the public with anti-bacteriological and chemical (ABC) masks should be managed and the distribution process overseen; the type of ABC mask that will protect the population in an emergency situation; the role of collective chemical protection gear in the protection package distributed to the population; and levels of medication stocks.

Layers of the Home Front Defense Policy

Measures to counter a threat to the home front comprise several layers (figure 14.1):

- *Attack prevention layers*, such as deterrence, attacks on launchers, and interception of surface-to-surface missiles
- *Damage control layers* in case of failure to prevent an attack, such as warning systems and passive protection

The two layers interface, and the overall combination provides a proper protection package to the population. In addition there is the component of "victim treatment," which is activated after adversarial offense measures have successfully penetrated the protective layers and caused casualties and damage.

Most of the layers of population defense were activated in Israel during Operation Iraqi Freedom.

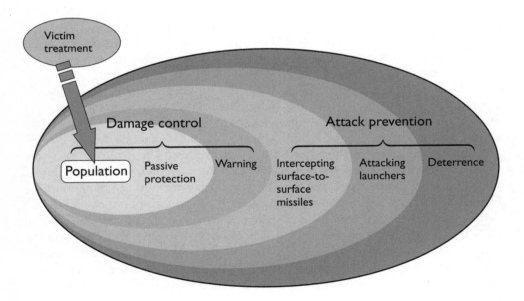

Figure 14.1 Protective Layers of the Home Front

Attack Prevention Layer

There was much effort on the part of Israel and the United States to ensure that the attack prevention layer would carry substantial weight in the protection package for the population in Israel.

- *Deterrence* consisted of ongoing, multidimensional activity of varied spheres (political, military–strategic, economic, and so on) intended to deter enemies from taking action against Israel. Out of all activities, it is not possible to isolate the ones directed towards Iraq and its intentions against the Israeli home front. In Operation Iraqi Freedom, components that were directed specifically to Iraq were added to overall activities, mainly verbal warnings voiced by American spokespersons.
- *Attacking launchers* involved activity by US and other forces in western Iraq to occupy areas from which launched missiles could reach Israel, as well as preparations for discovering and striking surface-to-surface missile launchers.
- *Intercepting surface-to-surface missiles* entailed deploying batteries of Arrow missiles and improved Patriot missiles and constituted the third layer of attack prevention.

Damage Control Layer

The main goal of this layer is to ensure that if a missile penetrates the attack prevention shield, the number of casualties in the population will be as low as possible.

The components of this layer are as follows:

- *Warning* – The effectiveness of the passive protection measures, that is, their ability to reduce damage in the event of failure to prevent the attack, depends on measures warning of the imminent attack. This is the component whose contribution to the layer of damage control is the greatest. Without warning, the most effective measures become useless. Warning enables the population to protect itself – to take cover, to put on a mask – even before the warhead strikes. The warning network deployed during Operation Iraqi Freedom included the radar of the Arrow batteries, the radar of the Patriot missile batteries, and warning from the network of American satellites.
- *Passive protection* – The protective measures against all types of chemical weapons include: various models of a gas mask, which provides good protection against chemical warfare agents that affect the respiratory system; a sealed shelter (APS, sealed room), which provides both an additional respiratory protective layer for the population, while reducing sensitivity in case of a protection failure by the mask,[2] as well as protection against persistent chemical warfare agents that penetrate through the skin; and treatment with medication in case of exposure to chemical warfare agents – at the first

stage, the personal syringe, and at the second stage, as part of the victim treatment layer, supplementary medical treatment by medical teams.

On the eve of the operation a decision was made by the Ministry of Defense to stop purchasing the Simplex (black rubber) masks and purchase a protective kit of a new type instead – the "Sapphire."[3] This is a new kit equipped with a blower, whose operation mechanism is similar to the protective hood ("Bardas"), the protective kit provided to children.

Victim Treatment Layer

This layer includes all the search and rescue operations and medical treatment. During the war the forces operating within this layer were deployed, but there was no need to operate them.

Assessing the Threat to the Population

In order to allocate resources efficiently for preparation of the home front for an emergency situation, a scenario for the home front should be created. The idea underlying the scenario is economic – what is the risk (set of threats) for which we are prepared to pay an insurance premium (resource allocation for protecting the home front). One such scenario, for example, prepared in 2001, characterized the conventional and non-conventional threat stemming from the countries in the region.[4] The aftermath of the 2003 war is an appropriate opportunity for examining the current existing threat to the Israeli home front. Significant changes in the threat will enable outlining a different scenario, which may in turn enable a reduction in the insurance premium that Israel pays for civil defense.

Table 14.1 Weapons Systems Posing a Threat to Israel[5]

Country	Weapon Systems	Characteristics
Syria	18 Scud-B launchers	200 missiles, 280 km; warhead weight 800–1,000 kg
	8 Scud C launchers	80 missiles, 550 km; warhead weight 500–700 kg
		350–400 missiles,
	18 Frog 7 launchers	70 km; warhead weight 500 kg
	18 SS-21 launchers	70 km; warhead weight 120 kg
Iraq*	5 al-Hussein launchers	20–30 missiles, 590–640 km; warhead weight 300 kg
Iran	1–3 Shehab 3 launchers	Several dozen missiles, 1,300 km; warhead weight 300 kg
Saudi Arabia	8–12 CSS-2 launchers	30–50 missiles, 2,700 km

* No verified information exists as to the number of missiles in Iraq after the 1991 Gulf War. The estimate presented here is the difference between the estimated number of missiles purchased and manufactured by Iraq and the estimated number of missiles fired by it (in training, towards targets in Iran, during the Gulf War in 1991, and the number of missiles destroyed by the inspectors).

The threat to the home front consists of four main components: the possession of surface-to-surface missile systems with a sufficient launching range by states in the region; the force of attack that can be generated from those systems, measured against the effectiveness of the attack prevention layer; the type of warhead (conventional, non-conventional); and political–strategic conditions enabling the threatening party to realize the potential threat.[6]

According to strategic assessments, by the end of the Gulf War in 1991 a small number of launchers and missiles remained in Iraq, as detailed in table 14.1. In other words, the Iraqi threat to the Israeli home front was already relatively small. Therefore, the removal of Saddam Hussein's regime in Iraq does not fundamentally change the potential severity of an attack on Israel.

Despite the fact that the threat of an attack by Iraqi missiles was relatively small, until Operation Iraqi Freedom was completed, the non-conventional threat from Iraq, and particularly the biological threat, constituted a core threat to the Israeli home front.

The biological warfare agents can be divided into three families, according to their effect mechanism:

- Toxins, which are similar in their harmful effects to chemical agents, but are based on a poison derived from a biological agent. They produce an immediate appearance of symptoms in people exposed to biological warfare agents of this type. Similar to chemical warfare agents, personal protection gear is highly effective against them.
- A second family is characterized by a non-epidemic biological agent, which is spread through the air and causes a disease upon penetrating the body. The most effective penetration is through the respiratory system. A person who is protected against chemical weapons is protected to the same degree against these biological weapons.
- A third family consists of epidemic agents. The disease spreads through contagion from one person to another. Therefore, the number of people infected increases with time, relative to the number of people exposed in the initial spread of the biological warfare agents.

Assessments name the biological agent that poses the greatest threat to Israel as anthrax, which belongs to the second family of biological warfare agents and was kept by Iraq in unknown quantities. Another biological agent, smallpox, which belongs to the third family of agents (epidemic agents), made headlines in the months preceding Operation Iraqi Freedom. Yet the very debate over whether or not to vaccinate the public testified to the low-intensity threat posed by this agent within the envelope of threats to the home front.

The ousting of Saddam Hussein's regime removed the Iraqi chemical and biological threat to Israel entirely. The remaining non-conventional threats against Israel consist of non-conventional terror, the Iranian effort to obtain nuclear weapons, and the chemical weapon systems in the hands of Syria.

The central characteristic of non-conventional terror is that the attack can only be detected through the appearance of victims or an outbreak of disease in the case of a biological agent. Therefore, passive protection gear such as an ABC mask, which is highly effective against armaments whose delivery is discerned and subject to advance warning (missiles and planes), is not effective in this case. Instead, the solution to a non-conventional terror threat is effective clinical detection and identification, treatment with medication, and in case of a biological agent, employing methods and measures for preventing the agent from spreading among a population that has not yet been exposed to it.

The expenditure on passive measures against a nuclear threat is prohibitive and therefore unfeasible. As to Syria, the magnitude of the non-conventional Syrian threat on the map of threats to Israel has been reduced. The fall of Saddam Hussein's regime and the US involvement in the Middle East have fundamentally changed the political–strategic conditions that enable Syria to make use of the chemical threat in its possession.

Thus, the deposal of Saddam's regime has created a new scenario for the preparation of the home front for emergency situations. The terrorist threat now stands at the core of the non-conventional scenario, while the threat posed by states has been significantly reduced.

Protective Measures

Personal Protection Kits

In-depth deliberations within the IDF in the wake of the 1991 Gulf War led to the decision that the protective kits would remain in the hands of the population, with a concomitant process of replacing masks to ensure that the population possessed protection kits in working order.

After Operation Iraqi Freedom, Israel faces a situation similar to conditions twelve years earlier: the ABC masks have been taken out of their sealed packaging, the filters' seals were removed and the filters were fitted into place, and the protective hoods and "babysitter" kits were activated and consumed electrical power, so that the remaining life-span of the batteries has been shortened. At this point two questions arise:

1 Should Israel initiate a process of replacing the protective kits, as was done in 1991?
2 Should the kits be left in the possession of the population, or should they be collected and stored in Home Front Command warehouses, to be distributed to the population only in an emergency situation?

The gas mask filters held by the public, even after being used, still have a high ability to absorb chemical warfare agents through the filtering mechanism of the active substances in the filter. Therefore, the public still has ABC masks that are effective and in proper working order, and there is no immediate need to refresh the protection gear. The apparent change in the characterization of the threat to the home front makes it possible to postpone the process of replacing the masks, at least in the short and medium terms.

Following the opening of the protection kits, one idea debated was that after Operation Iraqi Freedom the ABC masks would be collected and stored in Home Front Command warehouses, to be distributed to the population only in an emergency situation.[7] Such a solution is only possible if it guarantees protection availability to the population as of the first attack on the home front, and if its cost is no higher than the cost of having the public keep the masks in their homes. Moreover, an arrangement of this sort is fraught with difficulties. A decision to distribute the ABC masks that are located in storage warehouse becomes complex and intricate, and requires the intervention of the political echelon since such a decision, given at an inappropriate time, could create the impression that Israel is the party preparing to attack. Otherwise, it would not have a reason to protect its population. As a result, any decision to distribute the ABC masks would probably be delayed as much as possible.

The period of time required to distribute ABC masks to the population from the moment the decision is made until the distribution is completed could take weeks. In other words, while regional tension increases, protection kits that are stored in the Home Front Command warehouses and are slated to be distributed only in emergency situations might be unavailable to the citizens at the time of the first attacks on the home front. Conversely, if the kits were located in the citizens' homes, there would be no availability problem. Moreover, during the weeks of delivering the protection kits to the population there will be extremely heavy pressure on the distribution centers, significantly greater than the pressure experienced during the preparations for the recent war, when not all people came to replace their kits. The cost consideration of maintaining the ABC masks in a storage warehouse is relevant only if the Home Front Command could distribute the masks before the first attacks occur, a fairly unlikely scenario. In this case, storage warehouses are worthwhile if the overall cost is lower than maintaining the ABC masks at the citizens' homes. According to an initial examination of the major cost parameters, this is not the conclusion that is reached:

- Warehouses have storage space costs that do not exist when the ABC masks are stored in the citizens' homes.
- Collecting the protection kits would raise costs – personnel, transportation, and more.
- Insurance costs will rise for insuring all the ABC masks in stock as opposed to the cost of insurance for the operational stock only, as exists today.
- In contrast to the other parameters, operating the maintenance of a central storage is less expensive than operating a replacement network for the kits held at the homes, since it employs fewer personnel than at distribution centers.

The obvious conclusion is that at present and in the foreseeable future the ABC masks should be kept in the public's possession, until it is decided to replace the protection kits.

Gas Mask Protection

In the period leading up to Operation Iraqi Freedom the director general of the Ministry of Defense decided that only Sapphire masks would be purchased, rather than Simplex ABC masks (black rubber masks) because the protection method of the existing masks suffers from a number of failures. Some people refrain from using the mask due to discomfort, and some put on the masks incorrectly. Other concerns are the masks' incompatibility with the variety of facial structures among the population and their durability.

However, advanced personal protection measures against chemical warfare, such as the protective hood (Bardas or Sapphire), will not significantly lower the overall number of casualties in a case of chemical attack on the home front, relative to the number of casualties expected with the current ABC masks. Despite their technological advantage, the advanced masks trade one type of shortcoming for another. In the Sapphire mask the blower may stop working due to battery drain or some other electro-mechanical failure, which would result in a high probability of inhaling toxic substances. Similarly, a blower that has stopped working increases the concentration of carbon dioxide inside the mask, and endangers the life of the user even without exposure to chemical warfare agents. However, full power avail-ability for the blowers will increase their effectiveness to the full extent of their technical ability, while naturally increasing costs.[8] The proposed change in the characterization of the threat to the home front and the strategic respite that has emerged should be utilized to achieve the following goals:

- Examine the necessary technical changes in order to improve the blowers' power sources.
- Develop or locate purchasing sources abroad for a broader variety of "regular" ABC masks that are adapted to different facial profiles.
- Continue the development of masks that operate without a blower, are more comfortable to wear, have a significantly longer life-span, and use materials and technology that will lower their prices.

Once the new masks are developed or located abroad, should they be purchased and distributed to the entire population? It is clear that without replacing the masks, within a number of years the population will not possess working protection gear against a chemical threat. Despite the fact that the non-conventional threat from Syria has been marginalized, until peace agreements are signed probably no leader will decide that the population does not need ABC masks. In other words, Israel will continue to pay an insurance premium for a non-conventional threat of very low probability.

Therefore, it must at least be ensured that the insurance premium, that is, the overall expenditure for ABC masks, does not increase, but rather shrinks. If the product and all of its logistics is more expensive and its life-span is no greater than what exists today, the cost effectiveness of replacing all ABC masks to new models will drop. In such a case, distribution of the protective kits will have to be selective.

Collective Chemical Protection

During the preparations for Operation Iraqi Freedom a collective protection gear against chemical warfare agents, such as the Noah's Ark system, gained popularity. Advertisements promised good protection from chemical and biological warfare agents, which can relieve the users of the need to wear an ABC mask. However, such protection does not in fact obviate the need to distribute protection kits to the population, since it precludes the option for mobility outside the home. In addition, collective protection systems suffer from certain lapses.

For example, an individual or group that arrives at a shelter intended for more than one family after the doors have been closed could remain outside without protection, since no one staying in the shelter would risk opening the shelter doors and exposing all of its occupants to chemical warfare agents. This means that there is a high probability that the collective protection systems will actually cause a larger number of casualties than if people were protected only with individual gas masks. Such a failure is clearly less likely if the shelter is intended for one family only.

Maintaining the collective protection systems in working order is an essential condition for ensuring that their effectiveness remains at a high level, even years after they have been installed. This, of course, comes at a cost. If regular maintenance is not carried out, confidence in the system will be shaken and people will be required to wear a protection mask in conjunction. In such a case, the overall expenditure for protection is greater. The conclusion is that collective protection gear is not the ultimate solution, and its cumulative costs do not match the recommended scope of expenses for protecting the population. Thus it is not advised that the collective protection gear become part of the protection package provided by the state.

Medication Supply

The updated scenario to the home front makes it possible to consider the levels of medication stocks kept by the state. Medications are items that can be purchased in large quantities within a relatively short time. The change in the threat to the home front enables reducing stocks over time and remaining with a supply that is appropriate for a terror threat.

Assessment

The removal of Saddam Hussein's regime in Operation Iraqi Freedom brought about a strategic–political change that invites a review of civil defense expenditure, and in particular the scope of resources allocated to passive protection of the home front against a non-conventional weapons attack. The review yields eight principal conclusions:

1   In the post-Saddam reality the threat of terror stands at the core of the non-

conventional scenario, while the threat posed by states has been significantly reduced.

2   Unless the masks are replaced, within a number of years the population will not possess a working protection gear against a chemical threat. Despite the fact that the non-conventional threat from Syria has become marginal, the decision that the citizens of Israel do not need masks cannot be made until peace agreements are signed with Syria. Because Israel will continue to pay an insurance premium against a non-conventional threat of very low probability, the overall expenditure for gas masks must shrink rather than increase.

3   At the present stage, Israel should not replace protection kits.

4   The ABC masks should be left in the public's possession at the present and in the foreseeable future, until it is decided to replace them.

5   The diminishing threat to the home front as well as the strategic time slot that has opened up should be utilized:

   • To examine the necessary technical changes in order to improve the power sources for the blowers in the ABC masks

   • To develop or locate purchasing sources abroad for a broader variety of "regular" ABC masks that fit different facial structures

   • To continue the development of ABC masks that operate without a blower, are more comfortable to wear, have a significantly longer life-span, and are less expensive

6   If proposed new products and related logistics are more expensive and their life-span is no greater than what today's products offer, the cost effectiveness of changing the masks will drop. In such a case, distribution of the new protection kits will have to be selective.

7   Collective protection is not the ultimate solution. Its cumulative costs do not match the recommended scope of expenses for protecting the population, and therefore it is not recommended as part of the state-provided protection package.

8   The diminishing threat to the home front enables a reduction in the stock of medication against non-conventional threats to a size appropriate for a terror threat alone.

Notes

1   Yoel Marcus, "Don't Blabber, Don't Push," *Ha'aretz*, March 6, 2003.

2   Contrary to the publications in the press on the eve of Operation Iraqi Freedom, the gas mask is the central protective component against chemical warfare agents. A sealed shelter adds an additional level of protection, which assures that even if a certain failure takes place in the individual's defense, the overall protection package would compensate and provide a response.

3   Amnon Barzilai, "Defense Ministry to Exchange Gas Masks: Preparing for Immediate Production of the 'Sapphire,'" *Ha'aretz*, January 16, 2003.

4   David Klein, *Home-Front Defense: Examining the National Cost*, Memorandum No. 58, Jaffee Center for Strategic Studies, Tel Aviv University, April 2001.

5   Yiftah Shapir (ed.), *The Middle East Military Balance*, Jaffee Center for Strategic Studies, May 2003, www.tau.ac.il/jcss.

6   The analysis will focus on surface-to-surface missiles only, since it is simpler to stage a surface-to-surface missile attack on the Israeli home front than a plane strike. Israel's historical experience also shows that in previous wars, only a very small number of planes succeeded in striking the state's home front. Therefore, from the moment that the Arab states accumulated a critical mass of launchers and missiles, surface-to-surface missiles became the central threat to the home front. When adding the fact that the attacks on Israeli cities by surface-to-surface missiles in the 1991 Gulf War emphasized the vulnerability of the Israeli civilian home front to surface-to-surface missiles, the conclusion is reached that in planning, it is correct to treat surface-to-surface missiles as the central threat to the Israeli home front.

7   Amos Harel and Amnon Barzilai, "Security Establishment: Continue Walking Around with Protective Kits, Don't Disregard the Threat," *Ha'aretz*, March 23, 2003.

8   Power availability for operating the blowers can be obtained through one of the following options: (i) Installing a power connection on the protective kits so that they will be able to hook up to an electrical outlet. The battery in this case will serve as a backup in case the power supply is interrupted or if the user is on the street. It can be shown that the cumulative time for expected power shortages in emergency situations makes this proposal possible. (ii) Changing the type of battery used to operate the blower (for all models of masks) to a commercially available type of battery, and simplifying the method of changing the battery so that people will be able to do this on their own. Accordingly, citizens would be able to purchase batteries in stores and replace them by themselves. The demand that will arise for batteries in an emergency situation will provide local manufacturers and importers with economic motivation to provide them. (iii) The present solution is the State's maintaining a stock of batteries. This is the most expensive solution, due to the size of the required permanent stock, the relatively short shelf life of the batteries, and the fact that the type of battery is not suitable for many other uses and therefore cannot be sold elsewhere.

Chronology of the International Inspection Regime in Iraq, 1991–2003

Compiled by Ram Erez and Tamar Malz

1991

February 28
US President George Bush announces a ceasefire, ending the Gulf War.

March 2
United Nations Security Council (UNSC) adopts Resolution 686 ordering cessation of all Iraqi hostilities.

April 3
UNSC adopts Resolution 687 outlining provisions of ceasefire and setting up inspections. Saddam Hussein is ordered to destroy weapons and allow inspection of all weapons facilities by the United Nations Special Commission (UNSCOM).

April 6
Iraq accepts Resolution 687; US, UK, and France begin enforcing the northern no-fly zone covering territory north of the 36th parallel (Operation Northern Watch).

May 15
International Atomic Energy Agency (IAEA) conducts its first nuclear inspection in Iraq.

The chronology is based on the following sources: US Department of State, "Timeline of UN–Iraq–Coalition Incidents, 1991–2002," *International Information Program*, http://usinfo.state.gov/products/pubs/iraq/timeline.htm; "UNSCOM: Chronology of Main Events," *United Nations Special Commission (UNSCOM)*, http://www.un.org/Depts/unscom/Chronology/chronologyframe.htm; "UNMOVIC Chronology of Main Events," *United Nations Monitoring, Verification and Inspection Commission (UNMOVIC)*, http://www.un.org/Depts/unmovic/index.htm; Iraq Nuclear Verification Office (INVO), "Chronology of Main Events," *Worldatom – International Atomic Energy Agency (IAEA)*, http://www.iaea.org/worldatom/Programmes/ActionTeam/chronology.html, December 27, 2002; "Timeline – Iraq – A Chronology of Key Events," *BBC News* (online edition), http://news.bbc.co.uk/1/hi/world/middle east/737483.stm; "Timeline: Iraq – Special Report on Iraq," *Guardian Unlimited*, http://www.guardian.co.uk/Iraq/page/0,12438,793802,00.html; Seth Stern, "Timeline: The road to war in Iraq," *The Christian Science Monitor*, http://www.csmonitor.com/2003/0320/p02s01-woiq.html, March 20, 2003; "Spying on Saddam: Chronology," *Frontline*, http://www.pbs.org/wgbh/pages/frontline/shows/unscom/etc/cron.html.

June 9
UNSCOM begins its first inspection in Iraq.

June 17
UNSC adopts Resolution 699 approving UN Secretary-General's plan to eliminate Iraq's WMD programs.

June 28
UNSC presidential statement condemns Iraq for open violation of Resolution 687 in denying inspectors access.

June-September
Iraq consistently obstructs UNSCOM and IAEA inspections.

December 11
Iraq releases information on its nuclear program.

1992

February 28
UNSC presidential statement deplores Iraq's failure to disclose WMD programs.

July
UNSCOM begins to destroy large quantities of Iraq's chemical weapons and production facilities.

August 27
In response to Iraqi air strikes against its civilian population, coalition states create the southern no-fly zone below the 32nd parallel (Operation Southern Watch).

1993

January
Coalition forces launch air raids against radar sites in northern and southern Iraq in response to Iraq's increased military activity in the no-fly zones; US forces fire cruise missiles against industrial complex said to be linked to Iraq's nuclear weapons program.

June 27
US launches cruise missiles at Iraqi intelligence headquarters in retaliation for an Iraqi assassination plot against former US President Bush during his visit to Kuwait.

1995

April
UNSC adopts Resolution 986 on "Oil-for-Food" program.(Iraq did not accept this resolution until May 1996, and only in December 1996 was the resolution first implemented.)

July 1
Iraq admits for the first time the existence of a biological weapons program.

August 8
Saddam's son-in-law, Hussein Kamel, head of WMD program, defects. Kamel submits valuable information on Iraq's WMD programs.

August 17
Iraq acknowledges that its WMD program was more extensive than first admitted.

November 7
Iraq provides more information on its WMD programs.

1996

June 12
In response to consistent Iraqi refusal to allow UNSCOM access to military sites, UNSC adopts Resolution 1060. This resolution declares Iraqi actions as clear violations of UN resolutions and demands that Iraq grant immediate access to sites for inspection.

1997

September–October
Iraq blocks UNSCOM access to presidential sites.

October 29
Iraq states that it will no longer permit US personnel in UNSCOM and demands cessation of U2 surveillance flights.

November 13
Following Iraq's demand that all US inspectors leave within 24 hours, UNSCOM withdraws weapons inspectors.

November 20
Iraq agrees to let UNSCOM inspectors return.

1998

January 13–22
Iraq withdraws cooperation with UNSCOM, claiming too many members are American and British and denies UNSCOM access to presidential sites.

February 23
During the visit to Iraq by UN Secretary-General Kofi Annan, an agreement is reached allowing UNSCOM inspectors access to presidential sites.

October 31
Saddam ends cooperation with UNSCOM.

November 5
UNSC adopts Resolution 1205 ordering Iraq to resume cooperation with UNSCOM.

November 14
Saddam allows UNSCOM inspectors to return.

December 15–16
UNSCOM reports to UNSC that it is unable to continue inspections and withdraws its inspectors.

December 16–19
Operation Desert Fox: US–British air strikes target Iraq's weapons infrastructure.

December 19
Iraq declares that UNSCOM inspectors will never enter Iraq again.

1999

January 4
Iraq states it can no longer guarantee the safety of US and UK Oil-for-Food monitors.

February 3
UN Secretary-General orders US and UK Oil-for-Food monitors out of Iraq.

December 17
UNSC adopts Resolution 1284 that specifies conditions under which sanctions would be suspended. Under the resolution a new monitoring body is established to replace UNSCOM – the United Nations Monitoring, Verification and Inspection Commission (UNMOVIC).

2001

The UN and Iraq conduct several rounds of talks in an attempt to resume weapons inspections.

2002

January 29

In the State of the Union speech, US President George W. Bush defines Iraq as a member of an "axis of evil."

September 12
Addressing the General Assembly, President Bush calls on the UN to take proactive steps against Iraq; UNSC begins discussion on Iraqi non-compliance with UN resolutions.

September 17
Iraq announces that it will accept the return of inspections.

November 8
UNSC adopts Resolution 1441, which outlines provisions for enhanced weapons inspections (Iraq accepts this resolution on November 13).

November 18
UNMOVIC and IAEA inspectors arrive in Iraq.

December 7
In accordance with Resolution 1441, Iraq submits to the UN a 12,000-page report on its WMD programs. In this report Iraq states that it does not possess WMD.

2003

January 9
UNMOVIC Executive Chairman Hans Blix states that no "smoking guns" were found in Iraq. At the same time, he emphasizes that Iraq's report is incomplete.

January 19
President Bush offers Saddam Hussein immunity for leaving Iraq, avowing that such a step would prevent an attack on Iraq.

January 28
In the State of the Union speech, President Bush affirms that Saddam "is not disarming; to the contrary, he is deceiving."

February 5
In an attempt to make the US case against Iraq before the UNSC, Secretary of State Colin Powell accuses Saddam Hussein of deception and uses intelligence information to support the US claims.

February 10
A trans-Atlantic crisis in NATO over Iraq: France, Germany, and Belgium veto a US request for NATO to make plans to protect Turkey if Saddam attacks.

February 14
Hans Blix delivers a progress report to UNSC, arguing that Iraq is making an effort to disarm.

March 5
France, Germany, and Russia release a joint declaration stating that they would "not allow" further resolutions in the UNSC authorizing military action against Iraq.

March 7
The US, UK, and Spain present a revised UNSC resolution draft, giving Iraq an ultimatum to disarm by March 17; Mohamed ElBaradei, Director General of the IAEA, submits a report to the UNSC saying that there is no evidence that Iraq has a nuclear program.

March 16
The leaders of the US, UK, Spain, and Portugal meet in the Azores, giving an additional 24 hours for diplomacy.

March 17
The US and UK withdraw their UNSC resolution draft and call on the inspectors to leave Iraq; President Bush issues Saddam Hussein with a 48 hour ultimatum.

March 20
The war begins (on the evening of March 19–20).

The National Security Strategy of the United States of America

of the

United States of America

September 2002

The great struggles of the twentieth century between liberty and totalitarianism ended with a decisive victory for the forces of freedom—and a single sustainable model for national success: freedom, democracy, and free enterprise. In the twenty-first century, only nations that share a commitment to protecting basic human rights and guaranteeing political and economic freedom will be able to unleash the potential of their people and assure their future prosperity. People everywhere want to be able to speak freely; choose who will govern them; worship as they please; educate their children—male and female; own property; and enjoy the benefits of their labor. These values of freedom are right and true for every person, in every society—and the duty of protecting these values against their enemies is the common calling of freedom-loving people across the globe and across the ages.

Today, the United States enjoys a position of unparalleled military strength and great economic and political influence. In keeping with our heritage and principles, we do not use our strength to press for unilateral advantage. We seek instead to create a balance of power that favors human freedom: conditions in which all nations and all societies can choose for themselves the rewards and challenges of political and economic liberty. In a world that is safe, people will be able to make their own lives better. We will defend the peace by fighting terrorists and tyrants. We will preserve the peace by building good relations among the great powers. We will extend the peace by encouraging free and open societies on every continent.

Defending our Nation against its enemies is the first and fundamental commitment of the Federal Government. Today, that task has changed dramatically. Enemies in the past needed great armies and great industrial capabilities to endanger America. Now, shadowy networks of individuals can bring great chaos and suffering to our shores for less than it costs to purchase a single tank. Terrorists are organized to penetrate open societies and to turn the power of modern technologies against us.

To defeat this threat we must make use of every tool in our arsenal—military power, better homeland defenses, law enforcement, intelligence, and vigorous efforts to cut off terrorist financing. The war against terrorists of global reach is a global enterprise of uncertain duration. America will help nations that need our assistance in combating terror. And America will hold to account nations that are compromised by terror, including those who harbor terrorists—because the allies of terror are the enemies of civilization. The United States and countries cooperating with us must not allow the terrorists to develop new home bases. Together, we will seek to deny them sanctuary at every turn.

The gravest danger our Nation faces lies at the crossroads of radicalism and technology. Our enemies have openly declared that they are seeking weapons of mass destruction, and evidence indicates that they are doing so with determination. The United States will not allow these efforts to succeed. We will build defenses against ballistic missiles and other means of delivery. We will cooperate with other nations to deny, contain, and curtail our enemies' efforts to acquire dangerous technologies. And, as a matter of common sense and self-defense, America will act against such emerging threats before they are fully formed. We cannot defend America and our friends by hoping for the best. So we must be prepared to defeat our enemies' plans, using the best intelligence and proceeding with deliberation. History will judge harshly those who saw this coming danger but failed to act. In the new world we have entered, the only path to peace and security is the path of action.

As we defend the peace, we will also take advantage of an historic opportunity to preserve the peace. Today, the international community has the best chance since the rise of the nation-state in the seventeenth century to build a world where great powers compete in peace instead of continually prepare for war. Today, the world's great powers find ourselves on the same side—united by common dangers of terrorist violence and chaos. The United States will build on these common interests to promote global security. We are also increasingly united by common values. Russia is in the midst of a hopeful transition, reaching for its democratic future and a partner in the war on terror. Chinese leaders are discovering that economic freedom is the only source of national wealth. In time, they will find that social and political freedom is the only source of national greatness. America will encourage the advancement of democracy and economic openness in both nations, because these are the best foundations for domestic stability and international order. We will strongly resist aggression from other great powers—even as we welcome their peaceful pursuit of prosperity, trade, and cultural advancement.

Finally, the United States will use this moment of opportunity to extend the benefits of freedom across the globe. We will actively work to bring the hope of democracy, development, free markets, and free trade to every corner of the world. The events of September 11, 2001, taught us that weak states, like Afghanistan, can pose as great a danger to our national interests as strong states. Poverty does not make poor people into terrorists and murderers. Yet poverty, weak institutions, and corruption can make weak states vulnerable to terrorist networks and drug cartels within their borders.

The United States will stand beside any nation determined to build a better future by seeking the rewards of liberty for its people. Free trade and free markets have proven their ability to lift whole societies out of poverty—so the United States will work with individual nations, entire regions, and the entire global trading community to build a world that trades in freedom and therefore grows in prosperity. The United States will deliver greater development assistance through the New Millennium Challenge Account to nations that govern justly, invest in their people, and encourage economic freedom. We will also continue to lead the world in efforts to reduce the terrible toll of HIV/AIDS and other infectious diseases.

In building a balance of power that favors freedom, the United States is guided by the conviction that all nations have important responsibilities. Nations that enjoy freedom must actively fight terror. Nations that depend on international stability must help prevent the spread of weapons of mass destruction. Nations that seek international aid must govern themselves wisely, so that aid is well spent. For freedom to thrive, accountability must be expected and required.

We are also guided by the conviction that no nation can build a safer, better world alone. Alliances and multilateral institutions can multiply the strength of freedom-loving nations. The United States is committed to lasting institutions like the United Nations, the World Trade Organization, the Organization of American States, and NATO as well as other long-standing alliances. Coalitions of the willing can augment these permanent institutions. In all cases, international obligations are to be taken seriously. They are not to be undertaken symbolically to rally support for an ideal without furthering its attainment.

Freedom is the non-negotiable demand of human dignity; the birthright of every person—in every civilization. Throughout history, freedom has been threatened by war and terror; it has been challenged by the clashing wills of powerful states and the evil designs of tyrants; and it has been tested by widespread poverty and disease. Today, humanity holds in its hands the opportunity to further freedom's triumph over all these foes. The United States welcomes our responsibility to lead in this great mission.

THE WHITE HOUSE,
September 17, 2002

TABLE OF CONTENTS

I. Overview of America's International Strategy

"Our Nation's cause has always been larger than our Nation's defense.
We fight, as we always fight, for a just peace—a peace that favors liberty.
We will defend the peace against the threats from terrorists and tyrants.
We will preserve the peace by building good relations among the great powers.
And we will extend the peace by encouraging free and open societies on every continent."

PRESIDENT BUSH
WEST POINT, NEW YORK
JUNE 1, 2002

The United States possesses unprecedented—and unequaled—strength and influence in the world. Sustained by faith in the principles of liberty, and the value of a free society, this position comes with unparalleled responsibilities, obligations, and opportunity. The great strength of this nation must be used to promote a balance of power that favors freedom.

For most of the twentieth century, the world was divided by a great struggle over ideas: destructive totalitarian visions versus freedom and equality.

That great struggle is over. The militant visions of class, nation, and race which promised utopia and delivered misery have been defeated and discredited. America is now threatened less by conquering states than we are by failing ones. We are menaced less by fleets and armies than by catastrophic technologies in the hands of the embittered few. We must defeat these threats to our Nation, allies, and friends.

This is also a time of opportunity for America. We will work to translate this moment of influence into decades of peace, prosperity, and liberty.

The U.S. national security strategy will be based on a distinctly American internationalism that reflects the union of our values and our national interests. The aim of this strategy is to help make the world not just safer but better. Our goals on the path to progress are clear: political and economic freedom, peaceful relations with other states, and respect for human dignity.

And this path is not America's alone. It is open to all.

To achieve these goals, the United States will:

- champion aspirations for human dignity;

- strengthen alliances to defeat global terrorism and work to prevent attacks against us and our friends;

- work with others to defuse regional conflicts;

- prevent our enemies from threatening us, our allies, and our friends, with weapons of mass destruction;

- ignite a new era of global economic growth through free markets and free trade;

- expand the circle of development by opening societies and building the infrastructure of democracy;

- develop agendas for cooperative action with other main centers of global power; and

- transform America's national security institutions to meet the challenges and opportunities of the twenty-first century.

II. Champion Aspirations for Human Dignity

"Some worry that it is somehow undiplomatic or impolite to speak the language of right and wrong. I disagree. Different circumstances require different methods, but not different moralities."

President Bush
West Point, New York
June 1, 2002

In pursuit of our goals, our first imperative is to clarify what we stand for: the United States must defend liberty and justice because these principles are right and true for all people everywhere. No nation owns these aspirations, and no nation is exempt from them. Fathers and mothers in all societies want their children to be educated and to live free from poverty and violence. No people on earth yearn to be oppressed, aspire to servitude, or eagerly await the midnight knock of the secret police.

America must stand firmly for the nonnegotiable demands of human dignity: the rule of law; limits on the absolute power of the state; free speech; freedom of worship; equal justice; respect for women; religious and ethnic tolerance; and respect for private property.

These demands can be met in many ways. America's constitution has served us well. Many other nations, with different histories and cultures, facing different circumstances, have successfully incorporated these core principles into their own systems of governance. History has not been kind to those nations which ignored or flouted the rights and aspirations of their people.

America's experience as a great multi-ethnic democracy affirms our conviction that people of many heritages and faiths can live and prosper in peace. Our own history is a long struggle to live up to our ideals. But even in our worst moments, the principles enshrined in the Declaration of Independence were there to guide us. As a result, America is not just a stronger, but is a freer and more just society.

Today, these ideals are a lifeline to lonely defenders of liberty. And when openings arrive, we can encourage change—as we did in central and eastern Europe between 1989 and 1991, or in Belgrade in 2000. When we see democratic processes take hold among our friends in Taiwan or in the Republic of Korea, and see elected leaders replace generals in Latin America and Africa, we see examples of how authoritarian systems can evolve, marrying local history and traditions with the principles we all cherish.

Embodying lessons from our past and using the opportunity we have today, the national security strategy of the United States must start from these core beliefs and look outward for possibilities to expand liberty.

Our principles will guide our government's decisions about international cooperation, the character of our foreign assistance, and the allocation of resources. They will guide our actions and our words in international bodies.

We will:

- speak out honestly about violations of the nonnegotiable demands of human dignity using our voice and vote in international institutions to advance freedom;

- use our foreign aid to promote freedom and support those who struggle non-violently for it, ensuring that nations moving toward democracy are rewarded for the steps they take;

- make freedom and the development of democratic institutions key themes in our bilateral relations, seeking solidarity and cooperation from other democracies while we press governments that deny human rights to move toward a better future; and

- take special efforts to promote freedom of religion and conscience and defend it from encroachment by repressive governments.

We will champion the cause of human dignity and oppose those who resist it.

III. Strengthen Alliances to Defeat Global Terrorism and Work to Prevent Attacks Against Us and Our Friends

"Just three days removed from these events, Americans do not yet have the distance of history. But our responsibility to history is already clear: to answer these attacks and rid the world of evil. War has been waged against us by stealth and deceit and murder. This nation is peaceful, but fierce when stirred to anger. The conflict was begun on the timing and terms of others. It will end in a way, and at an hour, of our choosing."

President Bush
Washington, D.C. (The National Cathedral)
September 14, 2001

The United States of America is fighting a war against terrorists of global reach. The enemy is not a single political regime or person or religion or ideology. The enemy is terrorism—premeditated, politically motivated violence perpetrated against innocents.

In many regions, legitimate grievances prevent the emergence of a lasting peace. Such grievances deserve to be, and must be, addressed within a political process. But no cause justifies terror. The United States will make no concessions to terrorist demands and strike no deals with them. We make no distinction between terrorists and those who knowingly harbor or provide aid to them.

The struggle against global terrorism is different from any other war in our history. It will be fought on many fronts against a particularly elusive enemy over an extended period of time. Progress will come through the persistent accumulation of successes—some seen, some unseen.

Today our enemies have seen the results of what civilized nations can, and will, do against regimes that harbor, support, and use terrorism to achieve their political goals. Afghanistan has been liberated; coalition forces continue to hunt down the Taliban and al-Qaida. But it is not only this battlefield on which we will engage terrorists. Thousands of trained terrorists remain at large with cells in North America, South America, Europe, Africa, the Middle East, and across Asia.

Our priority will be first to disrupt and destroy terrorist organizations of global reach and attack their leadership; command, control, and communications; material support; and finances. This will have a disabling effect upon the terrorists' ability to plan and operate.

We will continue to encourage our regional partners to take up a coordinated effort that isolates the terrorists. Once the regional campaign localizes the threat to a particular state, we will help ensure the state has the military, law enforcement, political, and financial tools necessary to finish the task.

The United States will continue to work with our allies to disrupt the financing of terrorism. We will identify and block the sources of funding for terrorism, freeze the assets of terrorists and those who support them, deny terrorists access to the international financial system, protect legitimate charities from being abused by terrorists, and prevent the movement of terrorists' assets through alternative financial networks.

However, this campaign need not be sequential to be effective, the cumulative effect across all regions will help achieve the results we seek.

We will disrupt and destroy terrorist organizations by:

- direct and continuous action using all the elements of national and international power. Our immediate focus will be those terrorist organizations of global reach and any terrorist or state sponsor of terrorism which attempts to gain or use weapons of mass destruction (WMD) or their precursors;

- defending the United States, the American people, and our interests at home and abroad by identifying and destroying the threat before it reaches our borders. While the United States will constantly strive to enlist the support of the international community, we will not hesitate to act alone, if necessary, to exercise our right of self-defense by acting preemptively against such terrorists, to prevent them from doing harm against our people and our country; and

- denying further sponsorship, support, and sanctuary to terrorists by convincing or compelling states to accept their sovereign responsibilities.

We will also wage a war of ideas to win the battle against international terrorism. This includes:

- using the full influence of the United States, and working closely with allies and friends, to make clear that all acts of terrorism are illegitimate so that terrorism will be viewed in the same light as slavery, piracy, or genocide: behavior that no respectable government can condone or support and all must oppose;

- supporting moderate and modern government, especially in the Muslim world, to ensure that the conditions and ideologies that promote terrorism do not find fertile ground in any nation;

- diminishing the underlying conditions that spawn terrorism by enlisting the international community to focus its efforts and resources on areas most at risk; and

- using effective public diplomacy to promote the free flow of information and ideas to kindle the hopes and aspirations of freedom of those in societies ruled by the sponsors of global terrorism.

While we recognize that our best defense is a good offense, we are also strengthening America's homeland security to protect against and deter attack.

This Administration has proposed the largest government reorganization since the Truman Administration created the National Security Council and the Department of Defense. Centered on a new Department of Homeland Security and including a new unified military command and a fundamental reordering of the FBI, our comprehensive plan to secure the homeland encompasses every level of government and the cooperation of the public and the private sector.

This strategy will turn adversity into opportunity. For example, emergency management systems will be better able to cope not just with terrorism but with all hazards. Our medical system will be strengthened to manage not just bioterror, but all infectious diseases and mass-casualty dangers. Our border controls will not just stop terrorists, but improve the efficient movement of legitimate traffic.

While our focus is protecting America, we know that to defeat terrorism in today's globalized world we need support from our allies and friends. Wherever possible, the United States will rely on regional organizations and state powers to meet their obligations to fight terrorism. Where governments find the fight against terrorism beyond their capacities, we will match their willpower and their resources with whatever help we and our allies can provide.

As we pursue the terrorists in Afghanistan, we will continue to work with international organizations such as the United Nations, as well as non-governmental organizations, and other countries to provide the humanitarian, political, economic, and security assistance necessary to rebuild Afghanistan so that it will never again abuse its people, threaten its neighbors, and provide a haven for terrorists.

In the war against global terrorism, we will never forget that we are ultimately fighting for our democratic values and way of life. Freedom and fear are at war, and there will be no quick or easy end to this conflict. In leading the campaign against terrorism, we are forging new, productive international relationships and redefining existing ones in ways that meet the challenges of the twenty-first century.

iv. Work with others to Defuse Regional Conflicts

"We build a world of justice, or we will live in a world of coercion. The magnitude of our shared responsibilities makes our disagreements look so small."

President Bush
Berlin, Germany
May 23, 2002

Concerned nations must remain actively engaged in critical regional disputes to avoid explosive escalation and minimize human suffering. In an increasingly interconnected world, regional crisis can strain our alliances, rekindle rivalries among the major powers, and create horrifying affronts to human dignity. When violence erupts and states falter, the United States will work with friends and partners to alleviate suffering and restore stability.

No doctrine can anticipate every circumstance in which U.S. action—direct or indirect—is warranted. We have finite political, economic, and military resources to meet our global priorities. The United States will approach each case with these strategic principles in mind:

- The United States should invest time and resources into building international relationships and institutions that can help manage local crises when they emerge.

- The United States should be realistic about its ability to help those who are unwilling or unready to help themselves. Where and when people are ready to do their part, we will be willing to move decisively.

The Israeli-Palestinian conflict is critical because of the toll of human suffering, because of America's close relationship with the state of Israel and key Arab states, and because of that region's importance to other global priorities of the United States. There can be no peace for either side without freedom for both sides. America stands committed to an independent and democratic Palestine, living beside Israel in peace and security. Like all other people, Palestinians deserve a government that serves their interests and listens to their voices. The United States will continue to encourage all parties to step up to their responsibilities as we seek a just and comprehensive settlement to the conflict.

The United States, the international donor community, and the World Bank stand ready to work with a reformed Palestinian government on economic development, increased humanitarian assistance, and a program to establish, finance, and monitor a truly independent judiciary. If Palestinians embrace democracy, and the rule of law, confront corruption, and firmly reject terror, they can count on American support for the creation of a Palestinian state.

Israel also has a large stake in the success of a democratic Palestine. Permanent occupation threatens Israel's identity and democracy. So the United States continues to challenge Israeli leaders to take concrete steps to support the emergence of a viable, credible Palestinian state. As there is progress towards security, Israel forces need to withdraw fully to positions they held prior to September 28, 2000. And consistent with the recommendations of the Mitchell Committee, Israeli settlement activity in the occupied territories must stop. As violence subsides, freedom of movement should be restored, permitting innocent Palestinians to resume work and normal life. The United States can play a crucial role but, ultimately, lasting peace can only come when Israelis and Palestinians resolve the issues and end the conflict between them.

In South Asia, the United States has also emphasized the need for India and Pakistan to resolve their disputes. This Administration invested time and resources building strong bilateral relations with India and Pakistan. These strong relations then gave us leverage to play a constructive role when tensions in the region became acute. With Pakistan, our bilateral relations have been bolstered by Pakistan's choice to join the war against terror and move toward building a more open and tolerant society. The Administration sees India's potential to become one of the great democratic powers of the twenty-first century and has worked hard to transform our relationship accordingly. Our involvement in this regional dispute, building on earlier investments in bilateral relations, looks first to concrete steps by India and Pakistan that can help defuse military confrontation.

Indonesia took courageous steps to create a working democracy and respect for the rule of law. By tolerating ethnic minorities, respecting the rule of law, and accepting open markets, Indonesia may be able to employ the engine of opportunity that has helped lift some of its neighbors out of poverty and desperation. It is the initiative by Indonesia that allows U.S. assistance to make a difference.

In the Western Hemisphere we have formed flexible coalitions with countries that share our priorities, particularly Mexico, Brazil, Canada, Chile, and Colombia. Together we will promote a truly democratic hemisphere where our integration advances security, prosperity, opportunity, and hope. We will work with regional institutions, such as the Summit of the Americas process, the Organization of American States (OAS), and the Defense Ministerial of the Americas for the benefit of the entire hemisphere.

Parts of Latin America confront regional conflict, especially arising from the violence of drug cartels and their accomplices. This conflict and unrestrained narcotics trafficking could imperil the health and security of the United States. Therefore we have developed an active strategy to help the Andean nations adjust their economies, enforce their laws, defeat terrorist organizations, and cut off the supply of drugs, while—as important—we work to reduce the demand for drugs in our own country.

In Colombia, we recognize the link between terrorist and extremist groups that challenge the security of the state and drug trafficking activities that help finance the operations of such groups. We are working to help Colombia defend its democratic institutions and defeat illegal armed groups of both the left and right by extending effective sovereignty over the entire national territory and provide basic security to the Colombian people.

In Africa, promise and opportunity sit side by side with disease, war, and desperate poverty. This threatens both a core value of the United States—preserving human dignity—and our strategic priority—combating global terror. American interests and American principles, therefore, lead in the same direction: we will work with others for an African continent that lives in liberty, peace, and growing prosperity. Together with our European allies, we must help strengthen Africa's fragile states, help build indigenous capability to secure porous borders, and help build up the law enforcement and intelligence infrastructure to deny havens for terrorists.

An ever more lethal environment exists in Africa as local civil wars spread beyond borders to create regional war zones. Forming coalitions of the willing and cooperative security arrangements are key to confronting these emerging transnational threats.

Africa's great size and diversity requires a security strategy that focuses on bilateral engagement and builds coalitions of the willing. This Administration will focus on three interlocking strategies for the region:

- countries with major impact on their neighborhood such as South Africa, Nigeria, Kenya, and Ethiopia are anchors for regional engagement and require focused attention;

- coordination with European allies and international institutions is essential for constructive conflict mediation and successful peace operations; and

- Africa's capable reforming states and sub-regional organizations must be strengthened as the primary means to address transnational threats on a sustained basis.

Ultimately the path of political and economic freedom presents the surest route to progress in sub-Saharan Africa, where most wars are conflicts over material resources and political access often tragically waged on the basis of ethnic and religious difference. The transition to the African Union with its stated commitment to good governance and a common responsibility for democratic political systems offers opportunities to strengthen democracy on the continent.

V. PREVENT OUR ENEMIES FROM THREATENING US, OUR ALLIES, AND OUR FRIENDS WITH WEAPONS OF MASS DESTRUCTION

"The gravest danger to freedom lies at the crossroads of radicalism and technology. When the spread of chemical and biological and nuclear weapons, along with ballistic missile technology—when that occurs, even weak states and small groups could attain a catastrophic power to strike great nations. Our enemies have declared this very intention, and have been caught seeking these terrible weapons. They want the capability to blackmail us, or to harm us, or to harm our friends—and we will oppose them with all our power."

PRESIDENT BUSH
WEST POINT, NEW YORK
JUNE 1, 2002

The nature of the Cold War threat required the United States—with our allies and friends—to emphasize deterrence of the enemy's use of force, producing a grim strategy of mutual assured destruction. With the collapse of the Soviet Union and the end of the Cold War, our security environment has undergone profound transformation.

Having moved from confrontation to cooperation as the hallmark of our relationship with Russia, the dividends are evident: an end to the balance of terror that divided us; an historic reduction in the nuclear arsenals on both sides; and cooperation in areas such as counterterrorism and missile defense that until recently were inconceivable.

But new deadly challenges have emerged from rogue states and terrorists. None of these contemporary threats rival the sheer destructive power that was arrayed against us by the Soviet Union. However, the nature and motivations of these new adversaries, their determination to obtain destructive powers hitherto available only to the world's strongest states, and the greater likelihood that they will use weapons of mass destruction against us, make today's security environment more complex and dangerous.

In the 1990s we witnessed the emergence of a small number of rogue states that, while different in important ways, share a number of attributes. These states:

- brutalize their own people and squander their national resources for the personal gain of the rulers;

- display no regard for international law, threaten their neighbors, and callously violate international treaties to which they are party;

- are determined to acquire weapons of mass destruction, along with other advanced military technology, to be used as threats or offensively to achieve the aggressive designs of these regimes;

- sponsor terrorism around the globe; and

- reject basic human values and hate the United States and everything for which it stands.

At the time of the Gulf War, we acquired irrefutable proof that Iraq's designs were not limited to the chemical weapons it had used against Iran and its own people, but also extended to the acquisition of nuclear weapons and biological agents. In the past decade North Korea has become the world's principal purveyor of ballistic missiles, and has tested increasingly capable missiles while developing its own WMD arsenal. Other rogue regimes seek nuclear, biological, and chemical weapons as well. These states' pursuit of, and global trade in, such weapons has become a looming threat to all nations.

We must be prepared to stop rogue states and their terrorist clients before they are able to threaten or use weapons of mass destruction against the United States and our allies and friends. Our response must take full advantage of strengthened alliances, the establishment of new partnerships with former adversaries, innovation in the use of military forces, modern technologies, including the development of an effective missile defense system, and increased emphasis on intelligence collection and analysis.

Our comprehensive strategy to combat WMD includes:

- *Proactive counterproliferation efforts.* We must deter and defend against the threat before it is unleashed. We must ensure that key capabilities—detection, active and passive defenses, and counterforce capabilities—are integrated into our defense transformation and our homeland security systems. Counterproliferation must also be integrated into the doctrine, training, and equipping of our forces and those of our allies to ensure that we can prevail in any conflict with WMD-armed adversaries.

- *Strengthened nonproliferation efforts to prevent rogue states and terrorists from acquiring the materials, technologies, and expertise necessary for weapons of mass destruction.* We will enhance diplomacy, arms control, multilateral export controls, and threat reduction assistance that impede states and terrorists seeking WMD, and when necessary, interdict enabling technologies and materials. We will continue to build coalitions to support these efforts, encouraging their increased political and financial support for nonproliferation and threat reduction programs. The recent G-8 agreement to commit up to $20 billion to a global partnership against proliferation marks a major step forward.

- *Effective consequence management to respond to the effects of WMD use, whether by terrorists or hostile states.* Minimizing the effects of WMD use against our people will help deter those who possess such weapons and dissuade those who seek to acquire them by persuading enemies that they cannot attain their desired ends. The United States must also be prepared to respond to the effects of WMD use against our forces abroad, and to help friends and allies if they are attacked.

It has taken almost a decade for us to comprehend the true nature of this new threat. Given the goals of rogue states and terrorists, the United States can no longer solely rely on a reactive posture as we have in the past. The inability to deter a potential attacker, the immediacy of today's threats, and the magnitude of potential harm that could be caused by our adversaries' choice of weapons, do not permit that option. We cannot let our enemies strike first.

- In the Cold War, especially following the Cuban missile crisis, we faced a generally status quo, risk-averse adversary. Deterrence was an effective defense. But deterrence based only upon the threat of retaliation is less likely to work against leaders of rogue states more willing to take risks, gambling with the lives of their people, and the wealth of their nations.

- In the Cold War, weapons of mass destruction were considered weapons of last resort whose use risked the destruction of those who used them. Today, our enemies see weapons of mass destruction as weapons of choice. For rogue states these weapons are tools of intimidation and military aggression against their neighbors. These weapons may also allow these states to attempt to blackmail the United States and our allies to prevent us from deterring or repelling the aggressive behavior of rogue states. Such states also see these weapons as their best means of overcoming the conventional superiority of the United States.

- Traditional concepts of deterrence will not work against a terrorist enemy whose avowed tactics are wanton destruction and the targeting of innocents; whose so-called soldiers seek martyrdom in death and whose most potent protection is statelessness. The overlap between states that sponsor terror and those that pursue WMD compels us to action.

For centuries, international law recognized that nations need not suffer an attack before they can lawfully take action to defend themselves against forces that present an imminent danger of attack. Legal scholars and international jurists often conditioned the legitimacy of preemption on the existence of an imminent threat—most often a visible mobilization of armies, navies, and air forces preparing to attack.

We must adapt the concept of imminent threat to the capabilities and objectives of today's adversaries. Rogue states and terrorists do not seek to attack us using conventional means. They know such attacks would fail. Instead, they rely on acts of terror and, potentially, the use of weapons of mass destruction—weapons that can be easily concealed, delivered covertly, and used without warning.

The targets of these attacks are our military forces and our civilian population, in direct violation of one of the principal norms of the law of warfare. As was demonstrated by the losses on September 11, 2001, mass civilian casualties is the specific objective of terrorists and these losses would be exponentially more severe if terrorists acquired and used weapons of mass destruction.

The United States has long maintained the option of preemptive actions to counter a sufficient threat to our national security. The greater the threat, the greater is the risk of inaction— and the more compelling the case for taking anticipatory action to defend ourselves, even if uncertainty remains as to the time and place of the enemy's attack. To forestall or prevent such hostile acts by our adversaries, the United States will, if necessary, act preemptively.

The United States will not use force in all cases to preempt emerging threats, nor should nations use preemption as a pretext for aggression. Yet in an age where the enemies of civilization openly and actively seek the world's most destructive technologies, the United States cannot remain idle while dangers gather.

We will always proceed deliberately, weighing the consequences of our actions. To support preemptive options, we will:

- build better, more integrated intelligence capabilities to provide timely, accurate information on threats, wherever they may emerge;

- coordinate closely with allies to form a common assessment of the most dangerous threats; and

- continue to transform our military forces to ensure our ability to conduct rapid and precise operations to achieve decisive results.

The purpose of our actions will always be to eliminate a specific threat to the United States or our allies and friends. The reasons for our actions will be clear, the force measured, and the cause just.

VI. IGNITE A NEW ERA OF GLOBAL ECONOMIC GROWTH THROUGH FREE MARKETS AND FREE TRADE

"When nations close their markets and opportunity is hoarded by a privileged few, no amount—no amount—of development aid is ever enough. When nations respect their people, open markets, invest in better health and education, every dollar of aid, every dollar of trade revenue and domestic capital is used more effectively."

PRESIDENT BUSH
MONTERREY, MEXICO
MARCH 22, 2002

A strong world economy enhances our national security by advancing prosperity and freedom in the rest of the world. Economic growth supported by free trade and free markets creates new jobs and higher incomes. It allows people to lift their lives out of poverty, spurs economic and legal reform, and the fight against corruption, and it reinforces the habits of liberty.

We will promote economic growth and economic freedom beyond America's shores. All governments are responsible for creating their own economic policies and responding to their own economic challenges. We will use our economic engagement with other countries to underscore the benefits of policies that generate higher productivity and sustained economic growth, including:

- pro-growth legal and regulatory policies to encourage business investment, innovation, and entrepreneurial activity;

- tax policies—particularly lower marginal tax rates—that improve incentives for work and investment;

- rule of law and intolerance of corruption so that people are confident that they will be able to enjoy the fruits of their economic endeavors;

- strong financial systems that allow capital to be put to its most efficient use;

- sound fiscal policies to support business activity;

- investments in health and education that improve the well-being and skills of the labor force and population as a whole; and

- free trade that provides new avenues for growth and fosters the diffusion of technologies and ideas that increase productivity and opportunity.

The lessons of history are clear: market economies, not command-and-control economies with the heavy hand of government, are the best way to promote prosperity and reduce poverty. Policies that further strengthen market incentives and market institutions are relevant for all economies—industrialized countries, emerging markets, and the developing world.

A return to strong economic growth in Europe and Japan is vital to U.S. national security interests. We want our allies to have strong economies for their own sake, for the sake of the global economy, and for the sake of global security. European efforts to remove structural barriers in their economies are particularly important in this regard, as are Japan's efforts to end deflation and address the problems of non-performing loans in the Japanese banking system. We will continue to use our regular consultations with Japan and our European partners—including through the Group of Seven (G-7)—to discuss policies they are adopting to promote growth in their economies and support higher global economic growth.

Improving stability in emerging markets is also key to global economic growth. International flows of investment capital are needed to expand the productive potential of these economies. These flows allow emerging markets and developing countries to make the investments that raise living standards and reduce poverty. Our long-term objective should be a world in which all countries have investment-grade credit ratings that allow them access to international capital markets and to invest in their future.

We are committed to policies that will help emerging markets achieve access to larger capital flows at lower cost. To this end, we will continue to pursue reforms aimed at reducing uncertainty in financial markets. We will work actively with other countries, the International Monetary Fund (IMF), and the private sector to implement the G-7 Action Plan negotiated earlier this year for preventing financial crises and more effectively resolving them when they occur.

The best way to deal with financial crises is to prevent them from occurring, and we have encouraged the IMF to improve its efforts doing so. We will continue to work with the IMF to streamline the policy conditions for its lending and to focus its lending strategy on achieving economic growth through sound fiscal and monetary policy, exchange rate policy, and financial sector policy.

The concept of "free trade" arose as a moral principle even before it became a pillar of economics. If you can make something that others value, you should be able to sell it to them. If others make something that you value, you should be able to buy it. This is real freedom, the freedom for a person—or a nation—to make a living. To promote free trade, the Unites States has developed a comprehensive strategy:

- *Seize the global initiative.* The new global trade negotiations we helped launch at Doha in November 2001 will have an ambitious agenda, especially in agriculture, manufacturing, and services, targeted for completion in 2005. The United States has led the way in completing the accession of China and a democratic Taiwan to the World Trade Organization. We will assist Russia's preparations to join the WTO.

- *Press regional initiatives.* The United States and other democracies in the Western Hemisphere have agreed to create the Free Trade Area of the Americas, targeted for completion in 2005. This year the United States will advocate market-access negotiations with its partners, targeted on agriculture, industrial goods, services, investment, and government procurement. We will also offer more opportunity to the poorest continent, Africa, starting with full use of the preferences allowed in the African Growth and Opportunity Act, and leading to free trade.

- *Move ahead with bilateral free trade agreements.* Building on the free trade agreement with Jordan enacted in 2001, the Administration will work this year to complete free trade agreements with Chile and Singapore. Our aim is to achieve free trade agreements with a mix of developed and developing countries in all regions of the world. Initially, Central America, Southern Africa, Morocco, and Australia will be our principal focal points.

- *Renew the executive-congressional partnership.* Every administration's trade strategy depends on a productive partnership with Congress. After a gap of 8 years, the Administration reestablished majority support in the Congress for trade liberalization by passing Trade Promotion Authority and the other market opening measures for developing countries in the Trade Act of 2002. This Administration will work with Congress to enact new bilateral, regional, and global trade agreements that will be concluded under the recently passed Trade Promotion Authority.

- *Promote the connection between trade and development.* Trade policies can help developing countries strengthen property rights, competition, the rule of law, investment, the spread of knowledge, open societies, the efficient allocation of resources, and regional integration—all leading to growth, opportunity, and confidence in developing countries. The United States is implementing The Africa Growth and Opportunity Act to provide market-access for nearly all goods produced in the 35 countries of sub-Saharan Africa. We will make more use of this act and its equivalent for the Caribbean Basin and continue to work with multilateral and regional institutions to help poorer countries take advantage of these opportunities. Beyond market access, the most important area where trade intersects with poverty is in public health. We will ensure that the WTO intellectual property rules are flexible enough to allow developing nations to gain access to critical medicines for extraordinary dangers like HIV/AIDS, tuberculosis, and malaria.

- *Enforce trade agreements and laws against unfair practices.* Commerce depends on the rule of law; international trade depends on enforceable agreements. Our top priorities are to resolve ongoing disputes with the European Union, Canada, and Mexico and to make a global effort to address new technology, science, and health regulations that needlessly impede farm exports and improved agriculture. Laws against unfair trade practices are often abused, but the international community must be able to address genuine concerns about government subsidies and dumping. International industrial espionage which undermines fair competition must be detected and deterred.

- *Help domestic industries and workers adjust.* There is a sound statutory framework for these transitional safeguards which we have used in the agricultural sector and which we are using this year to help the American steel industry. The benefits of free trade depend upon the enforcement of fair trading practices. These safeguards help ensure that the benefits of free trade do not come at the expense of American workers. Trade adjustment assistance will help workers adapt to the change and dynamism of open markets.

- *Protect the environment and workers.* The United States must foster economic growth in ways that will provide a better life along with widening prosperity. We will incorporate labor and environmental concerns into U.S. trade negotiations, creating a healthy "network" between multilateral environmental agreements with the WTO, and use the International Labor Organization, trade preference programs, and trade talks to improve working conditions in conjunction with freer trade.

- *Enhance energy security.* We will strengthen our own energy security and the shared prosperity of the global economy by working with our allies, trading partners, and energy producers to expand the sources and types of global energy supplied, especially in the Western Hemisphere, Africa, Central Asia, and the Caspian region. We will also continue to work with our partners to develop cleaner and more energy efficient technologies.

Economic growth should be accompanied by global efforts to stabilize greenhouse gas concentrations associated with this growth, containing them at a level that prevents dangerous human interference with the global climate. Our overall objective is to reduce America's greenhouse gas emissions relative to the size of our economy, cutting such emissions per unit of economic activity by 18 percent over the next 10 years, by the year 2012. Our strategies for attaining this goal will be to:

- remain committed to the basic U.N. Framework Convention for international cooperation;

- obtain agreements with key industries to cut emissions of some of the most potent greenhouse gases and give transferable credits to companies that can show real cuts;

- develop improved standards for measuring and registering emission reductions;

- promote renewable energy production and clean coal technology, as well as nuclear power—which produces no greenhouse gas emissions, while also improving fuel economy for U.S. cars and trucks;

- increase spending on research and new conservation technologies, to a total of $4.5 billion—the largest sum being spent on climate change by any country in the world and a $700 million increase over last year's budget; and

- assist developing countries, especially the major greenhouse gas emitters such as China and India, so that they will have the tools and resources to join this effort and be able to grow along a cleaner and better path.

VII. Expand the Circle of Development by Opening Societies and Building the Infrastructure of Democracy

"In World War II we fought to make the world safer, then worked to rebuild it. As we wage war today to keep the world safe from terror, we must also work to make the world a better place for all its citizens."

PRESIDENT BUSH
WASHINGTON, D.C. (INTER-AMERICAN DEVELOPMENT BANK)
MARCH 14, 2002

A world where some live in comfort and plenty, while half of the human race lives on less than $2 a day, is neither just nor stable. Including all of the world's poor in an expanding circle of development—and opportunity—is a moral imperative and one of the top priorities of U.S. international policy.

Decades of massive development assistance have failed to spur economic growth in the poorest countries. Worse, development aid has often served to prop up failed policies, relieving the pressure for reform and perpetuating misery. Results of aid are typically measured in dollars spent by donors, not in the rates of growth and poverty reduction achieved by recipients. These are the indicators of a failed strategy.

Working with other nations, the United States is confronting this failure. We forged a new consensus at the U.N. Conference on Financing for Development in Monterrey that the objectives of assistance—and the strategies to achieve those objectives—must change.

This Administration's goal is to help unleash the productive potential of individuals in all nations. Sustained growth and poverty reduction is impossible without the right national policies. Where governments have implemented real policy changes, we will provide significant new levels of assistance. The United States and other developed countries should set an ambitious and specific target: to double the size of the world's poorest economies within a decade.

The United States Government will pursue these major strategies to achieve this goal:

- *Provide resources to aid countries that have met the challenge of national reform.* We propose a 50 percent increase in the core development assistance given by the United States. While continuing our present programs, including humanitarian assistance based on need alone, these billions of new dollars will form a new Millennium Challenge Account for projects in countries whose governments rule justly, invest in their people, and encourage economic freedom. Governments must fight corruption, respect basic human rights, embrace the rule of law, invest in health care and education, follow responsible economic policies, and enable entrepreneurship. The Millennium Challenge Account will reward countries that have demonstrated real policy change and challenge those that have not to implement reforms.

- *Improve the effectiveness of the World Bank and other development banks in raising living standards.* The United States is committed to a comprehensive reform agenda for making the World Bank and the other multilateral development banks more effective in improving the lives of the world's poor. We have reversed the downward trend in U.S. contributions and proposed an 18 percent increase in the U.S. contributions to the International Development Association (IDA)—the World Bank's fund for the poorest countries—and the African Development Fund. The key to raising living standards and reducing poverty around the world is increasing productivity growth, especially in the poorest countries. We will continue to press the multilateral development banks to focus on activities that increase economic productivity, such as improvements in education, health, rule of law, and private sector development. Every project, every loan, every grant must be judged by how much it will increase productivity growth in developing countries.

- *Insist upon measurable results to ensure that development assistance is actually making a difference in the lives of the world's poor.* When it comes to economic development, what really matters is that more children are getting a better education, more people have access to health care and clean water, or more workers can find jobs to make a better future for their families. We have a moral obligation to measure the success of our development assistance by whether it is delivering results. For this reason, we will continue to demand that our own development assistance as well as assistance from the multilateral development banks has measurable goals and concrete benchmarks for achieving those goals. Thanks to U.S. leadership, the recent IDA replenishment agreement will establish a monitoring and evaluation system that measures recipient countries' progress. For the first time, donors can link a portion of their contributions to IDA to the achievement of actual development results, and part of the U.S. contribution is linked in this way. We will strive to make sure that the World Bank and other multilateral development banks build on this progress so that a focus on results is an integral part of everything that these institutions do.

- *Increase the amount of development assistance that is provided in the form of grants instead of loans.* Greater use of results-based grants is the best way to help poor countries make productive investments, particularly in the social sectors, without saddling them with ever-larger debt burdens. As a result of U.S. leadership, the recent IDA agreement provided for significant increases in grant funding for the poorest countries for education, HIV/AIDS, health, nutrition, water, sanitation, and other human needs. Our goal is to build on that progress by increasing the use of grants at the other multilateral development banks. We will also challenge universities, nonprofits, and the private sector to match government efforts by using grants to support development projects that show results.

- *Open societies to commerce and investment.* Trade and investment are the real engines of economic growth. Even if government aid increases, most money for development must come from trade, domestic capital, and foreign investment. An effective strategy must try to expand these flows as well. Free markets and free trade are key priorities of our national security strategy.

- *Secure public health.* The scale of the public health crisis in poor countries is enormous. In countries afflicted by epidemics and pandemics like HIV/AIDS, malaria, and tuberculosis, growth and development will be threatened until these scourges can be contained. Resources from the developed world are necessary but will be effective only with honest governance, which supports prevention programs and provides effective local infrastructure. The United States has strongly backed the new global fund for HIV/AIDS organized by U.N. Secretary General Kofi Annan and its focus on combining prevention with a broad strategy for treatment and care. The United States already contributes more than twice as much money to such efforts as the next largest donor. If the global fund demonstrates its promise, we will be ready to give even more.

- *Emphasize education.* Literacy and learning are the foundation of democracy and development. Only about 7 percent of World Bank resources are devoted to education. This proportion should grow. The United States will increase its own funding for education assistance by at least 20 percent with an emphasis on improving basic education and teacher training in Africa. The United States can also bring information technology to these societies, many of whose education systems have been devastated by HIV/AIDS.

- *Continue to aid agricultural development.* New technologies, including biotechnology, have enormous potential to improve crop yields in developing countries while using fewer pesticides and less water. Using sound science, the United States should help bring these benefits to the 800 million people, including 300 million children, who still suffer from hunger and malnutrition.

VIII. DEVELOP AGENDAS FOR COOPERATIVE ACTION WITH THE OTHER MAIN CENTERS OF GLOBAL POWER

"We have our best chance since the rise of the nation-state in the 17th century to build a world where the great powers compete in peace instead of prepare for war."

PRESIDENT BUSH
WEST POINT, NEW YORK
JUNE 1, 2002

America will implement its strategies by organizing coalitions—as broad as practicable—of states able and willing to promote a balance of power that favors freedom. Effective coalition leadership requires clear priorities, an appreciation of others' interests, and consistent consultations among partners with a spirit of humility.

There is little of lasting consequence that the United States can accomplish in the world without the sustained cooperation of its allies and friends in Canada and Europe. Europe is also the seat of two of the strongest and most able international institutions in the world: the North Atlantic Treaty Organization (NATO), which has, since its inception, been the fulcrum of transatlantic and inter-European security, and the European Union (EU), our partner in opening world trade.

The attacks of September 11 were also an attack on NATO, as NATO itself recognized when it invoked its Article V self-defense clause for the first time. NATO's core mission—collective defense of the transatlantic alliance of democracies—remains, but NATO must develop new structures and capabilities to carry out that mission under new circumstances. NATO must

build a capability to field, at short notice, highly mobile, specially trained forces whenever they are needed to respond to a threat against any member of the alliance.

The alliance must be able to act wherever our interests are threatened, creating coalitions under NATO's own mandate, as well as contributing to mission-based coalitions. To achieve this, we must:

- expand NATO's membership to those democratic nations willing and able to share the burden of defending and advancing our common interests;

- ensure that the military forces of NATO nations have appropriate combat contributions to make in coalition warfare;

- develop planning processes to enable those contributions to become effective multinational fighting forces;

- take advantage of the technological opportunities and economies of scale in our defense spending to transform NATO military forces so that they dominate potential aggressors and diminish our vulnerabilities;

- streamline and increase the flexibility of command structures to meet new operational demands and the associated requirements of training, integrating, and experimenting with new force configurations; and

- maintain the ability to work and fight together as allies even as we take the necessary steps to transform and modernize our forces.

If NATO succeeds in enacting these changes, the rewards will be a partnership as central to the security and interests of its member states as was the case during the Cold War. We will sustain a common perspective on the threats to our societies and improve our ability to take common action in defense of our nations and their interests. At the same time, we welcome our European allies' efforts to forge a greater foreign policy and defense identity with the EU, and commit ourselves to close consultations to ensure that these developments work with NATO. We cannot afford to lose this opportunity to better prepare the family of transatlantic democracies for the challenges to come.

The attacks of September 11 energized America's Asian alliances. Australia invoked the ANZUS Treaty to declare the September 11 was an attack on Australia itself, following that historic decision with the dispatch of some of the world's finest combat forces for Operation Enduring Freedom. Japan and the Republic of Korea provided unprecedented levels of military logistical support within weeks of the terrorist attack. We have deepened cooperation on counterterrorism with our alliance partners in Thailand and the Philippines and received invaluable assistance from close friends like Singapore and New Zealand.

The war against terrorism has proven that America's alliances in Asia not only underpin regional peace and stability, but are flexible and ready to deal with new challenges. To enhance our Asian alliances and friendships, we will:

- look to Japan to continue forging a leading role in regional and global affairs based on our common interests, our common values, and our close defense and diplomatic cooperation;

- work with South Korea to maintain vigilance towards the North while preparing our alliance to make contributions to the broader stability of the region over the longer term;

- build on 50 years of U.S.-Australian alliance cooperation as we continue working together to resolve regional and global problems—as we have so many times from the Battle of the Coral Sea to Tora Bora;

- maintain forces in the region that reflect our commitments to our allies, our requirements, our technological advances, and the strategic environment; and

- build on stability provided by these alliances, as well as with institutions such as ASEAN and the Asia-Pacific Economic Cooperation forum, to develop a mix of regional and bilateral strategies to manage change in this dynamic region.

We are attentive to the possible renewal of old patterns of great power competition. Several potential great powers are now in the midst of internal transition—most importantly Russia, India, and China. In all three cases, recent developments have encouraged our hope that a truly global consensus about basic principles is slowly taking shape.

With Russia, we are already building a new strategic relationship based on a central reality of the twenty-first century: the United States and Russia are no longer strategic adversaries. The Moscow Treaty on Strategic Reductions is emblematic of this new reality and reflects a critical change in Russian thinking that promises to lead to productive, long-term relations with the Euro-Atlantic community and the United States. Russia's top leaders have a realistic assessment of their country's current weakness and the policies—internal and external—needed to reverse those weaknesses. They understand, increasingly, that Cold War approaches do not serve their national interests and that Russian and American strategic interests overlap in many areas.

United States policy seeks to use this turn in Russian thinking to refocus our relationship on emerging and potential common interests and challenges. We are broadening our already extensive cooperation in the global war on terrorism. We are facilitating Russia's entry into the World Trade Organization, without lowering standards for accession, to promote beneficial bilateral trade and investment relations. We have created the NATO-Russia Council with the goal of deepening security cooperation among Russia, our European allies, and ourselves. We will continue to bolster the independence and stability of the states of the former Soviet Union in the belief that a prosperous and stable neighborhood will reinforce Russia's growing commitment to integration into the Euro-Atlantic community.

At the same time, we are realistic about the differences that still divide us from Russia and about the time and effort it will take to build an enduring strategic partnership. Lingering distrust of our motives and policies by key Russian elites slows improvement in our relations. Russia's uneven commitment to the basic values of free-market democracy and dubious record in combating the proliferation of weapons of mass destruction remain matters of great concern. Russia's very weakness limits the opportunities for cooperation. Nevertheless, those opportunities are vastly greater now than in recent years—or even decades.

The United States has undertaken a transformation in its bilateral relationship with India based on a conviction that U.S. interests require a strong relationship with India. We are the two largest democracies, committed to political freedom protected by representative government. India is moving toward greater economic freedom

as well. We have a common interest in the free flow of commerce, including through the vital sea lanes of the Indian Ocean. Finally, we share an interest in fighting terrorism and in creating a strategically stable Asia.

Differences remain, including over the development of India's nuclear and missile programs, and the pace of India's economic reforms. But while in the past these concerns may have dominated our thinking about India, today we start with a view of India as a growing world power with which we have common strategic interests. Through a strong partnership with India, we can best address any differences and shape a dynamic future.

The United States relationship with China is an important part of our strategy to promote a stable, peaceful, and prosperous Asia-Pacific region. We welcome the emergence of a strong, peaceful, and prosperous China. The democratic development of China is crucial to that future. Yet, a quarter century after beginning the process of shedding the worst features of the Communist legacy, China's leaders have not yet made the next series of fundamental choices about the character of their state. In pursuing advanced military capabilities that can threaten its neighbors in the Asia-Pacific region, China is following an outdated path that, in the end, will hamper its own pursuit of national greatness. In time, China will find that social and political freedom is the only source of that greatness.

The United States seeks a constructive relationship with a changing China. We already cooperate well where our interests overlap, including the current war on terrorism and in promoting stability on the Korean peninsula. Likewise, we have coordinated on the future of Afghanistan and have initiated a comprehensive dialogue on counterterrorism and similar transitional concerns. Shared health and environmental threats, such as the spread of HIV/AIDS, challenge us to promote jointly the welfare of our citizens.

Addressing these transnational threats will challenge China to become more open with information, promote the development of civil society, and enhance individual human rights. China has begun to take the road to political openness, permitting many personal freedoms and conducting village-level elections, yet remains strongly committed to national one-party rule by the Communist Party. To make that nation truly accountable to its citizen's needs and aspirations, however, much work remains to be done. Only by allowing the Chinese people to think, assemble, and worship freely can China reach its full potential.

Our important trade relationship will benefit from China's entry into the World Trade Organization, which will create more export opportunities and ultimately more jobs for American farmers, workers, and companies. China is our fourth largest trading partner, with over $100 billion in annual two-way trade. The power of market principles and the WTO's requirements for transparency and accountability will advance openness and the rule of law in China to help establish basic protections for commerce and for citizens. There are, however, other areas in which we have profound disagreements. Our commitment to the self-defense of Taiwan under the Taiwan Relations Act is one. Human rights is another. We expect China to adhere to its nonproliferation commitments. We will work to narrow differences where they exist, but not allow them to preclude cooperation where we agree.

The events of September 11, 2001, fundamentally changed the context for relations between the United States and other main centers of global power, and opened vast, new opportunities. With our long-standing allies in Europe and Asia, and with leaders in Russia, India, and China, we must develop active agendas of cooperation lest these relationships become routine and unproductive.

Every agency of the United States Government shares the challenge. We can build fruitful habits of consultation, quiet argument, sober analysis, and common action. In the long-term, these are the practices that will sustain the supremacy of our common principles and keep open the path of progress.

IX. Transform America's National Security Institutions to Meet the Challenges and Opportunities of the Twenty-First Century

"Terrorists attacked a symbol of American prosperity.
They did not touch its source. America is successful because of the
hard work, creativity, and enterprise of our people."

President Bush
Washington, D.C. (Joint Session of Congress)
September 20, 2001

The major institutions of American national security were designed in a different era to meet different requirements. All of them must be transformed.

It is time to reaffirm the essential role of American military strength. We must build and maintain our defenses beyond challenge. Our military's highest priority is to defend the United States. To do so effectively, our military must:

- assure our allies and friends;

- dissuade future military competition;

- deter threats against U.S. interests, allies, and friends; and

- decisively defeat any adversary if deterrence fails.

The unparalleled strength of the United States armed forces, and their forward presence, have maintained the peace in some of the world's most strategically vital regions. However, the threats and enemies we must confront have changed, and so must our forces. A military structured to deter massive Cold War-era armies must be transformed to focus more on how an adversary might fight rather than where and when a war might occur. We will channel our energies to overcome a host of operational challenges.

The presence of American forces overseas is one of the most profound symbols of the U.S. commitments to allies and friends. Through our willingness to use force in our own defense and in defense of others, the United States demonstrates its resolve to maintain a balance of power that favors freedom. To contend with uncertainty and to meet the many security challenges we face, the United States will require bases and stations within and beyond Western Europe and Northeast Asia, as well as temporary access arrangements for the long-distance deployment of U.S. forces.

Before the war in Afghanistan, that area was low on the list of major planning contingencies. Yet, in a very short time, we had to operate across the length and breadth of that remote nation, using every branch of the armed forces. We must prepare for more such deployments by developing assets such as advanced remote sensing, long-range precision strike capabilities, and transformed maneuver and expeditionary forces. This broad portfolio of military capabilities must also include the ability to defend the homeland, conduct information operations, ensure U.S. access to distant theaters, and protect critical U.S. infrastructure and assets in outer space.

Innovation within the armed forces will rest on experimentation with new approaches to warfare, strengthening joint operations, exploiting U.S. intelligence advantages, and taking full advantage of science and technology. We must also transform the way the Department of Defense is run, especially in financial management and recruitment and retention. Finally, while maintaining near-term readiness and the ability to fight the war on terrorism, the goal must be to provide the President with a wider range of military options to discourage aggression or any form of coercion against the United States, our allies, and our friends.

We know from history that deterrence can fail; and we know from experience that some enemies cannot be deterred. The United States must and will maintain the capability to defeat any attempt by an enemy—whether a state or non-state actor—to impose its will on the United States, our allies, or our friends. We will maintain the forces sufficient to support our obligations, and to defend freedom. Our forces will be strong enough to dissuade potential adversaries from pursuing a military build-up in hopes of surpassing, or equaling, the power of the United States.

Intelligence—and how we use it—is our first line of defense against terrorists and the threat posed by hostile states. Designed around the priority of gathering enormous information about a massive, fixed object—the Soviet bloc—the intelligence community is coping with the challenge of following a far more complex and elusive set of targets.

We must transform our intelligence capabilities and build new ones to keep pace with the nature of these threats. Intelligence must be appropriately integrated with our defense and law enforcement

systems and coordinated with our allies and friends. We need to protect the capabilities we have so that we do not arm our enemies with the knowledge of how best to surprise us. Those who would harm us also seek the benefit of surprise to limit our prevention and response options and to maximize injury.

We must strengthen intelligence warning and analysis to provide integrated threat assessments for national and homeland security. Since the threats inspired by foreign governments and groups may be conducted inside the United States, we must also ensure the proper fusion of information between intelligence and law enforcement.

Initiatives in this area will include:

- strengthening the authority of the Director of Central Intelligence to lead the development and actions of the Nation's foreign intelligence capabilities;

- establishing a new framework for intelligence warning that provides seamless and integrated warning across the spectrum of threats facing the nation and our allies;

- continuing to develop new methods of collecting information to sustain our intelligence advantage;

- investing in future capabilities while working to protect them through a more vigorous effort to prevent the compromise of intelligence capabilities; and

- collecting intelligence against the terrorist danger across the government with all-source analysis.

As the United States Government relies on the armed forces to defend America's interests, it must rely on diplomacy to interact with other nations. We will ensure that the Department of State receives funding sufficient to ensure the success of American diplomacy. The State Department takes the lead in managing our bilateral relationships with other governments. And in this new era, its people and institutions must be able to interact equally adroitly with non-governmental organizations and international institutions. Officials trained mainly in international politics must also extend their reach to understand complex issues of domestic governance around the world, including public health, education, law enforcement, the judiciary, and public diplomacy.

Our diplomats serve at the front line of complex negotiations, civil wars, and other humanitarian catastrophes. As humanitarian relief requirements are better understood, we must also be able to help build police forces, court systems, and legal codes, local and provincial government institutions, and electoral systems. Effective international cooperation is needed to accomplish these goals, backed by American readiness to play our part.

Just as our diplomatic institutions must adapt so that we can reach out to others, we also need a different and more comprehensive approach to public information efforts that can help people around the world learn about and understand America. The war on terrorism is not a clash of civilizations. It does, however, reveal the clash inside a civilization, a battle for the future of the Muslim world. This is a struggle of ideas and this is an area where America must excel.

We will take the actions necessary to ensure that our efforts to meet our global security commitments and protect Americans are not impaired by the potential for investigations, inquiry, or prosecution by the International Criminal Court (ICC), whose jurisdiction does not extend to Americans and which we do not accept. We will work together with other nations to avoid complications in our military operations and cooperation, through such mechanisms as multilateral and bilateral agreements that will protect U.S. nationals from the ICC. We will implement fully the American Servicemembers Protection Act, whose provisions are intended to ensure and enhance the protection of U.S. personnel and officials.

We will make hard choices in the coming year and beyond to ensure the right level and allocation of government spending on national security. The United States Government must strengthen its defenses to win this war. At home, our most important priority is to protect the homeland for the American people.

Today, the distinction between domestic and foreign affairs is diminishing. In a globalized world, events beyond America's borders have a greater impact inside them. Our society must be open to people, ideas, and goods from across the globe. The characteristics we most cherish—our freedom, our cities, our systems of movement, and modern life—are vulnerable to terrorism. This vulnerability will persist long after we bring to justice those responsible for the September 11 attacks. As time passes, individuals may gain access to means of destruction that until now could be wielded only by armies, fleets, and squadrons. This is a new condition of life. We will adjust to it and thrive—in spite of it.

In exercising our leadership, we will respect the values, judgment, and interests of our friends and partners. Still, we will be prepared to act apart when our interests and unique responsibilities require. When we disagree on particulars, we will explain forthrightly the grounds for our concerns and strive to forge viable alternatives. We will not allow such disagreements to obscure our determination to secure together, with our allies and our friends, our shared fundamental interests and values.

Ultimately, the foundation of American strength is at home. It is in the skills of our people, the dynamism of our economy, and the resilience of our institutions. A diverse, modern society has inherent, ambitious, entrepreneurial energy. Our strength comes from what we do with that energy. That is where our national security begins.

Contributors

Ephraim Asculai worked for the Israel Atomic Energy Commission (IAEC) for over 40 years. In 1986, he was appointed to the International Atomic Energy Agency in Vienna, working on issues of radiation protection of the public. He participated in the Geneva deliberations leading to the conclusion of the Comprehensive Test-Ban Treaty, and following its approval, its verification mechanism. Dr. Asculai researches the proliferation and control of weapons of mass destruction in the Middle East.

Isaac Ben-Israel served in a number of roles in operations, intelligence, and research and development in the Israeli Air Force, reaching the rank of Major General. He has published extensively on various aspects of intelligence and national security. In addition to his appointment at JCSS, Prof. Ben-Israel is a member of the Department of Philosophy and the School of Government's Security Studies Program at Tel Aviv University.

Abraham Ben-Zvi, a member of the Jaffee Center's senior staff, is Head of the Security Studies Program at the School of Government and a former Chairman of the Department of Political Science at Tel Aviv University. He has published extensively on Israeli–American relations, issues of surprise attack, cognitive theory in international relations, and US foreign policy.

Shlomo Brom joined the Jaffee Center in 1998 after a long career in the IDF. His most senior post in the IDF was Head of the Strategic Planning Division in the Planning Branch of the General Staff. Brigadier General Brom participated actively in peace negotiations with the Palestinians, Jordan, and Syria. In 2000 Brom was named Deputy to the National Security Advisor, returning to JCSS at the end of his post.

Jonathan Cummings joined the Jaffee Center at the beginning of 2002. As the Bronfman Research Fellow of the Center's Andrea and Charles Bronfman Program on Information Strategy, he researches military–media relations and the evolution of public diplomacy doctrines.

Ram Erez is a research assistant who joined the Jaffee Center in 2001. A doctoral student at the Hebrew University in Jerusalem, he is engaged in a study on the factors influencing the formulation of national security doctrines, focusing on the conditions that impel states to alter these doctrines.

Shmuel Even joined the Jaffee Center in 1995 after a long career in the IDF's Intelligence Branch. He is an economist specializing in Middle East security issues. Dr. Even's recent publications deal with defense spending and with the world oil market.

Yair Evron is Professor Emeritus at the Department of Political Science at Tel Aviv University, where he continues to teach international relations. He has published widely on the Middle East as reflected through the prism of international relations, and has taught and been a visiting fellow at leading universities abroad.

Shai Feldman was appointed Head of the Jaffee Center in 1997, prior to which he was a Senior Research Associate since the Center's establishment. He is a member of the UN Secretary-General's Advisory Board on Disarmament Matters, the Scientific Advisory Committee of the Stockholm International Peace Research Institute (SIPRI), and other organizations. Dr. Feldman has written extensively on nuclear weapons proliferation and arms control in the Middle East, US policy in the region, American–Israeli relations, and the Middle East peace process.

Hirsh Goodman directs the Andrea and Charles Bronfman Program on Information Strategy at the Jaffee Center. He was vice president of the *Jerusalem Post* until January 2000, and the founding editor of the *Jerusalem Report*. For almost two decades Goodman covered defense issues for the *Post*, was a contributing editor to *US News & World Report*, and was a contributor to *The New Republic*. He has also written an official history of the Israeli Navy.

Mark A. Heller is Principal Research Associate at the Jaffee Center and editor of *Tel Aviv Notes*. He has been affiliated with the Jaffee Center since 1979 and has taught international relations at Tel Aviv University and at leading universities in the US. Dr. Heller has written extensively on Middle Eastern political and strategic issues. He is also currently a member of the Steering Committee of EuroMeSCo, the Euro-Mediterranean consortium of foreign policy research institutes.

Ephraim Kam, Deputy Head of the Jaffee Center, served as a Colonel in the Research Division of IDF Military Intelligence until 1993, when he joined the Jaffee Center. Positions he held in the IDF included Assistant Director of the Research Division for Evaluation and Senior Instructor at the IDF's National Defense College. He specializes in security problems of the Middle East, strategic intelligence, and Israel's national security issues.

David Klein is an operations research analyst and a strategic planning consultant, with experience in strategic planning in the IDF as well as in the private sector. His areas of expertise include civil defense measures, protecting the population in states of emergency, and emergency preparedness planning for public and private groups.

Anat Kurz has headed the Jaffee Center's Project on Low-Intensity Conflict since 1989. She has published extensively on insurgency related issues, and edited *Contemporary Trends in World Terrorism*. Her current research focuses on the institutionalization of popular struggles.

Emily B. Landau is director of the Jaffee Center's Arms Control and Regional Security Project. She has published on CSBMs, Arab perceptions of Israel's qualitative edge, Israeli–Egyptian relations, Israel's arms control policy, and the Arms Control and Regional Security (ACRS) working group. Her current research focuses on dynamics and processes in the Middle East and developments in arms control thinking.

Tamar Malz is a research assistant whose current study of Israeli strategic culture focuses on the manner and extent to which Israeli culture has affected the formulation and evolution of its deterrence strategy. She served as a research assistant to the Israel National Security Project and is presently enrolled as a doctoral student at the Hebrew University in Jerusalem.

Yoram Schweitzer joined the JCSS research staff as an expert on international terror. He has lectured and published widely on terror-related issues, and consults for government ministries on a private basis. His areas of expertise include the "Afghan Alumni" phenomenon and the threat posed by Bin Laden, suicide terrorism, and state-sponsored terrorism.

Index